658.84
THO

D1079054

Direct Marketing in Practice

The Chartered Institute of Marketing/Butterworth-Heinemann Marketing Series is the most comprehensive, widely used and important collection of books in marketing and sales currently available worldwide.

As the CIM's official publisher, Butterworth-Heinemann develops, produces and publishes the complete series in association with the CIM. We aim to provide definitive marketing books for students and practitioners that promote excellence in marketing education and practice.

The series titles are written by CIM senior examiners and leading marketing educators for professionals, students and those studying the CIM's Certificate, Advanced Certificate and Postgraduate Diploma courses. Now firmly established, these titles provide practical study support to CIM and other marketing students and to practitioners at all levels.

The Chartered
Institute of Marketing

Formed in 1911, the Chartered Institute of Marketing is now the largest professional marketing management body in the world with over 60 000 members located worldwide. Its primary objectives are focused on the development of awareness and understanding of marketing throughout UK industry and commerce and in the raising of standards of professionalism in the education, training and practice of this key business discipline.

Books in the series

Creating Powerful Brands (second edition), Leslie de Chernatony
  and Malcolm McDonald
Cybermarketing (second edition), Pauline Bickerton, Matthew Bickerton
  and Upkar Pardesi
Cyberstrategy, Pauline Bickerton, Matthew Bickerton and Kate Simpson-Holley
Direct Marketing in Practice, Brian Thomas and Matthew Housden
Effective Promotional Practice for eBusiness, Cathy Ace
eMarketing eXcellence, P. R. Smith and Dave Chaffey
Excellence in Advertising (second edition), Leslie Butterfield
Fashion Marketing, Margaret Bruce and Tony Hines
From Brand Vision to Brand Evaluation, Leslie de Chernatony
Innovation in Marketing, Peter Doyle and Susan Bridgewater
International Marketing (third edition), Stanley J. Paliwoda and Michael J. Thomas
Integrated Marketing Communications, Tony Yeshin
Key Customers, Malcolm McDonald, Beth Rogers and Diana Woodburn
Marketing Briefs, Sally Dibb and Lyndon Simkin
Market-Led Strategic Change (third edition), Nigel F. Piercy
Marketing Logistics, Martin Christopher
Marketing Plans (fourth edition), Malcolm McDonald
Marketing Planning for Services, Malcolm McDonald and Adrian Payne
Marketing Professional Services, Michael Roe
Marketing Research for Managers (second edition), Sunny Crouch
  and Matthew Housden
Marketing Strategy (second edition), Paul Fifield
Relationship Marketing for Competitive Advantage, Adrian Payne,
  Martin Christopher, Moira Clark and Helen Peck
Relationship Marketing: Strategy and Implementation, Helen Peck, Adrian Payne,
  Martin Christopher and Moira Clark
Strategic Marketing Management (second edition), Richard M. S. Wilson
  and Colin Gilligan
Strategic Marketing: Planning and Control (second edition), Graeme Drummond
  and John Ensor
Successful Marketing Communications, Cathy Ace
Tales from the Market Place, Nigel Piercy
The CIM Handbook of Export Marketing, Chris Noonan
The CIM Handbook of Strategic Marketing, Colin Egan and Michael J. Thomas
The Customer Service Planner, Martin Christopher
The Fundamentals of Corporate Communications, Richard Dolphin
The Marketing Book (fourth edition), Michael J. Baker
The Marketing Manual, Michael J. Baker
Total Relationship Marketing, Evert Gummesson

Forthcoming

Political Marketing, Phil Harris and Dominic Wring
Relationship Marketing (second edition), Martin Christopher,
  Adrian Payne and David Ballantyne

14558

Direct Marketing in Practice

Brian Thomas FIDM
and Matthew Housden MIDM

*Published in association with
The Chartered Institute of Marketing*

DUBLIN BUSINESS SCHOOL LIBRARY
13-14 AUNGIER ST
DUBLIN 2
01 - 417 7571/72

BUTTERWORTH
HEINEMANN

OXFORD AMSTERDAM BOSTON LONDON NEW YORK PARIS
SAN DIEGO SAN FRANCISCO SINGAPORE SYDNEY TOKYO

Butterworth-Heinemann
An imprint of Elsevier Science
Linacre House, Jordan Hill, Oxford OX2 8DP
225 Wildwood Avenue, Woburn, MA 01801–2041

First published 2002

Copyright © 2002, Brian Thomas and Matthew Housden. All rights reserved

The right of Brian Thomas and Matthew Housden to be identified as the authors of
this work has been asserted in accordance with Copyright, Designs and Patents Act
1988

No part of this publication may be reproduced in any material form (including
photocopying or storing in any medium by electronic means and whether
or not transiently or incidentally to some other use of this publication) without
the written permission of the copyright holder except in accordance with the
provisions of the Copyright, Designs and Patents Act 1988 or under the terms of
a licence issued by the Copyright Licensing Agency Ltd, 90 Tottenham Court Road,
London, England W1T 4LP. Applications for the copyright holder's written
permission to reproduce any part of this publication should be addressed
to the publishers

British Library Cataloguing in Publication Data
Thomas, Brian, 1938–
   Direct marketing in practice
   1. Direct marketing
   I. Title   II. Chartered Institute of Marketing
   658.8'4

Library of Congress Cataloguing in Publication Data
A catalogue record for this book is available from the Library of Congress

ISBN 0 7506 2428 0

For information on all Butterworth-Heinemann publications visit our website at:
www.bh.com

Typeset by Florence Production Ltd, Stoodleigh, Devon
Printed and bound in Great Britain by MPG Books Ltd, Bodmin, Cornwall

DUBLIN BUSINESS SCHOOL
LIBRARY
RECEIVED

- 8 MAY 2002

Contents

Acknowledgements   vii

1   How direct marketing works   1

2   Developing a direct marketing campaign   23

3   Taking the long-term view   34

4   Collecting customer information   56

5   Using your information   71

6   The marketing database   89

7   How to reach customers and prospects effectively   120

8   Direct marketing and the Internet   153

9   The importance of having an offer   178

10   How to increase responses through more effective creative work   191

11   The importance of testing   224

12   Evaluation, measurement and budgeting   254

13   Choosing and briefing suppliers   288

14   Where to go for more information   307

Glossary   325

Index   339

Acknowledgements

There are two kinds of supporters I want to acknowledge – those who helped and advised me whilst I was learning and plying my trade, and those who helped me in writing this book.

Firstly, although he died several years ago, I want to acknowledge the greatest influence on my business life – Peter Donoghue. Peter taught me most of what I know about marketing, segmentation and targeting, and generally helped me to understand how business works.

Secondly Graeme McCorkell – years ago I was a marketing director and Graeme was my advertising agent. Graeme filled in the gaps that Peter left and taught me lots of other very practical things about how to make advertising work.

Then there are those many people with whom I have worked running marketing departments and agencies over the past 30 years. I could fill a page with names but I guess the three who taught me the most were Jim Edgeley, Drayton Bird and Stewart Pearson.

Paul Robinson of SDM wrote the draft of the database chapter and Helen Trim of Chord9 wrote the Internet chapter for me. Many thanks to both of you.

On a personal level, I want to say a huge thank you to my wife and partner Karen (Lee), who helped, proof read, cajoled and put up with several ruined holidays so I could get it written.

Finally thank you to Matthew Housden who picked up both the book and me when we were sinking and helped me finish it off in a very professional way.

Brian Thomas

I would like to acknowledge the contribution of colleagues and students at the University of Greenwich and at the IDM.

I would also like to thank Brian Thomas for the opportunity to work with him – one of the country's most knowledgeable Direct Marketers.

Matthew Housden

Chapter 1

How direct marketing works

Introduction
  - Education
  - How direct marketing has developed
  - What about the new terminology?
  - The World Wide Web
- So what is direct marketing?
  - Is this not an invasion of people's privacy?
- Where does direct marketing fit into marketing?
- Why is direct marketing growing?
- Does this mean the end of broadscale or general advertising?
- Information – the driving force behind direct marketing
- Where does our information come from?
  - Market research
  - The customer database
- The power of integration
  - Making marketing cost-efficient
- The value of individual data
- Customer profiling and segmentation
  - Customer analysis
- What is junk mail?
- How testing and measurement can make us more efficient
- The marketing communications plan
Summary
Review questions
Exercises

INTRODUCTION

As I write this, I am on my way to Hong Kong and Sydney to run the second public pan-Pacific course for the Institute of Direct Marketing's Diploma in Direct Marketing. This started me thinking about how much has changed in the last 19 years.

Education

In 1982, when direct marketing was still the province of consumer mail order companies and three or four specialist agencies, Derek Holder had a vision. He felt it was time that direct marketing was taken seriously and he pioneered the Diploma in Direct Marketing. Almost single-handedly, he canvassed the few interested clients and agency companies, and it is a tribute to his selling skills that he managed to drum up 25 delegates for the first course.

A year or two later he conceived the Direct Marketing Centre, an organization dedicated to the sharing of knowledge and ideas amongst direct marketers. Slowly but surely, with the help of many able people, Derek's vision was developed into today's Institute of Direct Marketing, which now has more than 5000 members around the world.

There are now more than 800 delegates each year for the Diploma ranging from new graduates to senior managers in companies of all types. The course is run every year in more than a dozen venues around the UK, throughout the world by distance learning and now through public courses in Hong Kong and Australia. The autumn of 2001 saw the launch of the new IDM Interactive and Direct Marketing Diploma, the first professional qualification to embrace fully the impact of new technology in marketing.

Professor Derek Holder, the direct marketing world owes you a huge debt of gratitude for all you have done to raise the standards of direct marketing practice.

How direct marketing has developed

My second thought was about the way direct marketing has diversified. In the 1980s we saw the rapid growth of direct marketing in the financial services industry, and the adoption of the discipline across the whole of business to business. Today, we see fast-moving consumer goods (FMCG) companies, retailers, multi-national industrial conglomerates and the successful dot com companies, in fact every type of organization, using direct marketing to acquire and develop customers.

What about the new terminology?

Today it is not so fashionable to say 'direct marketing' – now we are supposed to say 'customer relationship marketing'. Data analysis has become 'data mining' and a centralized database has become a 'data warehouse' – except, of course, a database is now a 'customer relationship marketing system'. Even the good old 'Ladder of Loyalty' circa 1954 has had its name changed to the 'Pyramid of Propensity' – oh dear!

Happily for newcomers, and perhaps some experienced practitioners too, whilst the terminology changes almost daily, the principles have not really changed that much. However, the subject of my final thought is much more far-reaching.

The World Wide Web

This is the big new factor that is going to change things forever. As the technology becomes more user-friendly, and of course more familiar as the television set becomes the central household information system, we will see a huge increase in online communication and commerce.

Crucially, this will mean a dramatic change in the balance of power as customers start to select what information they are prepared to receive and in what format. Of course, many of the early e-commerce companies will not survive; indeed we have experienced a crash in the NASDAQ and much-hyped companies such as letsbuyit.com and lastminute.com are into liquidation or struggling to justify their share prices. It would not be surprising to see up to 80% of such start-ups fail as many were launched on a wave of e-commerce euphoria with little commercial experience behind them.

However, the Internet will not go away. It will become a central part of any company's communications with customers and prospects. There are many good new business models to follow and we need look no further than Dell, Novell, Federal Express and UPS to see examples of how the Internet can enable major changes in business practices and economics. More of this in Chapter 8.

Meanwhile, let's turn to the 1990s. In the early 1990s, after record-breaking losses, IBM had a change of management right at the top. One of the main problems was that the managers of IBM had become too remote from their customers. The new CEO Lou Gerstner is reported to have issued a decree to all his marketing people around the world saying, in effect: 'Within 3 years at least 50% of all your marketing money must be spent on direct marketing – or you're out of a job.'

The direct marketing trade press subsequently carried a report stating that in the first 3 years under Gerstner's leadership IBM had:

- reduced its sales force from 30,000 to 6000
- seen sales grow 12% faster than the industry average
- seen its direct marketing sales grow from zero to US$10 billion per annum.

No wonder that direct marketing is such a hot topic today. Everyone in marketing is talking about it. They may call it 'integrated marketing', 'one-to-one marketing', 'customer relationship marketing/management', 'loyalty marketing', 'personal marketing', 'database marketing' or some other buzz phrase, but what they are talking about is the fact that all marketers now have to include direct marketing skills in their armoury.

Even in its current form, direct marketing has been around for a long time, but it has really been with us since marketing began. Hundreds of years ago, a manufacturer of, for example, clothing or fine tableware, would use one-to-one marketing methods, seeking out selected customers, identifying their precise needs, and developing specific products to satisfy those needs.

After the first round of one-to-one marketing, came mass production, which, successfully it must be said, adopted the 'this is what we make, now go and buy it' approach. But today, as customers have become more affluent and more individualistic, they have also become more knowledgeable and more discerning, and the 'broad brush' approach does not work so well any more.

One of the reasons for IBM's change of fortunes in the early 1990s was Gerstner's abandonment of its former policy, quoted by one of their senior executives as 'We make, you take; we talk, you listen'. This policy would be commercial suicide today.

Happily, today's marketers have modern technology to help them deliver the more focused communications and service required whilst still dealing with a high volume of customers and prospects.

One expert recently defined direct marketing as 'Using tomorrow's technology to deliver yesterday's standards of service to today's customers'.

Direct marketing is a discipline, a subset of marketing, which permits us to carry out certain marketing tasks more efficiently. It does this by gathering, analysing and using information about individual customers and prospects. This information enables us to identify which of the people on our customer and prospect files are likely to be interested in a particular product, service or offer.

So what is direct marketing?

Direct marketing is a discipline, a subset of marketing, which permits us to carry out certain marketing tasks more efficiently. It does this by gathering, analysing and using information about individual customers and prospects. This information enables us to identify which of the people on our customer and prospect files are likely to be interested in a particular product, service or offer.

We can then select only those who will find our message appropriate and communicate with them alone, eliminating much of the wastage inherent in other forms of advertising. This is a major reason why direct marketing is so cost-effective. We can also use our customer information to develop 'profiles' and use these to identify the best sources of new customers. These processes are explained in detail in Chapter 5.

Is this not an invasion of people's privacy?

This is an area where there is still much misunderstanding – even among practitioners and those who seek to control our activities. The fact is that no sensible marketer would wish to alienate customers and prospects by abusing their trust. Nor would they want to waste money by writing to those who are not interested in a product or proposition.

The main concerns arise over the use of 'opt out' or 'opt in' statements on enquiry forms. Some supporters of a high level of data protection would like all advertisers to use the 'opt-in' option at all times. In this instance, the advertiser can only use the customer's name, address and other data when the customer positively opts in. To opt in a customer must tick a box agreeing that he or she would like to receive information about other products and services.

The majority of advertisers prefer the current minimum requirement – the opt-out version. To opt out the customer is obliged to tick the box if he or she does not want to receive such communications.

My personal view is that a compromise would be in order. In my experience, the majority of people who enquire about a product, or open a bank account, would be neither surprised nor offended if they received mailings offering similar products from the organization they approached in the first place.

On the other hand, they would rightly be concerned to find that their data, even minimal data such as their name and address and the fact that they enquired about skiing holidays, were passed on to some other organization wishing to sell them say, accident insurance.

UK data protection legislation remains in a state of flux as the Data Protection Registrar and various large consumer organizations debate the rights and wrongs of collecting and using customer data. There is also the ever-present threat of EU-wide legislation that will surely be more stringent than current UK law. All direct marketers must keep a close eye on these actions as, whatever the fine details, we are likely to encounter more confining rules and regulations.

I am not convinced that, in the long term, a more stringent standard would necessarily be in the interests of the consumer – whatever the newspapers say, many people actually like to receive offers of goods and services through the

To opt in a customer must tick a box agreeing that he or she would like to receive information about other products and services.

To opt out the customer is obliged to tick the box if he or she does not want to receive such communications.

post and, increasingly even over the telephone. The eventual challenge for our industry may well be to find a way of getting them to be bothered to tell us this.

We know, for instance, that when we use an opt-out box we get 10–15% of respondents ticking it. Critics say that if it were more prominent, a greater number would tick the box, but again I am not really sure about this. People who feel strongly about something tend to find a way of letting their feelings be known, and I believe that the majority of people who are concerned are either not responding to direct response advertisements and mailings at all or ticking the opt-out box already.

Whatever the outcome of the debate, the use of individual data will continue to be the primary weapon in the direct marketer's armoury.

Where does direct marketing fit into marketing?

Marketing is the process of identifying customer needs and satisfying them in a way which is acceptable to both parties – customers feel that their needs have been recognized and fulfilled at a fair price; the supplier makes a fair profit.

Let's begin by defining marketing.

Marketing is the process of identifying customer needs and satisfying them in a way which is acceptable to both parties – customers feel that their needs have been recognized and fulfilled at a fair price; the supplier makes a fair profit.

According to Peter Drucker, the aim of marketing is 'to make selling superfluous; to know and understand the customer so well that the product or service fits . . . and sells itself'. This statement, written in 1973, is also a fairly accurate definition of the objective of direct marketing.

Collecting and applying customer and prospect data enables us to:

- identify customer needs and wants more precisely
- communicate our proposed solutions more cost-efficiently.

In other words, direct marketing can support all aspects of the marketing process. It is not an alternative to marketing, but an integral part of it. If there is a difference between the two, it is that marketing tends to focus at the broader market level whilst direct marketing is more tightly focused at the individual level. It achieves this by using sophisticated information management techniques.

These techniques, in turn, require the use of computer systems and software, and modern direct marketers allocate a high priority to the task of developing their marketing databases. Fortunately, the constant reduction in the cost of PCs and the more user-friendly modern software make it possible to run highly sophisticated databases and information systems on low-cost hardware and software.

There is a feeling amongst many small business managers that sophisticated marketing databases are only really appropriate for large companies. This is not true; indeed it is arguable that the smaller the company the more important it is for it to know the preferences and buying behaviour of its customers. Without such tight focus, a business cannot gain maximum value from a limited promotional budget. Marketing databases are discussed at length in Chapter 6.

Why is direct marketing growing?

In the past, many people were content to buy new, untried products and services, based only on the advice of a salesperson. Knowledgeable buyers were few and far between. Today's buyers are much better informed and much more selective. There are number of reasons for this.

1 Choice – in almost every field there are more options available and more competitive prices offered to customers.
2 More information available – this started with *Which?* magazine but now there are many magazines in both consumer and business markets, carrying articles and features comparing the strengths and weaknesses of products available. Few people today would choose a new PC without first buying a couple of magazines that carry product test reports and offer skilled advice.
3 Greater pressure on consumer budgets – although most households tend to have more disposable income than they did 20 years ago, there is a greater range of goods that are now considered 'essentials' – few people would consider a television set and video recorder a luxury today. Business-to-business marketers are also finding their customers are experiencing greater pressure on costs than ever before, causing buyers of all types to be more selective.

The old reliable 'unique selling proposition' (USP) or 'single minded proposition' is a bit out of step with this situation. The USP was designed to persuade large numbers of people to buy, or at least change their attitudes about a product or service – all of them for the same reason.

Nowadays, we can say with confidence that whilst large numbers of people may buy a product, they do not all do so for the same reasons.

However, whilst buying patterns and preferences have been changing, the major advances in technology mean that companies can now identify the real needs and motivations of diverse groups of customers, and fulfil those needs cost-efficiently.

This means that an organization can afford to split its customers and prospects into 'segments' with similar needs and develop differential communications to each segment.

Direct marketers have not abandoned the idea of the USP, we have simply adapted it to our equipment and techniques, so that we can now develop a whole series of selling propositions which closely match the real needs of our specific customer segments.

Does this mean the end of broadscale or general advertising?

This does not mean that press and broadcast advertising is on the way out. However, it does mean that, in future, its role is more likely to be concerned with identifying new prospects than selling to existing customers.

This does not mean that press and broadcast advertising is on the way out. However, it does mean that, in future, its role is more likely to be concerned with identifying new prospects than selling to existing customers.

Once we know a customer's name and address, there are few logical reasons for communicating by general advertising. It will often be more cost-effective and more powerful to use direct mail, the telephone and face-to-face communication.

Having said that, we must recognize the power of mass media to reassure people and thus underpin our targeted efforts. A company trying to sell a high-ticket product to a prospect may be hugely persuasive to the office manager, but if the financial director has never heard of the company the order may not be forthcoming.

Information – the driving force behind direct marketing

Marketers have always used market research and published information sources with the intention of gaining a greater understanding of customer needs, wants and motivations.

What is different about direct marketing is the ability to take this difference down to the level of the individual. This ability enables us to become customer-focused in a much truer sense.

It also enables us to 'de-select' prospects for whom an offer would not be appropriate. This is an aspect of direct marketing that is rarely publicized by the data protection lobby, yet it is a key objective of any sensible direct marketer. For example, why on earth would we want to send information about lawnmowers to people without a garden? The only things that prevent us from being much more targeted and selective are the shortage of data available to us or, in some cases, the rules preventing us from using such data.

Of course, if we are going to use individual data to plan and execute campaigns, we have a great responsibility. We must make sure that our information is as accurate and up-to-date as possible.

of times faster than their predecessors, still required specialist IT operators and were distinctly user-unfriendly.

How microprocessors have changed the direct marketing world

Today, even a stand-alone desktop PC can carry out highly sophisticated data processing at very high speed and very low cost. Since the PC was introduced to the UK in 1983, developments have been astonishing.

Table 1.2 Processing speed and capacity

Machine		Processing speed	Capacity
1983 first PC	=	1	10 megabytes
1992 series 486	=	100+	1 gigabyte
Current series (Pentium IV)	=	10,000+	40 + gigabytes

Reference to megabytes and gigabytes is not very helpful, of course. Let's just say that the Pentium IV PC in the table above, which today could be bought for less than £1000, could quite easily run a business system with a database of more than 50,000 customers, giving a very high level of data analysis capability.

In 1965, Gordon Moore, co-founder of Intel, the company that manufactures Pentium microprocessor chips, said that computer power roughly doubles every 18 months. From 'Moore's law', Kahn extrapolates that 'by 2020 microprocessors will likely be as cheap and plentiful as scrap paper'. Recent forecasts from Gordon Moore are available at the Intel Web site on www.intel.com/pressroom/archive/speeches.

To demonstrate the power of the PC, let's consider a data analysis and profiling bureau I use. Their entire system is operated on a network of Pentium PCs and their clients are major household names with, in some cases, massive databases.

They will routinely run analyses of the UK electoral register (44 million records) with great speed and accuracy.

However, the benefits of microprocessor systems are not confined to bureaux. There are numerous user-friendly systems that enable marketing managers to carry out, at their desks, the sort of analyses that hitherto would have required a coded request to the IT department, and a wait of 3 to 5 days for the report to be produced.

Having the customer records on a PC database with some basic analytical features enables us to manage, integrate and analyse several types of data:

- customer and prospect addresses, fax, e-mail and telephone details
- customer and prospect values
- product needs/usage
- identities of decision-makers and budget-holders
- contact history – what did we send them and when?
- results of promotions – how did they react?
- attitudes towards our company and products
- attitudes towards and usage of competitive products.

General market information can be combined with individual customer data to create powerful marketing information.

Data is gathered from various sources:

- questionnaire responses
- advertising and mailing response forms and Internet registration
- telemarketing and sales force reports
- external databases operated by companies such as Claritas and Dun & Bradstreet.

General market information can be combined with individual customer data to create powerful marketing information.

We will discuss databases in more detail in Chapter 6, but the following is a good example of the imaginative use of data.

Example

A large office products manufacturer spent a great deal of time collecting information about the buying habits of both customers and prospects. Sales and customer service teams were asked to find out which other suppliers their customers and prospects used, and for which products. Many employees could not see the point of this work. The company was reluctant to 'go public' on the reasons because they had a major strategic use for the data.

When the story eventually leaked out, due to personnel changing companies, it became apparent that this company had stolen a real march on its competitors by collecting and using this data.

They set up a small team of specialists in each of their three regional offices. These teams comprised a marketing executive with database skills; a telemarketer and a salesperson. In addition to serving as a back-up team for colleagues who were ill, they spent their time gathering and analysing data. They were in effect 'commandos' waiting for a call to action. A typical scenario would be as follows.

A call would come in from a person in field sales. For example, 'Company C has had to withdraw a product in the North East Region because of a technical fault'.

Immediately, the team would swing into action. The marketing executive would pull off details of all companies in that area who had 'C' in the 'competitive supplier' field. These prospects would immediately be sent a mailing – largely pre-written and ready to be laser printed and addressed. The mailing was simply a letter and catalogue of products in the appropriate field.

The telemarketer would follow up these letters within 3 days of despatch, making appointments with any interested prospects. The salesperson would go along and sell products – fulfilling demand created by the rival company who could not now deliver.

Information and measurement

The database is at the centre of marketing communications planning.

Marketing communications have four main purposes:

- to initiate a relationship (prospecting)
- to develop the relationship into a sales transaction (conversion)
- to maintain the relationship (loyalty building)
- to resurrect a lapsed relationship (re-activation).

The marketing database is essential for efficient management of these tasks. It enables us to identify the right names for a particular communication, according to their potential value and their propensity to be interested in this offer. It tells us the right time to send it; even the right form of words to use based on our knowledge of the interests of the individual.

A publisher discovered that when writing to prospects with a subscription offer, copy tended to work better if it was written in the style of a publication currently read by the prospect. He found, for example, that an *Economist* reader would react better to more erudite 'educated' copy, whilst someone whose main reading was a sports magazine would respond better to a simpler approach.

Example

The database helps us record and analyse our responses by segment and gives us the information we need to prioritize and target future communications.

Obviously, if we are to rely on our database, the information it contains must be accurate and up to date. Unless this is so, it can sometimes be worse than having no information at all.

The database helps us record and analyse our responses by segment and gives us the information we need to prioritize and target future communications.

We use the data to make management decisions. So, if the data is bad:

- it simply helps us make bad decisions more quickly
- it reduces the accuracy of our targeting
- it clouds our judgement when analysing the outcome of our actions.

Not all traditional marketers are comfortable with the 'benefits' of accurate data. Although, undoubtedly, it helps us to keep improving our skills and our results, it also puts our decision-making skills on the line for others to see.

However, such concerns are far outweighed by the benefits – having close control of our activities enables us to identify weaknesses much more quickly and to correct them before we spend all our budget. Thus, the database leads to more effective and more profitable campaigns.

Ask any experienced direct marketer whether they would like to go back to the days before the user-friendly database – not 1 in 1000 would say 'Yes'. The database helps us continually to improve, bringing greater job satisfaction in the process.

The database enables precise testing of alternative ideas before we commit large amounts of money. A word of warning here – not all tests will work nor find a new 'winner'. There is a cost penalty in buying information. The investment is usually worth it, however, because the chances are that sooner or later you will find a result which produces enough incremental profit to pay for all your previous tests.

Note that you should not wait until you are in trouble to start testing. You may be perfectly happy with your results, but could you do better? It is certainly tempting to avoid the effort of setting up test programmes if you are not under pressure, yet this is precisely the time you should be testing. Successful direct marketing companies test not to solve problems but to pre-empt them.

A delegate studying for the Institute of Direct Marketing's Diploma said:

All this talk about testing is very interesting, but it's not the real world, is it? In my company we don't test but simply use our intelligence to select the right list segments and offers. And we make plenty of money.

All this talk about testing is very interesting, but it's not the real world, is it? In my company we don't test but simply use our intelligence to select the right list segments and offers. And we make plenty of money.

The only answer to this sort of naive comment is to point out that without testing you really do not know whether you are getting as much response, or making as much money as you might.

Direct marketing consultant Roger Millington tells the story of a publisher client, who for several years had been using the same incentive offer to attract new subscribers. Roger tried for 3 years to persuade him to test a new idea, but the publisher steadfastly refused, saying, 'My ads and mailings are profitable, so why should I risk money trying to do better?'

Roger eventually persuaded him to test the new offer against his current one and the new offer produced twice as many recruits. The publisher rapidly switched all his advertisements to the new offer, but consider what might have happened had he run the test 3 years earlier. His advertising budget would have bought twice as much business and, given the economics of publishing, his profit from this programme would have more than doubled.

> Example

The power of integration

We all want to increase the responses we achieve from customers and prospects, but what is the secret? There are not too many golden rules in marketing, but one that does generally apply is that careful integration of your marketing activities will produce a disproportionately beneficial effect.

When all the components of a communications campaign come together at precisely the right time, their effect can be considerably greater than the sum of their parts. There are several examples of this throughout this book but here is a taster:

An insurance broker tested the integration of telephone with a cross-sell mailing he had sent to existing policyholders. The purpose of the mailing was to persuade existing motor policyholders to consider insuring their homes with him; and existing 'home' customers to insure their cars with him.

Within 3 days of mailing he had a response of 5% – which some might think is quite good, but he felt was poor! He asked two of his office staff to follow up the non-respondents by telephone during the evenings of the following week. After the telephone campaign, he analysed the results. Almost 50% of the people mailed and telephoned had agreed to his offer.

> Example

Although this result seems remarkable, in fact it is not unusual when using this technique of mailing followed up by a telephone call. Many other companies have experienced similar uplifts in response. However, in common with all 'new' techniques, the more it is used, the less effective it may become.

You may be wondering how we can be sure that the uplift was caused by the telephone call. The answer is 'controlled testing'. To measure the precise effects of such variations, we need to set up control samples and, although this is covered in detail in Chapter 11, the subject is introduced briefly here.

If we have enough names on our database we might set up a three-way test:

1 Sample 1 receives neither the mailing nor the telephone call (this is our control sample).
2 Sample 2 receives the mailing but not the telephone call – comparing this with Sample 1 tells us how successful the mailing is on its own.
3 Sample 3 receives the mailing and the telephone call.

This simple matrix will help us to evaluate all parts of the test.

Note that before you set up a similar test, you should read Chapter 11, pp. 243–50, which will help you understand how reliable your test results are.

Making marketing cost-efficient

To make marketing work cost-efficiently, we have to say the right things to the right people at the right time. What do we mean by this?

Saying the right things

People react well to information that is interesting and relevant to their current needs. We need to provide relevant information, but we must also deliver it in a suitable way.

Reaching the right people

We are not in the business of 'junk mail' or junk anything – our aim is to send only relevant messages. This means we need to know which of the people on our list will find this message relevant right now. This calls for information about our customers and prospects and expertise in analysing the information to enable us to select the right people for this specific message.

Selecting the right time

Timing is much underrated as a marketing tool. The following example is from the insurance business.

Example

A UK direct insurance company historically recruited new customers for its motor policies by using 'cold' direct mail. Cold mailings are those sent to external lists with whom you have neither a relationship nor any natural affinity.

Such mailings sent to simple lists of motorists without any additional data on which to make selections produced a very low response – well under 1%.

The same advertiser found he could rent names of motorists from a lifestyle database company, but this time with a powerful additional factor – the month they renew their car insurance.

He now mails only those motorists whose insurance is due for renewal within the following two months and his average response has increased to more than 5%.

The value of individual data

As we can see, when we have access to real data about individual customers and prospects we can be much more selective. The fact that I am a freelance marketing consultant working from home tells you a lot more about me than the fact that I live in a detached house. Knowing my occupation, you could reasonably assume that I have a modern PC with a good printer and expensive software. I am also likely to have a fax, a telephone answering machine, a laptop computer and so on (probably several thousand pounds worth of business equipment). This is useful to know if you sell home security systems for instance.

Having individual information, enables us to be selective about:

- whom we communicate with
- when we speak to them
- what we say to them – tone, offer, style and so on
- how we ask them to respond/react.

In other words, we can segment our customers and prospects into clusters with similar needs, problems and characteristics, and develop messages that address individual issues, with relevant information at the time when it will be most useful.

Customer profiling and segmentation

Direct marketing can be an expensive process. A direct mailing might cost 100 times as much per 'contact' as an advertising campaign in a newspaper. Why then is it being used more and more by today's marketers?

The answer is that with direct mailing, apart from the fact that we can be more confident that the prospect has actually seen our advertisement, we can target individual clusters or segments with highly specific messages, and avoid much of the wastage associated with broadscale advertising.

Thus, although our mailing 'cost per thousand' may be £500 or even £1000, compared to perhaps £7 to £10 for a newspaper advertisement, the percentage of *good* contacts made within that thousand is likely to be very much higher than with broader forms of advertising.

How can we decide who fits into which cluster? The answer is by analysis and profiling.

Customer analysis

We start by analysing our best customers. What sort of households or businesses are they, where are they, how much do they spend with us, when do they renew, and so on.

According to Pareto's principle (or the 80/20 rule), 80% of revenue or profit typically comes from just 20% of customers.

The direct marketer's objective is to identify that 20%, analyse or 'profile' them and then use that profile to target other customers or prospects who have similar characteristics. This subject is examined in detail in Chapter 5.

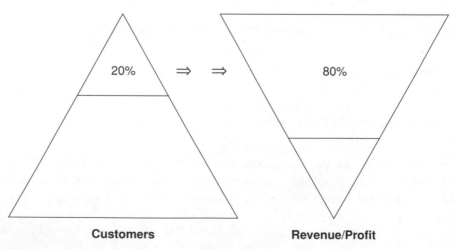

Figure 1.1   Pareto's Principle or the 80/20 Rule

What is junk mail?

Let's not fool ourselves, junk mail does exist. We see it every day in our homes and at work. We also see junk advertising and junk television commercials, but these do not invite the same level of criticism.

We do not need to go into the reasons why this is so. A better use of our time would be in getting rid of junk mail. How can we do this?

First, we must understand what junk mail is. Junk mail is not synonymous with direct mail, rather it is badly targeted, irrelevant direct mail.

The key to successful communication is relevance. Time after time research into the acceptability of direct mail comes up with the same finding, namely that direct mail is acceptable, even welcomed *providing the message is relevant*. As data is the key factor in achieving relevance, this emphasizes once again the crucial importance of the marketing database.

So direct marketing campaigns are designed to deliver the right message to the right person at the right time. As we saw earlier, integration of these elements will bring better returns, but without careful testing and measurement we will not achieve the optimum return on our investment.

Junk mail is not synonymous with direct mail, rather it is badly targeted, irrelevant direct mail.

How testing and measurement can make us more efficient

Every marketing activity we plan should be accompanied by a forecast of its results. We should then carefully measure the outcome against our forecast. This is easier in some cases than others, but it must always be attempted.

Direct response press advertisements will generally carry a code number on the reply form. If there is no reply form, we can use coded initials or names to identify the source of the enquiry. For example, in a test of three papers we could ask interested enquirers to telephone or write to:

- *Evening News*, Edward Jones
- *Weekly Gazette & Herald*, George Jones
- *Wiltshire Monthly*, William Jones.

Alternatively, telephone enquirers might be asked 'Where did you see our telephone number?' Having such information means that the next time we run an advertisement we can place it in the publication that is likely to deliver the best return for our investment.

Many organizations spend their marketing budgets according to habit, for example: 'We advertise in the *Echo* because we have always done so.' This is not a sound basis on which to build a business. Every marketing activity should be based on the likely return it is expected to achieve.

The marketing communications plan

This is the basis for achieving forecasts, by maximizing business from the most profitable customer groups and, thus, optimizing resources. The main driver of the plan is the budget.

The budget:

- identifies costs and expected profits associated with each activity
- lets us compare forecast with actual performance
- helps us decide between alternative strategies by predicting the business each will create.

Budgeting is covered in detail in Chapter 12.

SUMMARY

The budget:

- **identifies costs and expected profits associated with each activity**
- **lets us compare forecast with actual performance**
- **helps us decide between alternative strategies by predicting the business each will create.**

This chapter has explored the evolution of direct marketing. We have seen that whilst there have been recent changes in technology, the basic principles of direct marketing remain unchanged. Indeed, many of the new technology companies that have gone out of business may have survived if they had focused their minds and budgets on direct marketing principles. We have explored the benefits that IBM enjoyed from a commitment to direct marketing under Lou Gerstner.

This was followed by a definition of direct marketing and an exploration of direct marketing's links with traditional marketing. We have seen that direct marketing delivers the promise of marketing more effectively by focusing on individual behaviour and response. We have looked at the issues of data protection and privacy and the fact that trust between customer and company is crucial to the maintenance of the relationship.

We have explored the reasons for direct marketing's growth over the last decade, including the enormous changes in technology (most notably the increase in the processing power and capacity of PCs described by Gordon Moore of Intel). This was allied to changes in customer behaviour with choice, more information and ease of price comparison shown as fundamental.

It is clear that direct marketing depends on good data and information. We have looked at the various sources of information, including our own response files, and have explored the role of market research and its applications. Several examples were given of how companies use direct marketing information and marketing research to produce very effective direct marketing strategies.

The chapter went on to look at the role of the customer database and the links to the marketing communications planning process. We have seen that the process is central to the initiation, development, maintenance and resurrection of the customer relationship. We have seen the need for good and accurate data and have explored briefly the role of testing to produce efficient and effective marketing activity in terms of individual activity and equally in terms of the integration of direct marketing activity, for example the optimum combination of telephone and mail.

The chapter finished with an exploration of the communications process, looking at customer profiling and segmentation and analysis and the streaming of the right messages to the right people at the right time and to budget.

REVIEW QUESTIONS

1   Define direct marketing. What are its links to traditional marketing?

2   What are the key differences between direct and traditional marketing?

3   What are the reasons for the growth of direct marketing? How has IBM benefited from the use of a direct approach to customers?

4   What is Moore's law?

5   Explain briefly the role of information in the delivery of direct marketing.

6   What is the contribution of market research to the direct marketing process?

7   What were described as the two major barriers to the introduction of customer databases?

8   List five major applications of the customer databases.

9   What are the four key objectives of marketing communications?

10   Why do direct marketers test?

11   What is Pareto's principle and how is it used in customer analysis?

12   What is junk mail?

13   What are the three benefits of budgeting in marketing communications planning?

EXERCISES

Throughout the book I will draw on experiences in my career as a direct marketing specialist. It will be very useful for you to start your own case file.

To start this process, I would like you to collect three or four direct response advertisements from the press or from magazines. Follow their call to action; ring the call centre or follow the drive to Web. Make notes about the fulfilment process and the level of interaction allowed on the Web site. How competent were the call centre staff? This file of best practice (or even a rogues' gallery) will prove invaluable throughout your career.

Try to find examples for a range of industries and include consumer and business-to-business markets.

Chapter 2

Developing a direct marketing campaign

Introduction
- The campaign planning process
  - Specify the objective
  - One stage or two?
  - Identify the target audience and where to find them
  - Select the general communications approach
  - Decide on the best timing
  - Produce an outline creative plan
  - Book media
  - Produce the advertising material
  - Prepare to handle the response
  - Deliver the message
  - Record the details for measurement and evaluation
  - Acquisition or retention?
Summary
Review questions
Exercises

INTRODUCTION

In this chapter we will consider the planning of direct marketing campaigns, looking at each stage of the development process. However, before we can start to plan a campaign, we need to decide on our main priorities. Do we want to build the business we have with our existing customers or find new prospects and convert them into customers? The answer will often be 'both', but we need to get the balance right and to prioritize each phase of the plan.

The campaign planning process

The process of developing a campaign is quite straightforward. The essential steps are as follows.

Specify the objective

Ask yourself why you are running the campaign. Is it to:

- encourage enquiries from new prospects
- convert previous enquirers
- persuade previous customers to buy again
- sell more of the same products to existing customers (up-selling)
- sell additional products or services to existing customers (cross-selling)?

Clearly, each of the above objectives will require a range of strategies, some unique to the specific objective. Direct marketing objectives should always be quantified and have specific times allocated to them. Without this, progress cannot be measured.

We must make sure objectives are SMART.

We must make sure objectives are SMART.

- Specific – an objective is like a grid reference on a map; if it is not specific we will not know when we have achieved it.
- Measurable – we need not only a quantity, but also a time for achievement.
- Achievable – the classic version of the SMART mnemonic has 'achievable' here, but I prefer to use 'aspirational', believing that achievable and realistic are broadly the same thing. This version also makes people try harder in my opinion.
- Realistic – whilst giving people something to aim for, an objective must always be realistic, otherwise it can be counter-productive.
- Timed – as mentioned above, without a time attached there is no basis for measurement.

If a plan is to work, objectives should be clearly stated and communicated to all concerned.

One stage or two?

If we are writing to existing customers, we may well be able to achieve a sale or commitment from a single mailing – a one-stage process. The objective here might be 'to achieve 200 orders from our existing customers by the end of Q1 at a marketing cost per order of no more than £10'.

If, on the other hand, we are approaching entirely new prospects the process may be more complicated – a sensible objective here may be to persuade them to send for further information or to agree to a no-obligation trial. This is called two-stage marketing.

The objective here could be 'to achieve 500 enquiries by the end of Q2 from the subscriber list of *Personnel Manager Today* at a marketing cost of £15 per lead'.

We may then have a secondary objective relating to sales, which is 'to convert 25% of these enquiries into sales by the end of Q3'.

Identify the target audience and where to find them

- Who do we want to communicate with?
- Where are they?
- What is the best way of locating them? Do we have their names and addresses? Are they already on our database? Does someone else have a list available? We may be able to find other businesses that are targeting the same sort of people but not selling a competitive product. Can we reach them through advertisements in specialist media? For example, software manufacturers often locate prospects through advertisements in computer magazines or via Web sites.

The answers to these questions will help us decide how targeted the initial approach can be.

Select the general communications approach

You can select from broadscale media advertising, such as:

- television and radio
- Web sites or banner advertisements
- national newspapers and magazines

If we are writing to existing customers, we may well be able to achieve a sale or commitment from a single mailing – a one-stage process.

If, on the other hand, we are approaching entirely new prospects the process may be more complicated – a sensible objective here may be to persuade them to send for further information or to agree to a no-obligation trial. This is called two-stage marketing.

- specialist publications
- outdoor advertising, such as posters and bus sides.

Alternatively, you could choose from targeted communications, such as:

- direct mail
- e-mail
- door-to-door leaflet distribution
- telephone
- personal visits.

There could be a combination of broadscale and targeted communications.

Decide on the best timing

Next, we must spend some time establishing the correct timing for each individual prospect. If we know the right time, it is easier to make a highly specific approach – it is also more likely to be productive. For example, marketing of toys to the retail trade takes place in January or February. All parents will know that August to December is the time the retailers target their prospects.

In business-to-business marketing, a very productive time for marketing is at year-end, when very often there is budget available for discretionary activity.

Timing can also be important at the micro level (see the example of the insurance broker in Chapter 1 at p. 15). The timing of complementary messages can be tested and planned to achieve optimum response.

Produce an outline creative plan

Having decided on the right media and timing, we can now start to gather information, think up offers, and so on in preparation for writing copy or briefing an outside creative team.

Book media

- Book the advertising space – now we can talk to our agency or media owners direct about any help, advice or special deals they can offer.
- Assemble the mailing list – if this campaign is being organized in-house, we will input addresses into the computer to enable a mail merge with our letters. Alternatively, we may brief external suppliers to do this work.

Produce the advertising material

We must brief suppliers on:

- design and copy-writing where relevant
- artwork if necessary
- the ordering of additional supplies (such as envelopes)
- management of print, assembly and postage.

We must remember to include a way for prospects to respond. Ideally, we should offer them a choice, for example a coupon and reply-paid envelope, telephone and fax numbers, e-mail address and Web site details if there is one and it will be relevant to our prospects.

Prepare to handle the response

If we are asking people to send for more information, we will need to estimate how much response to expect. We can then produce enough 'response packs' to satisfy demand.

It is important to avoid keeping people waiting. This is a good rule in any circumstances, but it is vital when responding to enquiries. Prospects may have sent for details of two or three alternatives – the first one to respond has a better chance of getting the business.

When generating leads for follow up, speed is equally important. Leads should be passed directly to the sales or telemarketing people with any supporting information, for example what the respondent asked for, any special requests and so on. Salespeople may acknowledge the lead by telephone when making an appointment, but if this cannot be done promptly a written acknowledgement is advisable.

Deliver the message

Run the advertisement or send the mailing.

Record the details for measurement and evaluation

Future campaigns will be easier to plan, and more likely to succeed, if they are based on previous experience. The best approach is to develop a 'guard book' or computer 'guard file'. The book version is a large binder containing actual copies of each advertisement and mailing with details of costs, responses and, where relevant, conversions.

Of course, the details recorded will vary according to the activity, for example advertisement, mailing or telephone follow-up campaign. We can also

The best approach is to develop a 'guard book' or computer 'guard file'. The book version is a large binder containing actual copies of each advertisement and mailing with details of costs, responses and, where relevant, conversions.

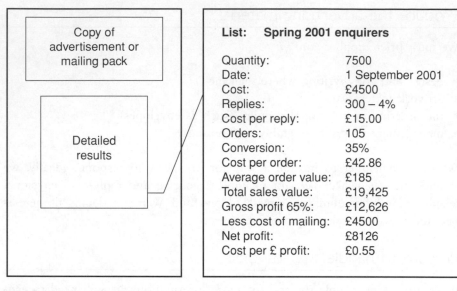

Figure 2.1 The Guard File

add in other costs such as sales-force time. The example shows a calculation of 'cost per £ profit'. Some prefer to use a ratio of cost to sales revenue – the choice is yours. Whatever you decide, the important thing is to have a basis for comparing results and selecting the best, most cost-effective, approaches for redeployment in future campaigns.

In addition to its historic importance, the guard book is a useful short-term measure to help in making tactical decisions such as selecting the right media, creative approaches, offers and so on, as the campaign progresses. It is essential that promotions be measured over the longer term too. See Chapter 12.

Note that with a scanner or digital camera you can develop a computer guard file that is an electronic guard book. Personally, I prefer the old-fashioned 'hard copy', as there is little 'touch and feel' about the computer version.

It can also be useful to put the results into a spreadsheet programme, such as Excel. This makes it easier to analyse results data and convert it into summaries and charts for presentation to colleagues.

Acquisition or retention?

A crucial question when planning a campaign is 'Should we concentrate on developing existing customers or locating new ones?' The answer will vary from one business to another and there are two further questions to be answered.

1 How well developed are our present customers, in other words how many of them are open to buy more or additional products?
2 How long can we afford to wait before we make a profit on a new customer? Do we have sufficient funding and sufficient confidence in our ability to retain customers to wait for a year or more to turn a new customer into profit? (See Chapter 3.)

The second question is the key to finding the balance between acquisition and retention strategies. If we can afford to wait for profit, we can clearly allocate more margin to promotions and, thus, recruit more new customers by making them a better offer.

There is another consideration in finding the correct balance, namely the actual cost of buying new customers. Research studies in the UK and the United States have shown that the cost of obtaining a 'conquest' sale (one from a new prospect) is between three and thirty times as much as the cost of achieving a repeat or renewal.

This means that, whatever we decide about the balance of the business, and however much time and money we devote to gaining new customers, we must first of all concentrate on maximizing the business we develop from existing and former customers.

The correct sequence of allocating the promotional budget is as follows.

This means that, whatever we decide about the balance of the business, and however much time and money we devote to gaining new customers, we must first of all concentrate on maximizing the business we develop from existing and former customers.

- Existing customers first – given the above cost factors it is essential that we concentrate first on retaining and developing existing customers before we start to allocate promotional funds to locating new prospects.
- Existing enquirers next – the second best source of business will be people with whom we already have a relationship, however slight. These people have already expressed an interest and they will always yield a better return per £ than any outside list of new prospects or any new advertising campaign. In this category we would also include people who used to buy from us but no longer do so. Unless they stopped buying because of a major problem the chances are that, sooner or later, they will look to change from their new supplier. A timely reminder may successfully resurrect a previously good relationship.
- New business last – note that I am not suggesting that getting new business is unimportant. I am simply stating that the best return on investment will come from promotions to existing contacts. Therefore, it makes sense to exhaust all possibilities of additional or renewal business from these before starting on the much riskier business of seeking entirely new customers. It is always worth taking any opportunity to build the prospect list by ensuring that any enquiries are recorded and not simply replied to and discarded.

It will be seen from the above that new business generation should be viewed as an investment – one which will pay back in the longer term rather than in the immediate future. In deciding on the optimum point of profit we will need to consider the following.

- Funding – do we have the financial resources to wait for profit?
- Competition – how much competition is there in this field? How strong is it in terms of price and offer?
- Development potential – what additional products do we have which could be cross-sold to the same customer, in other words, what is the potential for developing more business once we have sold them their first product?
- The promise – will our product or service live up to the promises we made? Will our customers feel they have been given good value for money when they come to consider repurchase? It is always easy to increase response to a prospect offer by lowering the price or increasing the incentive. However, if this raises unrealistic expectations we may find that future sales are disappointing.
- Level of service – can we afford to maintain or even increase our level of service to existing customers? What is our current retention percentage, in other words, how many customers continue to buy from us year after year?

There have been numerous recent studies into customer retention and loyalty and all have reached the same conclusion – many customers change suppliers because their existing one did not care enough about them. But how much is enough?

Customer satisfaction is clearly not enough these days. Studies show that whilst expressing satisfaction with a supplier, a large percentage of customers would happily shop elsewhere.

| Example | An electrical company reported that whilst 80% of customers stated they were quite satisfied with the present level of service, 70% said they would certainly consider using another supplier. In another study, a car manufacturer found that of all customers who changed to an alternative car, only 10% were dissatisfied. |

Customers today are more demanding and have a greater range of options to choose from than ever before. Today, therefore, customer satisfaction is the starting point not the objective: The objective should be customer delight.

How can this be achieved? Many studies show that it is added value that makes the difference.

Previously, a grocer would offer added value in his daily contacts with customers – popping in a couple of extra carrots after weighing and pricing your order; offering a little extra which stuck in the customer's mind because it was something 'he did not need to do'. Such an approach builds strong customer loyalty because it says, loud and clear 'I value your business'.

You should spend some time thinking about things you could do to increase your satisfaction rating in the perception of your own customers. Chapter 3 discusses ways in which we can develop relationships with customers and so increase their loyalty.

SUMMARY

This chapter has explored the processes involved in developing a direct marketing campaign. We have identified that we must first develop a clear understanding of the priorities of the business.

A ten-stage process was presented, covering the following elements:

1 setting objectives
2 identifying the target audience
3 media selection
4 timing
5 outlining the creative plan
6 booking media
7 producing communications material
8 response handling
9 delivering the message
10 measurement and evaluation.

We have discussed the need to make our objectives SMART (specific, measurable, aspirational (or achievable), realistic and timed).

The chapter has considered the need to identify and locate the target audience, including the use of bought-in lists.

Media options were discussed in relation to the characteristics of the target audience and the reach and impact of each medium.

We have looked at the importance of timing and recognizing the role of the intermediary in the selling process.

The process of communications development examined the production of the creative plan, booking of media and crucially preparing to fulfil any response. We discussed the importance of campaign measurement and evaluation and looked at the creation of the guard book.

The crucial question of the balance between acquisition and retention was discussed. The cost of acquiring customers was seen as a crucial factor in understanding the source of profit within a company.

The sequence of allocation of the marketing budget was discussed and we looked at the most profitable source of business, namely our existing customers. We then moved to existing enquirers and finally to new business as generally the most expensive source of business. In many cases, customers become more profitable over time and the conclusion was therefore that our aim should be to optimize profitability over time. We have seen that our ability to do this is dependent on our financial resources, the state of competition, our capacity to create value from the relationship through up-selling and cross-selling, and our ability to maintain customer satisfaction through ongoing customer service.

Finally, the issue of customer satisfaction through added value was discussed in relation to the retention of customers.

REVIEW QUESTIONS

1 What does the acronym SMART stand for?

2 List five objectives for a direct marketing campaign.

3 List the decision we must make when identifying our target market.

4 List two broadscale media and two targeted media.

5 List the four stages in the production of communications material.

6 What is the guard file? Why is it advisable to run a print version of this control mechanism?

7 Why is it important to target existing customers first?

8 Describe the sequence of allocating marketing communications budget.

9 What factors must we consider when deciding the optimum point of profit?

10 What is added value?

EXERCISES

List three companies you would recommend to friends or family. Why are you happy with their service? How do they provide you with satisfaction? What are the characteristics of these companies and how do they deliver added value?

Now list three companies with which you are dissatisfied. What has created this dissatisfaction?

What can you learn from this process?

Now think about your own company, or a company with which you are familiar. What factors would increase the satisfaction levels of your existing customers?

Chapter 3

Taking the long-term view

Introduction
- Developing and managing customer relationships
  - Customer retention is the key
- Back to your database
- What makes customers loyal?
- What do customers value in a relationship?
- Effect of reducing customer losses on new business requirements
- Customer life cycles
- Complainants may turn out to be your best friends
  - Customer satisfaction surveys
- Relationship marketing
- Customer communications
- Recovering your investment in retention marketing
  - Classification of customers
  - Segment analysis
  - Programme streaming
  - Communications planning
  - Testing and evaluating
- Two general rules for building loyalty
  - Develop dialogue
  - Make your database work for you
- Some basic loyalty techniques
  - Welcome
  - Dialogue
  - Helplines
  - Newsletters
  - Gifts and rewards
  - Timing of communications
  - Questionnaires
  - Extra value proposition
Summary
Review questions
Exercises

This chapter discusses the various ways in which you can develop relationships with your customers and so increase their loyalty. It is important to remember that loyalty is two way – you cannot treat your customers with disdain and expect unswerving loyalty in return.

Nowadays, loyalty campaigns alone are not enough to ensure continued success. The product must be right and the price must be considered reasonable – you do not need to be the cheapest, but if you are not you must work hard to make your customer feel that your service is worth the extra cost.

In other words, you must offer good value for money.

Developing and managing customer relationships

Today's successful companies seek a continuing relationship with their customers, not one based on occasional transactions. Of course, the costs of such an approach need careful management, but the objective must be to encourage the customer to enter into an ongoing relationship and, where possible, to extend this across several products and services.

Moving from a purely product-based approach enables you to communicate wider values to your customers – values related to style, ethos, service standards and attitude. Adopting such a customer-focused strategy enables you to maximize the lifetime value of each customer by anticipating needs and offering timely solutions. This involves a shift in emphasis in measuring success. Many companies have traditionally been preoccupied with making sales to new customers. As we have seen, this is not always the ideal approach when planning to build a business profitably.

Customer retention is the key

The enlightened company prefers to measure success by customer retention. Gaining a new customer is a considerable achievement, but it is only half the story. The profit comes from developing a relationship that leads to repeat or regular purchases, which are achieved at a lower marketing cost than the initial transaction.

Customer retention is not the only benefit of developing customer relationships. Many customers would be prepared to buy more than one type of product from a supplier they trust and cross-selling is cheaper and, therefore, more profitable than conquest selling.

The enlightened company prefers to measure success by customer retention. Gaining a new customer is a considerable achievement, but it is only half the story. The profit comes from developing a relationship that leads to repeat or regular purchases, which are achieved at a lower marketing cost than the initial transaction.

Existing customers can also exert a powerful influence over potential customers; they compare experiences regarding product satisfaction and customer service.

This is not to suggest that customer acquisition is not important; merely that customer development and retention are absolutely crucial. As I mentioned earlier, the greater the long-term customer value, the more you can afford to spend to acquire the customer in the first place.

Example

One large office equipment company places such high value on customer development that their sales and marketing managers' annual bonuses are largely based on the following two questions.

1 Of the customers you had a year ago, how many are still buying from you today?

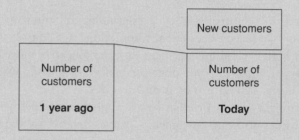

Figure 3.1
Measuring rate of customer retention

This measures the retention or renewal rate of customers. The more shallow the decline, the more valuable is the new business gained.

However, customer development is not just about retention. It is also important to grow existing customers. So the second question is as follows.

2 Compare the average value per customer now with that of the same group a year ago. How much has it grown?

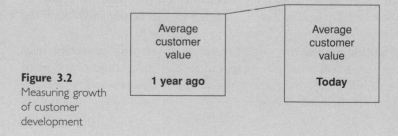

Figure 3.2
Measuring growth of customer development

Back to your database

Developing customers requires a differential approach. Not all customers will require the same information, nor will they respond to the same messages. Of course, the ideal timing will also vary for each customer.

Establishing differential customer development plans can be difficult and time consuming, unless the database can be made to do most of the work. Your database enables you to manage your customers in segments – based on customer type, amount of business, size of company, potential value or other factors, and to build a unique customer retention and development plan for each segment. It also enables you to measure the success of each plan precisely.

For each customer segment, you should develop a plan containing:

- forecasts of new product sales (cross-selling potential)
- forecasts of upgrade sales (up-selling potential)
- detailed action plans for exploiting these opportunities.

Careful database analysis can make it easier to study acquisition and retention by type of customer, value bands and so on. Databases are discussed in detail in Chapter 6.

Developing customers requires a differential approach. Not all customers will require the same information, nor will they respond to the same messages. Of course, the ideal timing will also vary for each customer.

What makes customers loyal?

1   Although loyalty is measured by behaviour it is really about customer attitudes. Recognizing loyalty can be difficult. Continued purchase tells you that customers are not unhappy, but by the time you have noticed that they have stopped buying it can often be too late to solve the problem. It is necessary to find a way of measuring customer attitudes before normal purchasing time, which of course varies from customer to customer.

2   You cannot keep track of customer attitudes without regular contact and feedback. Without direct feedback, you cannot hope to understand customer needs, attitudes and intentions.

3   Loyalty is not a one-way system. All of marketing consists of a two-way exchange between company and customer. Before you can expect loyalty you must offer it yourself. This means that, as discussed in Chapter 2, you must be prepared to 'go the extra yard' where necessary.

4   Loyalty cannot be developed by marketing communications alone. Every aspect of your business is a factor in building loyalty, from enquiry taking to delivery and after sales service – even a follow-up for non-payment must be made with courtesy and care.

5   It is impossible to develop customer loyalty without committed staff who share the objective of 'customer delight'. Loyalty and commitment of staff at all levels is a base requirement for developing and maintaining customer loyalty. Promises must be fulfilled; added value must be volunteered at every opportunity.

6   Customer loyalty is the logical outcome of caring about and delivering solutions for customer needs. 'Loyalty' obtained with discounts and incentives is very fragile and can easily be bought by competitors.

A loyalty programme is a continuing thing – a long-term commitment of time and resources.

A word of caution: you cannot go into this in the short term only. A loyalty programme is a continuing thing – a long-term commitment of time and resources. So, before you take the plunge, stand back and consider the following pertinent questions.

1   Have you quantified the benefits of investing in a loyalty programme? You need to calculate your present and potential customer retention rates in order to forecast the likely return on your investment. If you do not have the information or the experience to do this, you should consider testing your programme to a small discrete segment of customers.

2   Have you researched existing levels of customer satisfaction? You may already have a very high level of satisfaction and retention. If so, do not expect to achieve huge additional gains – you are already doing a lot of things right. If, on the other hand, your satisfaction ratings are very low, you may need more than a loyalty programme to put things right.

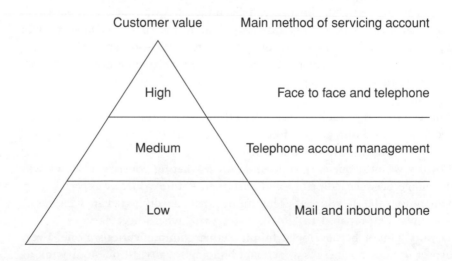

Figure 3.3   Tailoring communication to customer value

3 Have you defined the service requirements of your customers? Not all customers will require the same levels of service. Your objective is to allocate your resources in the most cost-efficient way. For example, try to segment your customers as shown in Figure 3.3.

Segmenting customers in this way enables you to use your resources in the most cost-effective way. Companies that have adopted this approach report that many customers who have transferred to telephone account management actually prefer it, as they can be sure that their contact is always available when they have a query.

Telephone account management implies a full service with regular communications from you to your customer. Low-value customers are dealt with solely by mail with the telephone available to them for queries – you would not generally make calls to these customers, except for specific promotional campaigns, research purposes and trouble-shooting.

4 Do you know what will improve your customers' loyalty and how this can be delivered cost-efficiently? You may be able to determine this from your customer satisfaction surveys. Alternatively, you may need to undertake wider research. Marketing research is discussed in Chapter 4.

5 Can you offer *genuine* benefits to your customers? Remember, these must be real benefits in the eyes of your customers. See the following list and the note about newsletters on p. 51.

Telephone account management implies a full service with regular communications from you to your customer. Low-value customers are dealt with solely by mail with the telephone available to them for queries – you would not generally make calls to these customers, except for specific promotional campaigns, research purposes and trouble-shooting.

What do customers value in a relationship?

When customers are asked to identify the factors that make them value a supplier, they generally list the following attributes.

- Good products at fair prices – not all customers seek the lowest prices. Many people realise that, at least to a certain extent, 'you get what you pay for'.
- Convenience and ease of access – they want to be able to get hold of you quickly and easily, especially when they have a problem. The 'take two aspirins and call me in the morning' approach is a sure way to lose customers.
- Effective and fast problem-solving – a quick sympathetic response to customers' queries and complaints is very important. Handling a customer's problem may be a routine, even boring, task to you, but that problem could be the most worrying experience of your customer's life.
- Privileged status as a *known* customer – they like to be recognized when they call.
- Appropriate contact and communication – they do not want to be bombarded with irrelevant mailings and telephone calls.

Happy customers tell their friends about the company, pay less attention to competitive offers, and also tend to be more receptive to offers of additional products.

- Anticipation of their needs – some call this being 'pro-active'. Whatever it is called, it is a key aspect of customer management.
- Professional friendly dialogue – all many customers want is the opportunity to discuss things with someone knowledgeable.

Happy customers tell their friends about the company, pay less attention to competitive offers, and also tend to be more receptive to offers of additional products.

Effect of reducing customer losses on new business requirements

Every business loses a percentage of its customers every year. Some of these losses are unavoidable, yet many could be avoided with better customer management. Let us suppose that you have 500 customers and your 7-year business plan requires you to grow your customer strength by 10% each year.

Your targets are indicated in Table 3.1. Let us see what the difference is in your recruitment targets between a customer retention rate of 70% and one of 85%.

As this table shows, if you can improve your customer retention by 15%, your marketing budget needs to buy 711 fewer recruits. If an average new customer costs you £75 to recruit, this represents a reduction of £53,325, which could pay for quite a lot of customer retention marketing with some left over to boost your profits.

Looking at this from the opposite point of view, losing an additional 15% of customers increases your recruitment requirement by 60%, which is a massive additional burden on your marketing budget.

Table 3.1 The impact of increased retention on new business requirements

	Now	Year 1	Year 2	Year 3	Year 4	Year 5	Year 6	Year 7	Cum. total
Customer strength required	500	550	605	666	732	805	886	974	–
New customers needed if 70% retained	–	200	220	242	266	293	322	354	1897
New customers needed if 85% retained	–	125	137	152	166	183	202	221	1186
Difference	–	75	83	90	100	110	120	133	711

Customer life cycles

Research across many markets indicates that customers have natural life cycles, just as products and complete industries have life cycles. Also some companies cease trading, in which case a customer 'life' may be determined by the effective life of that customer's company.

Research also tells us that many customer relationships are cut short without achieving their natural lifespan. A crisis or competitive intervention may be sufficient to break a productive relationship. For example, a study published in the 1980s showed that the natural lifespan of a transatlantic frequent business flyer relationship is about 5 years, after which the individual gets promoted or changes jobs. However, the study also showed that the customer might defect prematurely when the relationship reaches 'a moment of truth' and the airline does not recognize this, or fails to respond appropriately.

Such 'moments of truth' occur in all business relationships. Some may be predictable and so it may then be possible to anticipate and overcome them by delivering timely customer care messages.

A customer satisfaction survey carried out by an international airline identified the dangers of customer dissatisfaction over and above the business lost. It discovered that whereas a happy customer would tell four people about the airline, an unhappy customer would tell seventeen.

Example

Complainants may turn out to be your best friends

Many well-known companies report that former complainants generally turn out to be very good customers. It seems that a customer who complains is actually trying to let you know that they really would value the relationship if only you would recognize their problems and try to solve them. So it is vital to give your customers a channel to let you know when they are unhappy, *at the time of dissatisfaction*. Many companies run customer satisfaction surveys to a sample of their file and whilst this can be a valuable gauge of service and delivery levels it will not highlight specific cases of dissatisfaction.

If you positively encourage all customers to let you know their concerns, there will be two main effects:

- you will have a pile of complaints to deal with, some of which can be turned into future selling opportunities

- you will pick up cases of dissatisfaction at an early stage, when it is still relatively easy to put them right and this will help you increase customer retention.

There are really no infallible rules about customer retention. However, there are some general factors that apply to most situations:

1 The customer retention rate is the most decisive influence on marketing cost (as we have seen from the earlier example on p. 40). Remember that it costs most companies much more to replace a customer than to retain one.
2 Customer satisfaction can be measured through customer surveys. Many customers are quite willing, even keen, to tell you how to get it right.
3 The causes of customer losses can be established. A follow-up call to a lost customer can be an excellent investment. Not only will many of them tell you why they changed suppliers, a good telephone manner will encourage them to consider you favourably again, when their new supplier disappoints them in some way. This is a vital point. Existing satisfied customers cannot tell you why others are dissatisfied.
4 There is a strong correlation between absence of dialogue and customer loss rate. Much of the adverse feedback concerns the fact that companies give the impression that they do not want to know about customer problems and opinions. Simply keeping in touch can make a major difference to customers' willingness to repurchase. Consider the example from a major insurance company given in Table 3.2.

It can be difficult to measure the precise effect of a single marketing communication on customer attitudes, and it is necessary to analyse the strength of relationships continuously.

It can be difficult to measure the precise effect of a single marketing communication on customer attitudes, and it is necessary to analyse the strength of relationships continuously.

Table 3.2 The effect of contact frequency on retention rates

	Number of contacts in year	Retention rate (%)
All customers	0	63
	1	74
	2	80
	3	82
	4+	84
New customers	0	43
	4+	82

It may be possible, through customer surveys, to recognize critical points in the relationship (the 'moments of truth' mentioned earlier) which call for specific communications.

Customer satisfaction surveys

When researching customer satisfaction, an increasing number of businesses are approaching their entire customer file instead of just a sample.

There are two reasons why this is a good idea:

1 complaints can be picked up at a very early level – as we discussed earlier (p. 41), it is much easier to resolve a small concern than one which has been 'festering' for a long time
2 customers appreciate being asked – indications are that simply sending out a satisfaction survey can engender positive attitudes amongst customers.

The use of two-way marketing communications plays a valuable part in building and measuring the customer's view of the relationship. But why wait until you send out a survey? Every time you contact a customer you have the opportunity to encourage dialogue.

If you want your regular communications to help you build loyalty you must make sure that they are relevant to your customers. To make them relevant, ensure that every communication:

1 is useful and interesting to customers – they do not want to be told how successful or clever you are (it is amazing how often this mistake is made)
2 involves them – encourage them to reply; ask them to tell you what they think about your service and what they need from you that you are not supplying
3 helps them to get better value from you – offer useful advice on how they can get the most out of your relationship
4 is consistent – advertising, direct mail, telephone contacts and customer service people must all tell the same story.

The communications programmes described above are often called 'dialogue' or 'relationship marketing'. The aim of relationship marketing is not just to make customers think you are a good supplier. Your aim should be to make your customers value their relationship with you to the extent that they would not normally consider any other supplier.

Relationship marketing

The communications programmes described above are often called 'dialogue' or 'relationship marketing'. The aim of relationship marketing is not just to make customers think you are a good supplier. Your aim should be to make your customers value their relationship with you to the extent that they would not normally consider any other supplier.

The relationship marketing idea suggests that all customer touch points must be managed for customer delight. This means that relationship marketing places far more emphasis on the management of the networks of suppliers who impact on customers. It recognizes that a customer's view of a product is formed by a variety of influences not all directly controlled by the company.

The relationship marketing idea suggests that all customer touch points must be managed for customer delight. This means that relationship marketing places far more emphasis on the management of the networks of suppliers who impact on customers. It recognizes that a customer's view of a product is formed by a variety of influences not all directly controlled by the company.

Of course, you will not be able to lock in every customer for life, but this is not necessarily a bad thing. Building and maintaining strong relationships costs time and money and not all your customers will merit the extra investment.

The key is to identify those whose loyalty will repay the additional investment and concentrate your efforts there.

Providing added value to your customers can further strengthen the bond.

With added value, the objective is to make customers think 'They didn't need to do that'.

Example

I recently ordered some new business cards from Kall Kwik. When I collected my order, the manager gave me a booklet entitled 'Cash Management'. This was written specifically for small businesses by a well-known firm of accountants and funded by Kall Kwik. Although I am very happy with the advice of my existing accountant I was still very impressed that Kall Kwik should provide this entirely free of charge.

Such a booklet could be mailed or handed to your customers; mailed to prospects or offered as a premium in return for a sale or an enquiry.

Customer communications

There are two broad types of marketing communication:

1 customer care communication (or relationship-building communication)
2 sales-orientated communication – which is designed to sell or at least to initiate a selling process by generating leads.

Sales-orientated communication – is designed to sell or at least to initiate a selling process by generating leads.

Sometimes it is possible to combine these so that:

* customer care communications give customers the *opportunity* to send for sales information, although the sales content would be very 'soft sell'
* selling messages include a customer care content.

Where such combinations are possible, you can make your budgets work harder, but it is vital that you do not jeopardize the main purpose of each communication by trying to do too much.

Another key factor in relationship programmes is timing – the best customer care programmes are time-sensitive. Being sensitive to customer needs and buying cycles can make your promotional mailings much more productive.

Time-sensitive communications (or series programmes) are timed to coincide with critical customer life stages or 'moments of truth'. Therefore, the messages go to different customers at different times.

For example, a 'welcome' message may go to a new customer very soon after their first purchase. Another message may be timed to arrive shortly before they could be expected to re-order. The important point is that these communications should be timed according to the customer's requirements, and not to fit in with your sales or planning cycles.

You will also want to consider how your messages are delivered. Some selling messages may be better delivered face to face, whereas customer care messages will more usually be delivered by mail and/or telephone.

Finally, you will want to consider who should receive each message. In selling to consumers this may not be so important, but with business customers there may be differences between the ideal distribution of customer care and selling messages.

Although there may be one key decision-maker in a business, there may well be others who can block future orders.

One of the key advantages of direct marketing communications is their ability to deliver appropriate messages to each member of the decision-making chain. Messages can be varied whilst maintaining a consistency of style and tone.

The precise effects of a customer relationship programme are not so easy to measure in the short term. However, retention marketing is cheaper than customer acquisition. One never wants to lose a good customer, but as long as you are retaining a high percentage you are probably doing well in comparison with your competitors. In the 1980s, Price Waterhouse found in a survey that a 2% increase in customer retention is equivalent to a 10% reduction in costs.

> **Time-sensitive communications (or series programmes) are timed to coincide with critical customer life stages or 'moments of truth'. Therefore, the messages go to different customers at different times.**

> **It is vital to segment your customers and to target your retention marketing at those who have the propensity to repay your investment.**

Recovering your investment in retention marketing

Retention programmes cost money to develop and maintain. As mentioned earlier, they will not be cost-effective for every customer. It is vital to segment your customers and to target your retention marketing at those who have the propensity to repay your investment.

The five key stages in developing retention and loyalty are as follows.

Classification of customers

The first step is to segment your customers into categories, such as:

- business and consumer (where you serve both)
- high and low value
- percentage of their annual expenditure you already receive (share of customer)
- single and multi-product purchasing patterns
- payment performance
- lapsed customers – split into 'time since last order' bands
- property type – where relevant
- possessions (for example, for consumers it might be cars and other luxury goods and for businesses it might be type of equipment installed).

There are no fixed rules. You must apply your own segmentation according to the specific circumstances in your business.

Segment analysis

Here you will be concerned with the potential value of each type of customer. You should consider:

- profiles of those in each segment
- customer needs and expectations, and the costs of servicing their business
- potential lifetime value
- expected re-purchase rates
- acquisition costs and potential payback periods.

Programme streaming

The idea is to vary your investment level according to the segment analyses carried out above. You should also vary your strategy – what will be appropriate for one segment may be totally inappropriate for another.

Communications planning

Your objective should be a continuing programme of communications running through the following stages:

- welcome
- up-sell
- cross-sell
- prevention of dormancy and where this fails
- reactivation.

Testing and evaluating

If you have a large enough customer file, testing will answer many questions (see Chapter 11 for more information). However, even where testing is viable, you may also find it valuable to carry out some marketing research. Marketing research is discussed in Chapter 4.

Not all customers can be made loyal. It is a matter of basic character – some customers tend to be loyal (subject to good service, of course); others tend to be fickle or 'promiscuous' shoppers.

Research by one of the UK's largest direct marketing agencies indicates that, although still difficult, it may be easier to attract the loyal customers of another company than to change the basic attitudes of one's own fickle customers. This does not necessarily mean that it is a waste of time to try to build customer loyalty, simply that it will take a very strong bond to totally remove the chance of a customer being attracted to another supplier.

Two general rules for building loyalty

Develop dialogue

- Questionnaires can identify present and future needs, levels of satisfaction with products, service, delivery, and so on and generate warm feelings amongst your customers.
- Regular communication programmes, including welcome letters, special offers and incentives where relevant, can help you build good relationships.
- 'Personalized' communications are appreciated, but make sure it is true personalization and make sure the personalization is correct.
- Knowledge gained from such feedback can help you develop products, services, events and occasions which are valued by customers and prospects.

Make your database work for you

- Your database enables you to send effective, timely and appropriate communications.
- Tracking recency, volume and order details identifies cross-selling and up-selling opportunities, and incentive allocation where appropriate.

- Fast fulfilment of requests and orders builds customer confidence and satisfaction.
- Instant access to customer information enables you to deliver real personal service.

Some basic loyalty techniques

Welcome

Numerous researches have shown that welcoming new customers has a measurable effect on the level of renewals and repurchase. One major car manufacturer noted an increase in repurchase of 23% as a result of its welcome sequence.

Example

A major UK bank tested two ways of welcoming new customers:

- Control group: no welcome activity
- Group A: welcome letter
- Group B: same letter as Group A, but followed by a telephone call.

The customers were measured on their payment performance and repeat purchase of loan and/or investment products.

Although detailed results are confidential, the bank reported that over a 3-year period, customers in Group A performed better than those in the Control group, but Group B customers 'significantly out-performed those in the other two groups'.

The value of the 'welcome' stage is clearly recognized by many charities, which find this an effective opportunity to 'upgrade' new supporters.

Example

I recently sent a donation to the NSPCC and within 2 weeks I received a simple 'Thank you' letter from the Chief Executive, followed by an upgrade letter from the Appeals Manager.

The letter from the Appeals Manager said, in three simple paragraphs:

1 thank you again.
2 here is some more information (reassuring me that my money is being put to good use).

3 I hope to persuade you to think about other ways you can help us.

They enclosed a form for me to sign up for a regular donation, but they also say they plan to telephone me 'shortly' to talk about it. They pre-empt the possibility that I might see this as unwelcome by giving me a form to return to say I do not wish to be called.

I do not know the results of this programme but I am sure it works very well.

Dialogue

Customers want to tell you when they are happy and when they are not. Making this process simple and friendly increases the level of dialogue between you and your customers. It also increases the number of complaints. Most of all it increases renewal and repurchase.

Developing the relationship across more than one product is in itself beneficial to retention.

Another well-known bank compiled a study into customer retention. It showed the following odds of a customer changing banks:

Example

Table 3.3 Effect of share of customer on retention rates

Accounts held	Odds against changing
Current account only	Evens
Savings only	2 : 1
Savings and current	10 : 1
Savings, current and loan	18 : 1
4 accounts	100 : 1

This example demonstrates the increased grip one has on a customer by extending the business across more than one product line. This tends to hold true in most businesses and it highlights the benefits of cross-selling.

So, selling additional products to a customer not only increases your revenue, it also locks in your customer more strongly.

Helplines

These are generally beneficial, but are especially significant in a field where customers are apt to be confused by jargon and technical detail. Sadly, many helplines are not very helpful. I find this particularly so in the field of finance as the following experience demonstrates.

Example

I telephoned a company that had previously financed a computer lease for me to ask if it could do the same for my new machine. The young man wanted to show me how much he knew about finance and launched into a description of the several different ways in which the deal could be financed. I interrupted gently to tell him that I did not really want to know all the technical details, but simply ask 'Can you finance the deal?' He took immediate umbrage and said, 'Well if that's your attitude, thank you for your call' and hung up. Clearly, a man in the wrong job! Needless to say, I found another supplier.

Software suppliers usually offer helplines, but I find two main problems with these. First, they tend to take a long time to answer, although whether this is due to staffing levels or the fact that most queries take a long time to answer I am not sure. Second, they are often staffed by 'nerds'. Whilst I appreciate that it takes a 'techie' to answer a technical question, these people do not seem to grasp that if I telephone with a question it is because I do not understand the intricacies of computer speak. They usually manage to make me feel that I am completely stupid. I think some training in 'user-friendliness' would be helpful here.

Example

A good example of the helpline is that set up in the mid 1980s by Nestlé in France to advise mothers of young babies about health and nutrition. The company reported that this and other similar customer focused initiatives has enabled them to increase their share of the very competitive baby food market from 26% to 43%.

The telephone should not just be considered as an 'inbound' tool however. Calls made to customers to see if they are happy are sometimes called 'cuddle calls'. A brief call, asking, 'Is everything all right? Do you have any problems?' can work wonders for customer loyalty. You can also be lucky and achieve a major gain as the following example shows.

A small computer retailer in Belfast delivered a new laser printer to a customer. One week later the marketing executive telephoned the customer to ask if everything was OK. The customer replied, 'Well the printer is fine, but we are not sure if our carpet will ever recover'.

Apparently, when loading the printer with toner, there was a major spillage and their cream carpet ended up with a large black stain on it.

The marketing executive sent round a firm of cleaners who lifted, cleaned and refitted the carpet. This cost around twice as much as the profit on the laser printer and she was in trouble with her sales manager.

Not for long, however, because the customer was so impressed that he telephoned the television station that ran a feature on the computer retailer with the message 'If it's customer service you are looking for, this is the company to buy from'. Since then business has never been so good!

> **Example**

Newsletters

These have their place, but they are often misused. Customers do not want to read about your luxurious new offices, they want to know how to get more out of the product they bought from you. Make sure your 'news' is of interest to them not just to the employees of your company.

The European subsidiary of a large international company opened a huge new warehouse on the Continent. This cost more than US$4 million and, naturally, it was very proud of this facility. The head office marketing department produced a newsletter announcing the new facility under the headline: 'New US$4 million warehouse now open – most modern in Europe.'

> **Example**

Before it mailed this, the UK marketing department asked my opinion. 'Burn it' was my response. My reason for this wasteful advice was that the company already had a reputation for high prices (and for very high quality products it must be said). What was not needed was something that might cause customers to say, 'That's why they are so expensive'.

What was needed was a headline that demonstrated a benefit for the customers. After some discussion with the operations director, we eventually came up with the crucial fact that the greater efficiencies of the warehouse would reduce the average delivery time of 5 days to 3 days. Now we had a headline: 'New warehouse reduces delivery times by 40%.' Not surprisingly, this had greater customer appeal.

So, although it must be prepared with care, a good newsletter can have a major impact on a customer's attitude towards you. It can also have a powerful impact on sales.

<table>
<tr><td>Example</td><td>In the 1990s, the Marketing Director of Heinz UK said that the newsletters it was sending to its customers generated a sales increase of 3% – a huge shift for an FMCG company. Of course, it is important to ensure that costs are controlled so that any gains made are achieved cost-efficiently, and Heinz has since dramatically reduced this programme.</td></tr>
</table>

Gifts and rewards

These have their place, but remember that a customer who can be bought by a gift can be bought by someone else offering a better gift. Try to think of gifts as a 'Thank you' rather than a 'Please'. Several studies in the last 20 years have shown that, whilst short-term customer behaviour can be changed by rewards, once the rewards stop, buying behaviour often reverts to its original pattern.

Some studies suggest that if you are able to offer a gift that is relevant to your product, there is a better chance of a longer-term attitude change.

Third-party offers

Third-party offers are where you are able to offer something funded or part-funded by a third party. For example, you may be able to do a deal with your local theatre and offer seats at a special discount to selected customers. Such offers are a chance to give your customers a special extra value opportunity.

Third-party offers are where you are able to offer something funded or part-funded by a third party. For example, you may be able to do a deal with your local theatre and offer seats at a special discount to selected customers. Such offers are a chance to give your customers a special extra value opportunity.

There are currently numerous offers of free weekend breaks at hotels. Many customers are becoming suspicious of such offers as they usually require the participant to buy meals in the hotel restaurant. Of course, the accommodation is free so the offer is genuine. However, if you had not intended to go away for a weekend, it still represents a cost to you.

So if your offer is a genuine no-strings attached discount, make sure you say so, loud and clear.

Timing of communications

Time communications to suit your customers not your sales department. Remember that customers buy according to their time cycles not yours. Do not mail all your customers at the same time because it is convenient to you.

Relevance relates to timing as well as to content. Phasing your mailings in this way also eases the load on your call centre, enabling it to give a better service too.

A related point concerns ad hoc communications. If you can send people some information that is appropriate to them, they will appreciate this far more than a stock mailing.

An alternative to the 'cuddle call' mentioned earlier (p. 50) is the 'love letter'. This is a similar approach, but by mail. Of course, you cannot afford to overdo this. Your customers will not appreciate being bombarded with such notes.

Questionnaires

As mentioned earlier, customers appreciate being asked, complaints are identified early and products and services can be developed which are exactly what customers need.

Extra value proposition

The extra value proposition (EVP) or added value item (such as the booklet on cash management given away by Kall Kwik) can be hugely beneficial in retaining business.

SUMMARY

This chapter has looked at the value of customers to the company over time. We have seen that loyalty is a 'two-way system' – loyalty to customers generates loyalty from customers. We have seen that profit comes from customers who transact with the company over time and that levels of profitability generally increase over time. That said, all companies need to acquire customers. However, a balance between acquisition and retention is required and the greater the customer value over time, the more we can afford to acquire them in the first place.

In managing this process, the database provides us with an invaluable tool, segmenting customers and helping identify plans to develop these segments.

We have explored the six factors to consider when developing customer loyalty:

1 explore attitudes as well as behaviour
2 communicate on a regular basis
3 be loyal to your loyal customers

4 all customer touch points should be managed to foster loyalty
5 highly motivated staff are vital to the delivery of customer satisfaction
6 loyalty must be deeper than a response to price discounts.

We have seen that there has to be a long-term approach to the development of loyalty. There are five questions to ask.

1 What quantified benefits accrue to the organization through the introduction of a loyalty programme?
2 What are existing levels of satisfaction?
3 What are the service requirements of your customers?
4 How can you deliver loyalty cost-efficiently?
5 What genuine benefits can you offer your customers?

The chapter has explored the aspects that customers value in a relationship and how providing these and retaining more customers can have a significant effect on profitability.

The value of encouraging complaints has been identified as a key source of feedback on your activities. High levels of customer satisfaction will not always lead to loyalty, but they are a good indicator of potential. We have seen that the process of measuring customer satisfaction is crucial for four reasons:

1   retention is the key to profitability
2   customers will tell you what they want
3   the causes of defection can be established
4   the absence of dialogue can cause dissatisfaction.

The key to the process is to make each communication consistent, relevant and involving, with the potential always to add value to the relationship.

The five-stage process of establishing a retention programme was given as:

1 classification of customers
2 segment analysis
3 programme streaming
4 communications planning
5 testing and evaluation.

We have seen the importance of the database driving appropriate timely interaction with our best customers.

Finally, the chapter has explored some simple but effective devices for encouraging and developing loyalty.

1   Where does profit come from? Describe the contribution of retained customer to cost revenues and profit.

2   Describe the role of the database in evolving a retention strategy.

3   List six factors that make customers loyal.

4   What are the five things a company should do before investing in a loyalty programme?

5   What do customers value in a relationship with a company?

6   Why should companies encourage complaints?

7   What are the five stages of a retention programme?

8   Why is it important to encourage dialogue with customers?

9   Discuss the importance of measuring customers' satisfaction levels.

10   What are the two types of customer communications?

11   According to Price Waterhouse, a 2% increase in retention will reduce cost by how much?

12   What are the five elements of the communications planning process in delivery of a retention programme?

13   List and critically assess five loyalty building techniques.

EXERCISES

Consider the five stages of communications planning in delivery of a retention programme. Gather and analyse marketing material which you think attempts to deliver against each of the five stages. How effective do you think they are in encouraging loyalty?

Explore how the retention process might work in each of the following businesses:

- a small car dealership
- a large pharmaceutical company
- a marketing consultancy.

What are the differences and similarities in establishing loyalty across these sectors?

Chapter 4

Collecting customer information

Introduction
- What information do you need?
  - Consumers
  - Lifestyle data
  - Business-to-business information
- How to obtain the information
  - Collecting information from existing customers
  - Gathering information through external research
  - Using the Internet for information gathering
  - Warnings about gathering information via research

Summary

Review questions

Exercises

One of the main benefits of gathering customer information is that it enables you to segment customers into groups of a similar kind. Database analysis will help you select those segments that are more likely to buy or buy additional products. It will also highlight those less likely to buy, and enable you to quantify the potential from each segment.

INTRODUCTION

As discussed in Chapter 1, direct marketing relies for its success on the collection and application of information. Without detailed information, we are not able to focus on the right customer groups or segments, and without this focus we cannot take advantage of the power of direct communications.

This chapter will discuss:

- the types of information you should gather about your customers and prospects
- the sources and methods of obtaining such data.

You may be wondering how, with costs already so high and margins under threat, you can afford to develop a more sophisticated marketing system. Can you afford to increase the frequency of customer communications? First, you cannot afford not to. If you do not do all you can to lock in your customers, a competitor may lure them away. Second, you do not need to communicate with all customers in the same way or with the same frequency. Third, by focusing on specific segments, with highly relevant offers, you will increase your return on investment, despite perhaps spending more on the overall programme.

Example

A UK bank used to send around 70 promotional mailings a year to its customers. Return on investment was adequate, but not exciting. In 1999 the bank sent almost 400 mailings, each to a carefully selected segment of the customer base. This programme increased the cost per customer contact but generated more than 200% increase in return on investment.

One of the main benefits of gathering customer information is that it enables you to segment customers into groups of a similar kind. Database analysis will help you select those segments that are more likely to buy or buy additional products. It will also highlight those less likely to buy, and enable you to quantify the potential from each segment.

You can then focus your main additional marketing efforts on those who will provide the greatest return on the investment.

What information do you need?

First, we will consider what customer information might be useful to you and then discuss how you can get hold of it. Chapter 5 will look at some ways in which you may be able to use the data you have gathered.

Consumers

- Name and address – the obvious starting place. It is vital to have accurate complete details here.
- Transactional information – this is what products they have bought from you, what they enquired about and what you offered them in the past.
- How long have they been a customer? The longer you have had them, the more chance you have of retaining their business.
- Property type – there are a number of these systems (such as ACORN and MOSAIC) and you will find further details in Chapter 5. Property type can be a very useful indicator for lots of products. Its main limitation is that it deals with properties rather than people and it relies on the premise that people who live in the same types of house will have the same needs, wants and buying characteristics. Whilst this may be broadly true, you only have to compare yourself with your next-door neighbour to see that it is a huge generalization. Property type indicators would be quite accurate in identifying high and low value areas – they are less good at identifying the characteristics of individual occupants. There are other property descriptors that may also be helpful, for example do they have a garage, is the property detached, semi-detached or terraced and is there a garden?
- Household composition – this is the number of adults, the number of children and their relationships to each other. It is often important to know the ages of the various occupants.

Transactional information – this is what products they have bought from you, what they enquired about and what you offered them in the past.

Household composition – this is the number of adults, the number of children and their relationships to each other.

Lifestyle data

Although geodemographic systems such as ACORN and MOSAIC can be very useful in broad targeting and evaluation of customer types, they are limited by the fact that they do not deal with individuals.

Psychographic or 'lifestyle' data, on the other hand, is about individuals. Its limitation is that not all UK households are represented on the various lifestyle databases.

Collectively, the various lifestyle companies now have detailed volunteered questionnaire information on up to 40% of UK adults. There are many duplicates across the various lifestyle databases, but Claritas (the largest UK practitioner) now claims to have detailed information on more than 75% of UK households.

This information covers details of products preferred across a wide range of consumer areas from holidays to toothpaste and cars to insurance. These databases also contain information on age, income, occupation and so on.

The lifestyle companies have worked in partnership with other organizations such as the Henley Centre to produce some very sophisticated profiling techniques (for more on profiling see Chapter 5 and pp. 126–7).

Business-to-business information

The above classifications relate to consumers, but similar information is available for business-to-business marketing using classifications such as the following.

- Business type (perhaps by industry code) – it is often productive to segment businesses into industry types.
- Company size, including the number of employees and/or the size of the turnover. Clearly, this could be a highly relevant factor for certain products and services. A car fleet supplier would obviously want to segment a prospect file based on the number of employees, or ideally on the number of employees with company cars.
- Age – in this case, the age of the business. Although it may not seem relevant, it is in fact very important, as the following example demonstrates.

Example

One major marketer, in a search for new business prospects, studied its most recent new customers analysing the significance of 30 different business factors. These included turnover, assets, number of employees and industry type. The most significant factor in identifying propensity to purchase was 'number of years since founded'.

The company was able to identify a clear relationship indicating that when a business reached a certain age customers were much more likely to be interested in their products.

A business database can be enriched with a wide variety of additional information such as sales per employee, growth rate and so on.

How to obtain the information

Information can be sourced:

1 internally, that is by asking your existing customers and prospects via the sales force or by telephone or postal questionnaire if you do not yet have a database (if you have a database, your information gathering will start here)

2 externally, that is from sources such as the register of electors, lifestyle databases, credit reference houses and business information brokers (such as Dun & Bradstreet and Experian), rented databases (mailing lists), advertisements and leaflet drops; data is also available from industry studies and omnibus surveys

3 through original marketing research – using a range of techniques that will be discussed later in this chapter.

Collecting information from existing customers

Train employees to gather information at every opportunity

Every employee must understand the power of up-to-date information and be encouraged (preferably), coerced, or if necessary forced to gather data at every opportunity.

When a customer telephones (almost regardless of the reason for the call), you should try to complete the missing fields in your database. Most customers, when approached politely, are prepared to give basic information about their circumstances, their properties, the number of cars they own and similar details.

This is so important that many successful companies incentivize their employees to ensure that this happens.

Specific questionnaires

Have you ever asked your customers, formally, what they think about your service? How many do you think would respond to a printed questionnaire – 5%, 10%, 25% or more?

It may be surprising to learn that many companies receive more than 50% response to a customer questionnaire. Of course, to achieve such high levels of response your survey must be 'customer focused' – that is, asking questions which are seen to be relevant and giving good reasons why you would like to have the information.

Many companies use additional 'sweeteners' to encourage people to respond and there is no doubt that these can work. However, you may not wish to pay for hundreds of free gifts, nor to provide a prize for a free draw.

Fortunately, it is not absolutely necessary to do these things to generate a good response.

In face-to-face and telephone research the interviewer relies on skill and charm to persuade the respondent to participate. The intended respondent does not know what questions are in store and a mini relationship is developed during the interview. In this way a skilled questioner can elicit a remarkable amount of sensitive information, even information about personal hygiene and sexual matters.

However, it is not possible to develop the relationship so cautiously in print. With printed questionnaires, recipients tend to read the whole thing before deciding whether to fill it in. So how can you persuade more people to fill in your questionnaire?

One of the most effective techniques is to find a way of making the questionnaire more interesting and relevant to the recipient. If you can identify some specific interest of an individual, you may be able to use this.

An oil company is planning to send a questionnaire to a file of company car drivers to discover their opinions of the standards of service at your stations. It could build in a question or two that would be of specific interest to them such as:

Example

From time to time, the oil industry has an opportunity to give motor manufacturers its views on the additional safety and security features which have been developed for cars recently. To make sure we take account of your own views, would you mind giving us a few moments to complete the following section?

Please tick the box that most closely reflects your view.

All new cars should now be fitted with:

	Agree strongly	Agree	Neither agree nor disagree	Disagree	Disagree strongly
Air bags for driver and front passenger	☐	☐	☐	☐	☐
Anti-lock Braking Systems (ABS)	☐	☐	☐	☐	☐

Figure 4.1 Questionnaire design

Although such questions may have little bearing on the main information being sought, they can increase response to a survey by 20–25%. This may sound surprising, but it is simply the application of one of the basic rules of communication, namely make it interesting and more people will read and react to it.

When designing a questionnaire, consider the following points.

1 Make it easy. Do not ask people to spend a long time writing out answers. You should give as many pre-printed options as you can, asking respondents to simply tick the box that is closest to their view, like the example above. It is also a good idea to leave a line or two at the end of each question for that small percentage who feel so strongly about something that they wish to write some additional comments. Such comments cannot easily be quantified for analysis, but can be noted and reported for further action where necessary. This is also an excellent source of testimonials.
2 Make it relevant by using special interest questions (like the example above).
3 Promise a benefit. For businesses, it might be a copy of the outline findings. Often you can promise a general benefit, such as: 'Your answers will enable us to provide you with a better service, more closely aligned with your needs.'
4 Do not make it too glossy. It should look like a research document, not a promotional leaflet.
5 Give clear instructions where necessary. Do not leave anything to chance. Give worked examples for more complex questions.
6 Break it up, with prominent section headings where necessary.
7 Do not cram it the questions. Large type and plenty of white space will make it look easier to fill in – this means more people will do so.
8 Leave room for discretion. If you are asking for personal information such as a person's age, some may be reticent to complete the questionnaire. Rather than deterring them from returning the questionnaire, reassure them that you would still like to hear from them, even if there are certain questions they cannot or do not wish to answer.

Have you tried to profile your own customers? Perhaps not, because of the general lack of data in most databases. However, as we know, direct marketing succeeds because it helps to eliminate wastage by focusing on the individuals or segments with the most potential. Profiling and data analysis is one of the ways in which this wastage can be identified.

Have you tried to profile your own customers? Perhaps not, because of the general lack of data in most databases. However, as we know, direct marketing succeeds because it helps to eliminate wastage by focusing on the individuals or segments with the most potential. Profiling and data analysis is one of the ways in which this wastage can be identified.

Gathering information through external research

Traditionally, direct marketers have ignored marketing research, believing that their testing programmes provided all the information necessary. This view has slowly changed but there are still many diehards who cling to the view that research is money wasted.

The following are just some of the ways a direct marketer could use research.

1 To learn about customers – their needs, wants and buying patterns, and who else they buy from and why.
2 To group customer by typology, for example organized/disorganized; sophisticated tastes/simple tastes; and older and affluent/younger aspiring.
3 To measure attitudes towards the company and its products – research can help us measure those things beyond raw response data, for example did our mailing make people think differently about us?
4 To find out what positioning we have achieved in the market place – a company may want to be thought of as the 'Rolls Royce of services', but if its customers and prospects think of it as a Fiesta, it needs to know.
5 To identify prospects – that is people or companies having the same needs or inclinations as our best customers.
6 To understand buying processes and decision-making – especially in business-to-business marketing.
7 In planning campaigns, business development, new products, pricing and so on.
8 To identify trends in the market place – good planners need to stay ahead or at least abreast of what is happening out there.
9 To monitor competitors and their marketing activities.
10 To refine communications – ensuring that people understand and relate to what we say.
11 To measure the effectiveness of non-response activities. Although it is easy to count responses and even to measure the quality of those responses, some communications are designed to change attitudes rather than attract replies. The only way of measuring their effectiveness is research.

There are broadly two kinds of marketing research – desk research and original research.

Desk research

Desk research or secondary research is that which is already available – you simply have to locate it and read it. Some is available free of charge, other studies can be subscribed to.

Desk research or secondary research is that which is already available – you simply have to locate it and read it. Some is available free of charge, other studies can be subscribed to.

Industry statistics

Although these are not always of much practical use to an individual business, they can help to explain trends. They include:

- trade associations often produce periodic high level market analyses
- stockbroker reports can also be very useful
- independent companies produce annual analyses of DTI returns for various industry sectors; you will see these quoted in the trade press relating to your own industry, and you will often be able to buy all or part of one of these reports
- DTI returns are available either direct from a company or from Companies House; a company's annual reports and accounts often contain commentary/statistics on the broader industry involved
- various market research companies (such as Mintel, Market Assessment and Keynote, Datamonitor) produce annual reports on various industry sectors.

Public domain data

In addition to individual company and industry sector reports, there is much general information available from the government and most of this is free of charge or reasonably priced. The Office of National Statistics publishes a catalogue of all its publications – these include:

- Family Expenditure Survey
- General Household Survey
- The National Food Survey.

Eurostat, the statistical service of the European Union, also publishes a vast array of data for member countries. Much of this is now accessible online.

Other government reports provide information regarding populations and household compositions by area and major conurbation.

Register of electors

The annual electoral roll is published every February and is available for viewing at your local authority headquarters. There is likely to be a charge made, especially if you want to make copies of any data, depending on the policy of your local authority.

An alternative, and more user-friendly source of electoral roll data is one of the main data supply companies such as Experian (owners of MOSAIC) and CACI (who ACORN run). (See Chapter 14 for their contact details.) Such companies can supply information on tape or CD-Rom for quite a modest cost.

Companies House records

When looking for information about businesses, Companies House is a good source. However, its records contain simple raw data that is not always very user-friendly. Commercial companies such as Dun & Bradstreet, Market Location and others offer the same data but in a more tailored format. Keep an eye on Companies House, however, as it has recently become much more alert to commercial opportunities. (For contact details see Chapter 14.)

Rented mailing lists

There are approximately 6000 consumer and business lists available to rent in the UK. All can be selected by postcode so it is possible to select names and addresses down to quite a small area. You can find more information about rented lists in Chapter 13.

Original research

Original (or primary) research is that which you can do yourself. Original research has two broad classifications – quantitative and qualitative. Quantitative research asks and hopes to answer the questions 'How much?' or 'How many'. Qualitative research asks the question 'Why?' and explores, for example, the deeper reasons behind the customer's purchase of a particular brand.

The database can provide a lot of data on what customers do – what they buy and when and to which promotional messages they respond. What the database will not tell us is why they behave in this way. The use of qualitative research in direct marketing can add a great deal to understanding of customers.

The weakness of the database, of course, is that we know this information about our existing customers only. The use of marketing research can help put the database in context.

Not all businesses can afford to commission large industry-wide surveys, but the customer and prospect questionnaires discussed earlier are examples of original research.

Build your own mailing lists

Not all businesses want huge mailing lists, and if your requirements are quite specific, you may want to consider building or locating your own lists. The possibilities include the following.

- Direct response advertising – you can often generate quite large numbers of enquiries in this way. Chapters 7–9 include many ways of ensuring good response from advertising.

> Original (or primary) research is that which you can do yourself. Original research has two broad classifications – quantitative and qualitative. Quantitative research asks and hopes to answer the questions 'How much?' or 'How many'. Qualitative research asks the question 'Why?' and explores, for example, the deeper reasons behind the customer's purchase of a particular brand.

- Loose inserts – despite what critics say, inserts will generally produce more replies than display advertisements. Look at how many major direct response advertisers use them. They measure results very carefully and only repeat what works well for them.
- Localized insert campaigns – even small advertisers can use inserts. Many local newspapers and 'freesheets' accept inserts and they are usually very cost-effective. Some national newspapers now offer the facility to insert leaflets down to the level of a local wholesaler – making national newspaper insert campaigns available to local advertisers.
- Door-to-door distribution of leaflets – this is a realistic way of gathering prospect details. You cannot select specific households, but you can choose streets or areas containing the sort of properties you would like to reach.
- Telephone directories – these are more useful for business addresses of course. Note that some publishers now print copyright warnings in their directories, stating that the names and addresses may not be used for mailing purposes. Take the advice of your solicitor before copying any directory listings into your computer.
- Members of clubs/associations – you could try to organize a PI deal with them. A PI deal is a US term standing for 'per inquiry'. You arrange to pay the mailing list providers a small amount, say £1 for every reply you get from your mailing. Some national publishers and television stations accept these deals, so there is no reason why clubs and associations would not. Naturally, they would expect to have sight of your mailing material and a right to refuse permission if it does not meet with their approval.
- Previous customers (unless you had some sort of disagreement with them). They may have left you because they were offered a better deal. If their new supplier is not able to match the introductory deal, or their service is not so good as yours, these people may be prepared to come back to you.
- Existing customers – many businesses have great success with what are called member get member offers. Member get member (MGM) offers are also called 'referral offers', 'friend get a friend' and 'recommend a friend' schemes. The basic premise is that people's friends have similar lifestyles and, therefore, similar needs for products and services. This certainly holds true in the mail order industry, where such a scheme can be a very good source of new prospects. Furthermore, the new names tend to convert better and pay better than the average new prospect. Many business-to-business marketers also find this technique works well.

Using the Internet for information gathering

Many of the techniques described above can be managed or at least started online through the use of the Internet.

Most secondary sources of data from government statistics to the services of Claritas and Dun & Bradstreet are available online and can be accessed remotely. Certainly, almost all list brokers can be contacted via their Web sites and most allow the online construction of list selections.

Online businesses have a real advantage in collecting customer information as the use of cookies (a device which allows a site provider to recognize the browser's machine), allows them to track buyer progress through a Web site.

They can also use online surveys to measure many things, including customer satisfaction with the site. For example, Dell has a pop-up rating scale, allowing customers to rate the page.

The use of e-mail surveys to gain information, rather like the fax a generation ago, is currently achieving very high response rates, although this might fall as consumers become more concerned with the effects of unsolicited e-mail communication (sometimes called 'spam').

The Internet is not a panacea for information gathering, but it does allow access to a vast range of published data and to certain groups of customers particularly in business-to-business markets. A key point in consumer markets is that the penetration of Internet in the home is still relatively low at around 40% of households and this is skewed towards the middle-class affluent market. It may be appropriate to use if this is your target market, but it is not suitable for all products.

Warnings about gathering information via research

Data protection

The 1998 Data Protection Act is more rigorous in the way that data is held and used. It puts into law the idea of informed consent and transparency. If you are in any doubt consult the Data Protection Registrar or get legal advice.

Statistical reliability

If you are using research simply to add information to your database, most of the above techniques can be used safely. However, if you want to use it to give you a clear picture of the state of a market place with a view to making accurate forecasts of likely take-up for a new product or offer, for example, you must enlist specialist help and be fully aware of the need to assess sample sizes and statistical validity.

Your own in-house research or planning department might well be able to help. If not, a useful starting point is the Market Research Society (contact details are provided in Chapter 14), which publishes a list of member organizations free of charge. All members of the Society must abide by a rigorous code of conduct.

Marketing research is a minefield for the uninitiated, and sometimes even for those who should know better. Beware of industry publications telling you things such as 'Average response to direct mailings in the UK in 1996 was 8%'. This may be true, based on the samples polled in the study concerned, but it can be highly misleading. Not having such a high average with my own mailings, I investigated this study and discovered that the 'average' was made up of:

- two insurance company mailings producing around 1%
- one publisher's mailing that achieved 5%
- two financial services mailings generating 3.5%
- one mailing for a major soft drinks brand offering free drinks vouchers to teenagers that generated 52% response.

The researcher had simply accumulated all these results and reached the impressive average of 8%!

So, beware of such statistics, unless the report gives details of how the figure was arrived at. The Direct Mail Information Service publishes figures annually and, to emphasize the above point, it not only publishes details of the number of mailings incorporated into the study, but also shows averages in total and separately with the especially large responses removed. This gives a much clearer picture, although you should still be very wary of assuming that your own mailings would generate similar responses.

In 1999, another nameless industry 'research' study quoted: '60% of UK businesses are "millennium ready".' This study was carried out amongst thirty businesses in UK across six business sectors. Eighteen of them said they were ready – hardly a representative sample of the entire UK.

So the lesson when conducting or even interpreting research is to seek professional advice at an early stage. Alternatively, you could buy a good specialist book. (See the recommendations in Chapter 14.)

SUMMARY

This chapter has looked at the role of information in the creation of direct marketing strategies and how it should be gathered, analysed and acted upon.

We have seen that in order to construct workable segments we need to gather information in several key areas. We need to have access to two broad types of data:

- consumer data – who are our customers and where do they live?
- lifestyle data – how do they live?

In business-to-business marketing, similar data is required. We need to know where the businesses are and other characteristics (such as the size and type of company) in order to be able to market effectively to them.

We have seen that some data is available in-house and other information can be obtained externally either through a range of secondary sources or through the use of marketing research.

Information has been indentified as a key asset to the business and staff should recognize its value and seek to gather and to record information at every opportunity.

The day-to-day operation of the business gives a great many opportunities to gather data, but we have also looked at the use of questionnaires and explored the characteristics of good questionnaire design. These included:

* simplicity
* relevancy
* reward for completion
* clear instructions
* easy to read and complete.

We have also seen the need to manage questions of a sensitive nature.

The chapter went on to list the multiple uses to which this data is put. For example, we can:

* learn about customer needs and buying behaviour
* create market segments – group customers by typology
* measure attitudes to our products and services
* establish our brand position
* identify future customers
* start to understand the buying decision process
* identify trends in the market place
* monitor competitor activity
* refine our communications
* measure the effectiveness of other non-response activity.

There followed an exploration of the different types of marketing research, looking at secondary (desk) research and primary (original) research.

We looked at the different sources of secondary information including government data and those lists available commercially.

We have seen that original research can be described as qualitative or quantitative and have noted the benefits of the two approaches. The applications of original research were considered, particularly in list building.

We have reviewed the role of the Internet in information-gathering at all stages.

Finally, we have pointed out the necessity of complying with the Data Protection Act and of using professional researchers for certain research tasks.

REVIEW QUESTIONS

1   What is the value of customer data?

2   What is the benefit of segmentation?

3   What are the two broad types of data we need in consumer markets?

4   What information do we need to acquire in business-to-business markets?

5   Where is information available?

6   What are the two broad types of marketing research?

7   What are the two broad types of original research?

8   List five characteristics of a good questionnaire.

9   List five uses of market research.

10   What are the five types of secondary data available to direct marketers?

11   How can we build our own mailing lists?

12   What are cookies?

13   What organization manages the market research profession in the UK?

EXERCISES

Select a company of your choice. Using the Internet, find out as much as you can about this company and its markets. What are the strengths and weaknesses of the Internet as a research tool?

Go to the Dun & Bradstreet Web site (www.dunandbradstreet.com). What are the benefits of the online service it provides?

Chapter 5

Using your information

Introduction
- Segmentation
  - Segmentation enables selectivity
- The use of profiling
  - Profiling factors
- Types and sources of external data
  - How the demographic systems work
- Ladder of loyalty
  - Uses of the ladder of loyalty

Summary

Review questions

Exercises

INTRODUCTION

This chapter will look at some of the ways the information you have gathered can be used to increase your business.

There are two main reasons for gathering data:

1 to enable customer and prospect segmentation
2 to permit companies to more closely tailor products, offers and messages to the recipients.

Segmentation

Segmentation is the sub-division of large customer and prospect files into smaller groups (segments).

Example

An office products company may segment into:

- companies with and without an IT department
- size bands – having up to 50 employees, having 51–100 employees and so on
- independent vs part of a larger group (possible variations in purchasing procedures)
- industry sectors, perhaps by SIC Code or other codes, such as Duns Number
- transactional history – types of product bought, timing, frequency, enquirers only and no history (for example added to list by sales force)
- source of first enquiry.

Such segmentation would enable this company to decide who to contact and what level of information to send about a new product (for example technical or non-technical material).

Segmentation is the sub-division of large customer and prospect files into smaller groups (segments).

A business with no affiliates will present a different opportunity to one which is part of a large multi-national group with a head office elsewhere in the UK or abroad, and perhaps a centralized purchasing or accounting function in a remote location.

Customers and prospects might break down into segments such as:

- location (for example distance or drive time to a retail site)
- owner/occupiers of large detached houses with no children

- owner/occupiers of large detached houses with children, further segmented by ages
- people who rent similar properties
- people with smaller homes
- garden or no garden
- house or flat
- households with two or more cars
- ownership of various luxury goods
- purchasing patterns – by products, value, frequency and so on
- type of occupation
- professionals, such as doctors and dentists
- self-employed people
- gender and age.

Even this brief list shows the number of possibilities. Once you have your market place segmented like this, you can see how your marketing might vary. You would quite possibly want to offer different products to prospects in the various segments.

Segmentation enables selectivity

Even though direct communication may not be competitive with mass media in terms of cost per thousand, its greater selectivity makes it the most cost-efficient choice in many cases.

You cannot achieve this selectivity without detailed information. The ideal starting position is to know who will be interested and when they are likely to be in a buying situation. Targeting is not only about people, but also about their situations. Remember the example (on p. 15) of the insurance company that multiplied its response by five simply by getting the timing right.

If you were able to sub-divide the people in each of your segments according to their own personal timing preferences, you would be even better equipped to send powerful, relevant communications that generate maximum response.

There are several ways to decide whom to select from a list or audience.

Database analysis
Obviously, if you have detailed individual information on each prospect, this is the best way to select. Your database will enable you to:

- identify the overall pool of prospects for a particular product
- select those who should be in the market during a particular week or month
- take account of additional data about their buying methods, drawn from records of previous transactions or questionnaire responses

- devise attractive offers to fit their circumstances (for example, you would not send the same offer to a company with the potential to buy a 50 portion pack as you would to a company which uses 5000 a day)
- draw up profiles of your best customers and use these to identify good segments of other lists or target audiences (profiling is explained in more detail on p. 75).

Testing

This involves mailing external lists or running advertisements or inserts and analysing the replies. Testing is covered in Chapter 11. Respondents can be 'profiled', enabling you to target more of the same. Where time and budget permit, this is much more reliable than making assumptions about who will be interested.

| Example |

A company selling fleet management services approached a direct marketing specialist for advice. It had tried direct mail for prospecting, but had found that it produced almost no response. The specialist asked, 'To whom are you sending your mailings?' The company replied, 'The fleet manager of course'.

The specialist pointed out tactfully that, although it may seem logical, fleet managers were entirely the wrong audience. They are the people who will lose their jobs if the company adopts the service.

A simple analysis of their advertisement responses produced the answer – the people who are interested in outsourcing fleet management services are the financial directors.

Once the company started targeting financial directors, direct mail, previously not viable, became their most cost-efficient medium for new business prospecting.

Research

This may be by postal questionnaire or over the telephone. Asking the question 'Who in your company will be interested?' can be highly beneficial. Note that when you use this approach with businesses, you must make sure that you are asking someone who really knows. Simply asking the telephonist or receptionist will not always work. Whereas receptionists will know the answer to 'What is the name of your marketing director?', they cannot be expected to answer the question 'Who in your company is responsible for deciding on the purchase of security software?'

As discussed elsewhere, many purchasing decisions in a business are made by a committee called a decision-making unit (or DMU). When it comes to identifying the members of a decision-making unit for a major purchase, the best person to ask is usually the managing director's secretary or the senior secretary at that location.

Intuition or judgement

Unless this is based on some evaluation of real events, it remains guesswork. As we saw from the fleet management example above, assumptions can be dangerous.

The use of profiling

Profiling is the act of identifying a characteristic which appears to be common or more prevalent than the average amongst customers. This factor can then be used to select a sub-group of prospects or customers who are more likely to be interested in a specific product, offer or message.

(In the fleet management example above, the relevant characteristic was the job title – financial director.)

Profiling factors

Business profiling can relate to company size, number of employees, annual turnover, geographic location, financial year-end, title or job function of contact, number of locations, size of company car fleet, even the number of meals served in the staff restaurant. There are many possibilities, depending on the types of products or services you sell.

Similarly consumer profiling can relate to household composition (children/no children), property type (large/small, garden/no garden, ACORN or MOSAIC type), geographical location, and so on.

Note that not all profiling has to be related to such inanimate matters. Attitudinal factors can be very important too. Households could be typified by their attitudes towards home computing for instance; businesses could be sub-divided by their public attitudes towards the environment, and so on.

If you are able to isolate such factors, they can be very helpful in targeting the right segments, reducing wastage and, thus, your costs.

Sometimes the targeting factor is very simple as in the following example.

Dave and Maureen Lindsay run Helping Hands, a property management, repair and refurbishment business in Normandy.

Dave produces very low cost mailings that work well because they are targeted at exactly the right people.

Example

The target market is English people who own holiday properties in Normandy. Their customers have a number of problems:

- they are rarely in France and need someone to keep an eye on their property and garden
- they do not speak very good French and so have difficulty in organizing basic repairs and maintenance
- they are worried about the standards of work if they are not around to supervise.

Dave and Maureen assembled a list using two main sources:

- rented list from Brittany Ferries, which runs 'The French Property Owners' Club' (because its members own a property in France, they travel more frequently and thus qualify for discounts on car ferries)
- recommendations (MGMs) – Dave and Maureen get a high percentage of their work from friends of customers.

The mailing is very simple, consisting of two pages of A4 paper copied through a fax machine (see Figure 5.1).

Here is another example:

Example

A company running high-quality expensive seminars was worried about declining delegate numbers and asked for advice on how to improve response to its mailings. It had eighteen seminars scheduled for the following 6 months and was planning to promote these through six mailings (each detailing three seminars) to its entire list of 22,000 names. As it had not carried out any detailed analysis of this list or of its attendees, its list of previous attendees was profiled by a specialist company. The specialist discovered that:

- 75% of all previous attendees came from companies with more than 200 employees – such companies represented 14% of the list
- the next 15% came from companies having 100–200 employees, which was a further 8% of the list.

This was all the information the company needed. It changed the emphasis of its mailing programme as follows:

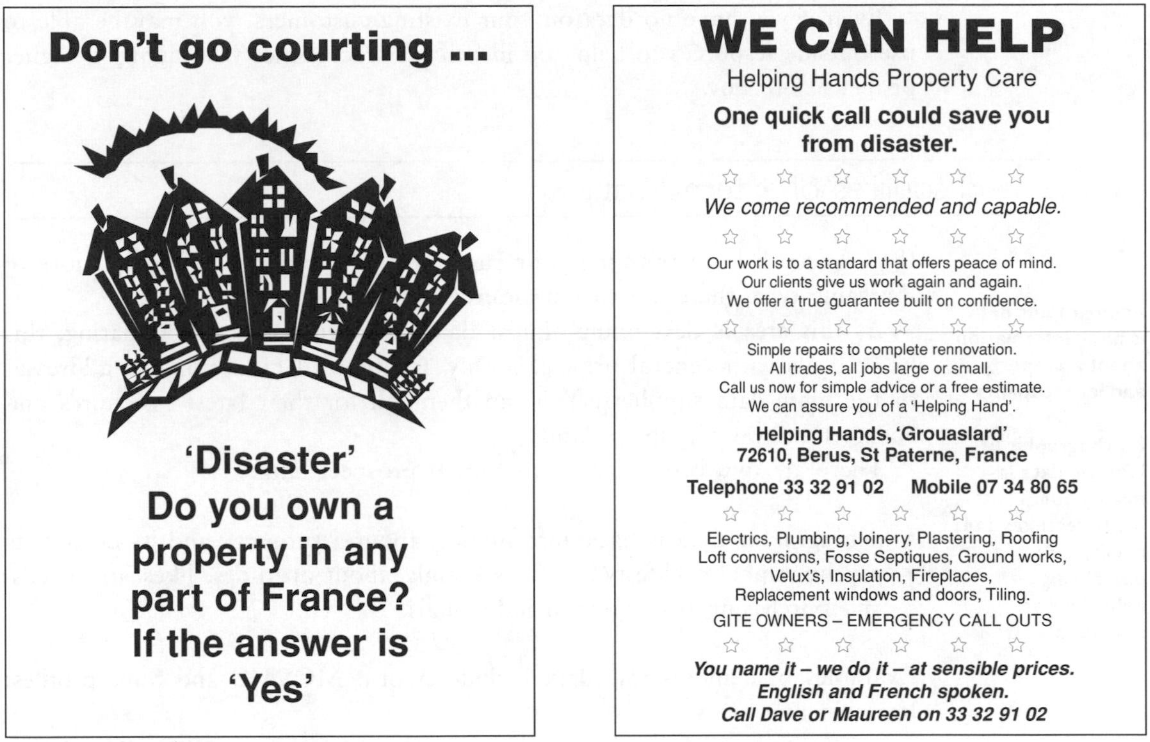

Figure 5.1 Helping Hands Property Care marketing

- Every one of the top 22% was telephoned. The call was followed by selective mailings covering the seminars in which they were interested. Each mailing was followed up by a further telephone call. This increased the marketing costs to this group by around 400%.
- The balance received a single mailing with the full eighteen-seminar programme inviting telephone or fax enquiries for more information about any seminars in which they were interested. The marketing cost for this group (78% of the list) was reduced by 80%.

The net result was a 20% increase in bookings and a 15% reduction in marketing costs. All because a single key profiling factor was identified – company size.

Now, if you start thinking about your own business, can you identify any factors that will help you select those prospects likely to be better customers for you?

Even if you have no data on your existing customers, you may be able to use outside resources to help you identify characteristics that signify a higher propensity to buy.

Types and sources of external data

Demographic data is basic information about a property and its occupants

Psychographic or lifestyle data is mainly about attitudes, likes and needs, and purchasing behaviour of individuals.

If you need help in profiling your customers and, indeed, in finding more of the same type, there are various sources of help.

As this area is developing almost daily and needs constant updating, this book deals with general principles only. Chapter 14 gives you the addresses of the main data suppliers. You can then call for their latest brochures and ensure that you are up to date.

There are two broad types of external prospect data:

• demographic data is basic information about a property and its occupants
• psychographic or lifestyle data is mainly about attitudes, likes and needs, and purchasing behaviour of individuals.

Examples of demographic data include Acorn, MOSAIC and Superprofiles. Its main uses are to:

• refine lists (for example a list could be compared to the electoral roll to check that a name is still current at that address)
• select the most likely segments from external lists – this could be done by comparing property types like the example on p. 81
• gain a better understanding of a market place – knowing the household composition and property type of your best customers gives you a clearer view of your prospects.

How demographic systems work is discussed a little later in this chapter (see p. 79).

Examples of psychographic systems are the National Shoppers Survey, Prizm, Behaviour Bank, the Lifestyle Selector, Lifestyle Focus and Facts of Living Survey. The main uses of these types of data are as follows.

• Data enhancement – you can send your own list to a lifestyle bureau and it will add information to those records that they can match with records on their own databases. In practice, this is not always a very high percentage (see p. 79).
• Profiling – another interesting option is to have your own best customers profiled by the lifestyle company. It will then offer you additional names and addresses of people on its databases who match your customer profile. You could send these people a mailing to identify those interested in your

products. Again a good offer would help to maximize your response (see Chapter 9 for discussion on offers). Many companies who have used this 'matching' process to find new prospects from the lifestyle database have had great success. However, many of these lists are being heavily mailed and, at the time of going to press, there is some evidence that response rates may be starting to fall.

One of the weaknesses of lifestyle data is that it is self-selecting. Only a certain proportion of people are willing to spend time filling in a highly detailed questionnaire about their living and shopping habits. However, it is more often seen as a weakness by classic market researchers than it is by direct marketers. It is not improbable that someone who is prepared to fill in the questionnaire is more likely than average to respond to an offer in a mailing or direct response advertisement.

A greater weakness has been that only a proportion of UK individuals is represented on these databases. Claritas now claims to have completed lifestyle questionnaires on 75% of UK households, but this probably still represents less than 50% of the adult population. This is why many marketers have been disappointed with the level of individual matches found.

In other words, if you have Mr James Brown on your customer file but Mrs Margaret Brown filled in the lifestyle questionnaire, although there will be a match at the address level there will be no match at the individual level.

Claritas says that it needs a minimum of 300 matches for it to develop a usable profile of your customers. If the individual match rate is less than 50%, you will need to supply more than twice this number to achieve a basic profile.

This basic process would be enough to identify new prospects with approximately similar profiles, but a larger number would be safer. Strategic Data Management, one of the UK's leading data analysis bureaux, advises its clients to provide enough names to achieve at least 1000 matches.

In other words, the more customers you already have, the easier it is to harness the power of the lifestyle database.

How the demographic systems work

Demographic systems such as ACORN and MOSAIC are based on the same starting information – the National Census that takes place every 10 years.

Census information is gathered in blocks of households called enumeration districts (EDs). An ED contains approximately 150 households and the data about it relate to the block not to any individual property. Every household in an ED can be identified by postcode although the process is not exact, especially in densely populated areas.

Census information is gathered in blocks of households called enumeration districts (EDs). An ED contains approximately 150 households and the data about it relate to the block not to any individual property. Every household in an ED can be identified by postcode although the process is not exact, especially in densely populated areas.

There are 150,000 EDs in the UK, so to be of use to the marketer they need to be grouped into larger units. These are given names typifying the occupants so, using ACORN as an example, we find six broad groupings covering broad life stages:

- A – Thriving
- B – Expanding
- C – Rising
- D – Settling
- E – Aspiring
- F – Striving.

Each of these breaks down into two or more sub-groups. So we see in B – Expanding that there are two sub-divisions:

- Type 4 – Affluent Executives, Family Areas
- Type 5 – Well-off Workers, Family Areas.

These break down again into several further groups. Type 4 — Affluent Executives, Family Areas sub-divides into:

- 4.10 – Affluent working families with mortgages
- 4.11 – Affluent working couples with mortgages
- 4.12 – Transient workforces, living at their place of work.

Type 5 – Well-off Workers, Family Areas contains:
- 5.13 – Home-owning family areas
- 5.14 – Home-owning family areas, older children
- 5.15 – Families with mortgages, younger children.

It must be stressed here that although in addition to the basic census data, personal data is used to identify the predominant characteristics of an ACORN ED, it is still only the general characteristics of the area we are observing. Thus, if we mailed every house in ED Type 5.13 – Home-owning family areas, whilst we would expect to reach a good percentage of homes occupied by families, a large number of them would not fit the pattern. We may find perhaps that families occupied 60% of the households, in other words 40% do not fit the pattern.

Geodemographic systems are therefore more useful to describe the general characteristics of an area than to target an individual household for a mailing. This is not to say they are without value – let's take an example.

If we are wishing to target well-off families with teenage children, we could mail ACORN Type 5.14 and reach a good proportion of our target. If nationally only 20% of homes contain teenagers, then compared to an untargeted mailing we should expect to do three times as well using ACORN.

This would still not be as good as knowing the composition of each address and selecting only those that we know contain teenagers.

You could also send your customer list to CACI or Experian to have it ACORN or MOSAIC coded. This will identify the predominant property types of the people who are buying your products. You can then target households in similar properties for a mailing or perhaps a leaflet distribution.

Although ACORN and MOSAIC do not offer the precision of lifestyle data there is an advantage for small marketers in that every household in the UK can be matched. So unlike the case with the lifestyle companies, a sample sent for ACORN or MOSAIC coding will achieve virtually a 100% match. So a smaller sample will yield a result.

As was stated earlier, the basic difference between the two methods is that the geodemographic systems such as ACORN and MOSAIC simply match property types and they do not deal with actual people. The lifestyle or psychographic systems deal with actual people and therefore the resulting matches are more accurate.

Business marketers will find that companies such as Experian and Dun & Bradstreet can offer a similar service for them. You will find the addresses of these companies in Chapter 14.

The following example will expand on this process.

Housesafe wants to find new customers for its home security devices – alarms, security lighting and so on. It decides to test lifestyle lists and also try ACORN or MOSAIC. Here is a procedure it could use.

> Example

- Identify its best customers – it would need to have at least 600 names, but as mentioned earlier on p. 79 a greater number would give more statistical validity.
- Contact one or more of the lifestyle companies and ask them for a quote to evaluate its data and identify how many names they have that match its best customer profile.
- After analysing the data, they will be able to tell Housesafe how many similar names they can provide it with.
- This same customer sample could also be sent to the owners of ACORN (CACI) or MOSAIC (Experian), although as explained earlier, it would not be necessary to have so many names in this case.
- Housesafe can then plan to produce and send a test mailing in two or more simultaneous batches – the lists provided by the lifestyle company and those provided by CACI (ACORN) and/or Experian (MOSAIC).

The response devices of each should be coded separately, so that Housesafe can tell which half of the test produces the best response. If it encloses a response form, it can simply print a code on it – 1 = Batch 1; 2 = Batch 2.

For telephone responses, the company will need to be a bit more imaginative. Unique telephone numbers would be ideal – failing that it could still print its codes in the response area, but it will have to ask callers to quote the code when they ring. Some will not remember it and may not have kept that piece handy.

It is very important to do this coding exercise, as the company needs to know which is its best source for 'roll out', that is sending a larger mailing to the remainder of the more productive list.

As mentioned earlier, if Housesafe really has no information to help it target prospects, it will probably need to use direct response advertising to generate enquiries. Once it has some enquiries, it can analyse these and this will improve its targeting in the future.

Some marketers think that these techniques are relevant only to large businesses with huge marketing budgets, but this is not so. In fact, the opposite is nearer the mark. When funds are limited, it is even more important to target carefully and gain the maximum value for every pound spent.

Remember that profiling and targeting are not just for prospecting. You can increase the profitability of your existing customer activities by careful segmentation – targeting those most likely to be interested in a particular offer, or at a particular time.

Ladder of loyalty

The ladder of loyalty is a useful device to help you highlight the differences between various types of people and help you produce appropriate communications for each.

The ladder of loyalty is a useful device to help you highlight the differences between various types of people and help you produce appropriate communications for each. Such communications will be better received because they recognize the status of each person and deliver relevant messages.

You can categorize your own customers and prospects according to their positions on the ladder, shown in Figure 5.2.

There has been speculation about the value of the ladder of loyalty. The ladder analogy implies progress towards the end position of advocate. Research has shown that there is movement up and down the ladder and that some customers jump on at advocate stage! However, the descriptors, reflecting the degree of connection with a company and its products, remain very useful.

```
┌──────────────────┬
│                  │
│     Advocate     │
│                  │
├──────────────────┤
│                  │
│     Customer     │
│                  │
├──────────────────┤
│                  │
│    Considering   │
│                  │
├──────────────────┤
│                  │
│    Prospects     │
│                  │
├──────────────────┤
│                  │
│     Suspects     │
│                  │
├──────────────────┤
│                  │
│                  │
└──────────────────┴
```

Figure 5.2 The ladder of loyalty

Salespeople can use the ladder to help them allocate their time, devise appropriate contact strategies for individual prospects according to their potential, and decide what and how much to tell people about their products.

The ladder can be just as useful in helping you to decide what and how much to tell the people to whom you are communicating.

On the bottom rung are **suspects**. **Suspects** are those people who should be in the market, but about whom you have no information (other than perhaps their names and addresses). This segment will include many people who are totally unaware of your services. So in the car insurance example on p. 15 the general list of motorists which produced 1% response is a list of suspects.

Prospects are those about whom you know enough to be able to say they are likely to be in the market place now. From the same example on p. 15 knowing the renewal dates enabled the company to change the category from suspect to prospect. This distinction is hugely important. Remember that this segment produced more than five times as much response as the basic 'suspects', that is those without renewal dates. Prospects include those who know about your services but who have not yet got round to doing anything about it. Perhaps they do not realize quite how well you can satisfy their needs?

Next we have those who are '**considering**' giving you some business. These could also be called 'non-converted enquirers'. They are very probably considering other suppliers at the same time. It is essential that you send them all the information they require and perhaps even follow up your information pack with a helpful telephone call or reminder.

Suspects are those people who should be in the market, but about whom you have no information (other than perhaps their names and addresses). This segment will include many people who are totally unaware of your services.

Prospects are those about whom you know enough to be able to say they are likely to be in the market place now.

Customers have bought at least one product from you. Assuming they are satisfied that you have delivered what you promised these people are potential advocates.

Customers have bought at least one product from you. Assuming they are satisfied that you have delivered what you promised these people are potential advocates. You may find it advantageous to encourage this process by sending an MGM offer. Here you would ask customers to send you the names of people who might also be interested in your products. These offers can be incentivized and this often produces more recommendations, but see the cautionary tale below.

Advocates are regular customers who are so pleased with your service that they tell their friends and colleagues. Advocates should be nurtured carefully – they are worth far more to you than the profit from their own orders. They will usually not need incentives to recommend you to others, although a suitably restrained incentive offer *may* prompt them into action. This should be approached with extreme care however, as the following example shows.

Example

The marketing director of a very up-market furnishings company, which had numerous shops and a thriving mail order business, tested an incentivized MGM offer.

The customer list contained many titled people and in fact the company had the Royal Warrant for supplying members of the Royal Family.

Although the incentivized MGM offer attracted many positive responses, it also received several complaints. Typical of these was the lady who said, 'If I want to share my suppliers with my friends I will do so without the need for bribery. Please remove my name from your mailing list.'

Advocates are regular customers who are so pleased with your service that they tell their friends and colleagues.

What exactly do we mean by 'prospects'? The term 'suspect' is a fairly clear description meaning someone about whom we know very little, or perhaps someone who knows little about us. The term 'prospect', on the other hand, can have several meanings. In fact, any person on any rung of the ladder could be described as a prospect for something. Those on the bottom rung are prospects for an initial order; advocates are prospects for repeat purchase or sales of additional products. So, with the exception of this section, the term 'prospect' is used throughout this book to mean someone who has the potential to buy from your next promotion.

Uses of the ladder of loyalty

There are two main uses.

1   To help us decide what to say, in other words to develop relevant copy and offers. Clearly, if you are communicating with suspects, it will be necessary to tell that person about the value of a particular type of product

or service. They are probably aware that it exists, but it had not assumed any sort of priority for them.

2   To help decide how and where to say it – to enable us to select an appropriate medium for the communication.

Unless you know enough about them to target a relevant segment (who happen to be in the market at present, say), it may not be cost-effective to send a direct communication to them all. You may opt to start with a broad-scale media approach using television, press or even posters with a very simple offer to tempt those interested to declare their interest.

This is why many direct insurance companies, such as Admiral, start with broadscale advertising. It would not be cost-efficient to mail every householder every month when they only buy the product once a year. A broad approach, using something like 'Save money on your insurance – call 0800 000 000 for details' will generally prove more cost-effective in such cases.

Once people have responded to such an offer, they identify their interest and become prospects. In sending for their information pack, they will have given their renewal date and perhaps the name of their existing insurer. The advertiser can now send them a highly targeted relevant offer that has a much better chance of being accepted.

The existing 'prospects' group is already segmented by such key factors and these will only be communicated with at appropriate times.

Those considering your product are probably beyond the need for basic product information – they already have this. They may still react well to additional detail relevant to their specific situation, and a rationale for preferring yours to a competitive product.

Customers may not need fully detailed product information, although this will not always be the case. Research in many fields shows that customers do not get the best out of products they buy because they are not totally aware of all that the product can do. This is especially true in the case of PC software for example.

At the top of the ladder are the advocates – customers who are so impressed by your products and service that they tell their friends and colleagues about it. You do not need to explain to these customers why they should buy your products – they would be insulted if you did.

Communications to advocates should be to say 'Thank you for your business' and to give information about new developments or make special offers to encourage continued business and recommendations.

From the above descriptions two key considerations emerge:

1   people will need different levels and amounts of information according to their place on the ladder

2 the same person could be on different rungs according to the specific product you are promoting.

This is an over-simplification, of course. An advocate who has regularly bought Product A from you, may not be aware of Product B and, thus, could be classified as unaware. However, there is a strong relationship already established, and hopefully some information on your database, which will help you to sell Product B to this person. In this sense, they should be classified much higher than the average 'suspect'.

The important thing is that you should use these descriptions to help you to identify the right people, the right messages, and the right timing for a specific product or offer. However, do not forget the huge value of the relationship you have with existing customers.

Note that common sense is a useful ally when deciding how tightly to target best prospects – 100% response to a mailing may be highly interesting, but if you have mailed only forty people, you will not build your business very quickly.

So, whilst it is important to try to improve cost-efficiency, you must also keep an eye on the overall number of sales needed to cover costs and make a contribution to your profits.

SUMMARY

This chapter has looked at how the information we gather deliberately or simply as a result of our business activities can be used to enhance customer focus and satisfaction.

We have seen that the main reason for gathering data is to segment the market, enabling better tailoring of the product messages and offers to customers.

We have looked at a range of segmentation possibilities in a range of markets including consumer and business to business and have explored the four ways of creating market segments:

- database analysis
- testing
- marketing research
- intuition or judgement.

We saw that intuition or judgement was the most risky. Where possible, one or more of the other three methods should support the use of intuition.

We have looked at the use of profiling in business-to-business markets. Some of the key segmentation variables used are:

- size
- number of employees
- number of locations
- financial year-end
- size of car fleet.

The range of possibilities reflects the products sold.

One way of managing the process of segmentation is to buy in services. We have learned that there are a number of services supporting the direct marketer in this task. External services are classified into two areas.

1   Demographic – the main uses of these data are to refine lists, to help selections from external lists and to gain a better understanding of our customers and markets. Examples include ACORN and MOSAIC.
2   Psychographic or lifestyle – the main uses are data enhancement and profiling. Examples include the Behaviour Bank and the Lifestyle Selector.

The chapter has looked in detail at how the demographic systems work and some of the output from the ACORN system. The advantages of demographic systems were discussed, including the fact that there is virtually a 100% match with these systems as all homes are coded. The disadvantage was seen to be the relative lack of precision in the demographic systems. ACORN and MOSAIC deal with property types not people. We saw that Experian and Dun & Bradstreet offer similar profiling services for business-to-business markets. There was a worked example of how to apply these systems in practice.

We have looked at the ladder of loyalty and explored how it helps by segmenting customers into relevant groups. We saw that the ladder of loyalty describes the relative position of customers in terms of their relationship to the company. They may be:

- advocates
- customers
- considering purchase or non-converted enquirers
- prospects
- suspects.

Each of these categories was defined and an indication of the different direct marketing approaches to each was given. The ladder of loyalty helps us to decide what to say to customers and how and where to say it.

Finally, it has been seen that segmentation allows us to identify the right people, the right messages and the right time for a product or offer.

REVIEW QUESTIONS

1   Why should we gather data about customers?

2   Define segmentation.

3   List five consumer segmentation variables.

4   What are the four ways of creating marketing segments?

5   What are the two types of external data available for profiling?

6   What are the three main uses of demographic data?

7   What are the two main uses of lifestyle data?

8   What is an enumeration district?

9   Who provides profiling services to business-to-business markets?

10   List five rungs of the ladder of loyalty.

11   What is an advocate and what are the implications of this description for direct marketing?

12   How should direct marketers use the concept of the ladder of loyalty?

13   What is the main purpose of segmentation?

EXERCISES

Describe the market segments that are available to a company in one of the following markets:

- travel
- desktop PCs
- beauty products
- financial services.

What are the main segmentation variables used in dividing the market? What impact do these variables have on:

- products
- offers
- media choice
- messages?

Chapter 6

The marketing database

Introduction
- Targeting and segmentation
  - Regression analysis
  - CHAID and cluster analysis
  - Neural networks
  - Doing it yourself
  - Using the data – a summary
- Development of customer relationships
  - What data do you need?
  - Where does the data come from?
  - The continuing need for data
  - How can you capture the data?
  - How can data be kept up to date?
  - The importance of de-duplication
  - How can the data be used?
- Microcomputer hardware
  - Chips, storage and memory
  - Summary
- Microcomputer software
  - Building your database on a PC
  - Summary
- External data sources
  - Demographics
  - Lifestyle data
  - Data warehousing and data mining

Summary
Review questions
Exercises

INTRODUCTION

Although, as mentioned in Chapter 1, it is now fashionable to talk about customer relationship management systems, rather than databases, this chapter will continue to refer to a marketing database.

Most marketers today consider it to be an essential part of their armoury, and would consider those not having a database to be behind the times. This opinion is put forward by most marketing people regardless of rank, job function or technical knowledge. But what exactly is a marketing database and is this view justified?

Most computer systems in use today were originated between 1960 and 1985. This was before the use of customer data for marketing purposes became prevalent. Consequently, in the early 1980s, when marketing database theory was in its infancy, systems were designed primarily to handle customer transactions and billings rather marketing requirements.

To this day in many companies, marketing is still viewed as an ancillary task – a bank's system centres around customer accounts, a newspaper's system around circulation and printing, and so on. Thus, the marketing function is seen as peripheral to the central system of most companies, and this will probably remain the case for some years to come.

The purpose of a marketing database is to enable marketers to use the company's data for marketing purposes.

The purpose of a marketing database is to enable marketers to use the company's data for marketing purposes. This may seem blindingly obvious, but a 1996 report by the Henley Centre stated that whilst 76% of UK companies claim to have a marketing database, fewer than 8% of them are organized to obtain significant benefits from it. You may feel that a 1996 study is a little out of date, but feedback from my seminar delegates in 2000 tells me that little has changed.

In order for a database to be useful to marketers, it must be capable of being viewed from a customer basis rather than an accounts basis. Thus, if Mrs Jones, a bank customer, has a current account, a mortgage and a gold card, the bank is able to plan its marketing in the light of her total business with it rather than having a variety of accounts each of which is viewed as a separate entity. Apart from enabling more cost-efficient marketing programmes, it also prevents the bank from looking incompetent in the eyes of its better customers, namely those with more than one strand of business with it.

The marketing database usually stands separate from a company's central system. A bank's marketing database would take data from the various customer accounts records and merge them into a separate data area. This avoids the marketing functions impinging on the day-to-day activities of running the bank and assembles the data in a way that facilitates the marketer's requirements.

Of course, there are other possible sources of data. In some cases, data is automatically gathered on a customer-by-customer basis as part of another business function. For example:

- part of a customer care system – people may ring a helpline number if they experience problems with a product or service
- a sales force management system – where salespeople visit prospects and these are converted to customers
- part of a facilities management system – where direct debits and standing orders are processed for, say, a charity.

The reality then is that there are many types of marketing databases. As long as you have a means of assembling data for marketing purposes, you can claim to have a marketing database. What really counts is how the data is used. Used in the right way, data is an extremely powerful tool, as we will be shown in the rest of this chapter. Consider this example of Sodastream.

Based in Peterborough, Sodastream manufactures and distributes machines and concentrates that are used to make fizzy drinks. Sodastream has a customer care system originally designed to:

Example

- answer the queries of customers requiring help in operating the machines
- provide information for customers wishing to buy more concentrates.

This is an excellent example of a system designed to serve essential business functions that has evolved into a marketing database. In fact its use as a marketing tool is beginning to outstrip its original purpose. It is a good example of how customer problems can be turned to a company's advantage.

The marketing database is used to further relationships with customers. The initial contact may be negative – the customer may have a problem with the machine. The system enables this to be dealt with smoothly and ensures that remedial action takes place; a spare washer is despatched, a money-off voucher is given in compensation and so on.

Once Sodastream has logged the customer details on the marketing database, it can use this information to build the relationship. It may offer further benefits such as money-off vouchers for new products, advice of forthcoming promotions and entry into prize draws.

The data can also be used to produce reports for other departments in the company; Quality Control can see where problems are arising. Marketing can look at, for example, age and consumption habits of specific segments of the customer base. One of the most important functions of the marketing database is to provide easily understood and actionable reports for a range of audiences within Sodastream.

By combining data from promotions with sales records, Sodastream has developed a powerful weapon to help with both strategic and tactical marketing.

When planning a promotion at a Liverpool supermarket, it was able to use the data to:

- identify customers in the vicinity through postcode selections
- refine this list by selecting people with certain buying patterns, perhaps selecting those within 5 miles of the store who last bought a drinks maker more than 2 years ago.

Pareto's principle or the 80/20 rule states that 80% of a company's business comes from just 20% of its customers.

This is broadly true of most businesses and Sodastream is no exception. Its aim is to sell drinks-making machines, then concentrates to be used in the machines, and eventually replacement machines, thus perpetuating the sales cycle.

In practice, buyers of the machines do not all exhibit the same behaviour. Some use them briefly and then lapse; others who receive them as gifts may never use them; a third category are regular users. Each of these segments requires a different approach. Some will receive frequent communications and promotions; others may not prove worth any investment at all. The marketing database enables Sodastream to manage these differing relationships efficiently.

The principles of customer segmentation can be applied in most countries and Sodastream has been able to apply its UK learning to achieve similar levels of success in other European countries.

In summary, the marketing database enables Sodastream to:

- develop customer relationships on a selective, cost-efficient basis
- provide regular high-quality relevant reports to its colleagues
- select sub-sets of customers based on individual data
- target those most likely to be appropriate for a particular communication or offer
- manage different segments of customers according to their potential
- apply its UK learning to develop overseas markets.

Targeting and segmentation

Consider British Airways Holidays (BAH). This is a subsidiary of British Airways that offers top-class holiday packages to the discerning traveller. These packages are designed to appeal to the more affluent customer who is more concerned with quality than price.

Example

The BAH marketing database is made up of data from a variety of sources including information on previous bookings. We can consider how this might be used.

When selecting an audience for a Caribbean holiday promotion, BAH will consider customers' previous buying patterns. Would it offer this holiday to someone who went there last year? Yes, of course, this would be a good selection. What about those who went last month? Probably not a good selection unless their buying pattern shows us that they take several holidays a year.

Buying patterns are powerful predictors. If you took a holiday in June last year, the chances are you will consider June again this year. If you have visited Paris, Rome and Amsterdam in recent years, an offer on a holiday to Prague may well appeal.

Clearly, concurrency of data and timing of offer are key factors. With an efficient marketing database, BAH can make the right offer to the right customers at the right time. Such precision leads to greater relevance and, thus, more cost-efficient marketing programmes.

By planning well-targeted campaigns like these, you can forecast how much you are going to spend and what the likely response to your promotion will be. This enables fairly accurate forecasting of sales and return on investment.

In addition to its customer database, BAH has a database of people who are likely to be good prospects. This was made possible by profiling its existing customers. A major advantage of building a good marketing database is the ability to identify prospects. We will see later in this chapter how you can select good prospects by matching them to a profile of your current best customers.

In summary, segmenting and targeting specific customers means BAH can:

- ensure that its communications are relevant and, therefore, more likely to succeed
- develop and offer more appropriate products and services
- improve the effectiveness of all customer contacts
- identify better prospects
- increase the accuracy of its forecasts
- increase the productivity of the marketing expenditure.

Having looked at some of the benefits of targeting and segmentation, we can now turn to how it can be achieved. There are a number of statistical techniques in common use. We will not study them in detail here, rather discuss them from a marketing perspective.

Regression analysis

Regression analysis is a technique that scores individuals according to their characteristics. Study of previous behaviour enables us to allocate plus or minus scores in relation to this particular event.

Regression analysis is a technique that scores individuals according to their characteristics. Study of previous behaviour enables us to allocate plus or minus scores in relation to this particular event.

For example, our analysis of previous customers may show us that people who take expensive holidays tend to:

- have taken one before
- live in larger houses or at least in certain postcodes
- be over 40 years of age
- have children at private schools
- have a household income of more than £40,000 per annum.

We can consider a study into the likelihood of a prospect responding to the offer of a Caribbean holiday. We may find this can be forecast as follows:

- add 50 if they have booked a luxury holiday before
- add a further 50 if this was in the Caribbean
- subtract 35 if they are aged less than 40
- add 40 if they earn more than £50,000 per annum.

By applying this scoring method to every relevant characteristic of every prospect on file, we can confidently predict that those with the highest scores are the ones most likely to respond to the offer.

Such analyses are carefully developed and tested based on historical data, and then monitored during use to ensure their continuing accuracy.

Regression analysis is a good tactical tool, delivering a highly targeted set of prospects for a given offer.

CHAID and cluster analysis

On a more strategic level, we may consider the use of tools such as CHAID and cluster analysis. These aim to allocate semi-permanent codes to customers which are then broken down into segments having similar needs and behaviour.

So instead of reviewing the entire file for prospects for our holiday offer, we may have previously segmented the base into groups, some of whom are more likely to be interested in such offers.

For instance, we may derive a 'Type A1 – High income, loyal customers'. This works in a similar way to the popular demographic coding systems such as ACORN and MOSAIC, but in this case it is applied to your own customer data rather than to a type of property.

In order to understand the workings of CHAID, we can consider an example of a bank wishing to sell ISAs.

At present, 8% of the bank's customers have an ISA and it wishes to increase this to 10%. The CHAID model is fed say 30,000 customer records containing data on:

> **Example**

- number of ISAs
- household income
- size of mortgage
- years as a customer.

The CHAID software considers all of the given variables and determines which is the most important in this case.

Let's say it establishes that the most significant factor is 'years as a customer'. It further sub-divides this factor into less than 1 year with the bank; 1–5 years as a customer; more than 5 years as a customer. It may then identify something like the following:

- less than 1 year as a customer – only 3% have an ISA
- 1–5 years – 8% have an ISA
- more than 5 years – 12% have an ISA.

The CHAID model then moves on to the next stage which is to take each of these three segments and consider the next most significant variable in each instance. It may ascertain that in the most loyal customer segment (more than 5 years with the bank) the next best discriminator is mortgage size. People in this segment with mortgages of more than £100,000 may have a 14% take-up of ISAs.

By breaking down each segment into its significant variables, a number of potentially good sub-segments may emerge. For example, we may find that, although 'semi-loyal' customers (with the bank 1–5 years) are not of interest as a whole group (only 8% have an ISA), those in this group who have mortgages of more than £150,000, and household incomes of £65,000 or more are much better prospects. The model may show that 15% of those in this sub-set have an ISA.

CHAID segments are easy to understand and apply. We know exactly what characteristics we are seeking and we then select our target audience according to these factors.

Furthermore, we can brief our creative people on these characteristics so that they can write relevant copy. We can also feed back the information to the computer programmers so they can apply the segmentation to their files.

When using CHAID, it is important to set out a detailed plan of what is mailed to whom and when. Otherwise one group of prospects may well come up again and again and receive too many mailings whilst another may not be mailed enough.

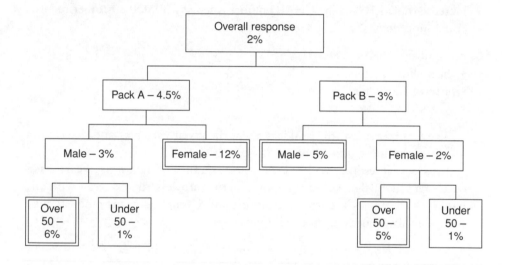

Figure 6.1 The CHAID Analysis of Response

Note how the CHAID model continues to break down the responses according to those making a significant difference.

In Figure 6.1, with a response requirement of 5% neither test pack produces enough response on its own. However, once pack A responses are split into Male and Female we can see that Females receiving Pack A responded at 12%. Males on the other hand produced a disappointing 3%. However, males over 50 years of age responded at 6% so they can be mailed too.

Meanwhile, Males responded at exactly 5% to Pack B, whilst only those Females aged over 50 will be worth mailing again.

Cluster analysis is also a powerful strategic tool. The cluster analysis model deals with general characteristics rather than specific variables.

Cluster analysis is also a powerful strategic tool. The cluster analysis model deals with general characteristics rather than specific variables.

In the same way that ACORN and MOSAIC typify property, cluster analysis breaks down customers into types. So we may see more general descriptions such as:

- loyal customers with a large spread of products
- struggling 'nest builders'.

Such classifications would be used strategically across the entire product range rather than to select propensity to buy a particular product like an ISA. This method has many of the advantages of CHAID, but it is not so easy to understand.

Neural networks

Neural networks are the latest technique to appear in this sector. They apply artificial intelligence within a statistical model.

We tell the model who is an ISA customer and feed in all of the other data about those people. In effect, the model asks questions of the sample in order to determine who is likely to be a good ISA prospect.

With most of these techniques, we base our predictions on the behaviour of those who responded to previous offers.

The main disadvantage of neural networks is that they work by splitting the response or behavioural sample into three discrete samples. In marketing we are often dealing with quite low response rates and splitting these responses into three means that there is sometimes a real paucity of data.

Rather than trying to explain how this technique works, it can simply be said that given enough data it seems to be comparable with the other techniques. As our understanding and usage of artificial intelligence develops, it may become the best of these tools in the future.

Neural networks are the latest technique to appear in this sector. They apply artificial intelligence within a statistical model.

Doing it yourself

It is possible to use the above techniques on your own PC using a number of statistical analysis packages. The most common statistical analysis packages are SPSS and SAS. These are off-the-shelf packages that are relatively user friendly and cost-effective.

It is important to understand that the main skill in data analysis is not in running the software, but in understanding the data.

For example, the data from a recent petrol station promotion seemed to indicate that there were lots of youngsters driving around in expensive cars. In fact, they were mainly teenage respondents to a CD promotion who filled

The most common statistical analysis packages are SPSS and SAS. These are off-the-shelf packages that are relatively user friendly and cost-effective.

out questionnaires with a mixture of personal preferences (musical tastes) and household data (family car). The lesson here is to know your data and understand its implications before submitting it to the model.

To use these statistical analysis packages you will need at least a basic knowledge of statistics. Most marketers will not need to use all the features, but they will include advanced statistics, modules, coefficients and so on. If you are not familiar with such techniques, you should have someone trained in statistics by your side when running these models.

Using the data – a summary

Any model derived should be actionable. It is no use finding that sales of your drinks increase during hot weather if you are not able to make use of that fact. You cannot affect the weather of course, but such knowledge may enable you to use the weather forecasts to prepare for more rapid production and distribution when demand is likely to rise. Findings must make sense – remember your conclusions will have to be explained to colleagues, creative agencies, bureaux and so on.

Summarizing this section we have looked at:

Regression analysis – a statistical modelling technique used mainly for tactical mailings.

CHAID – an analysis tool that creates your own customer typology, often for a specific product or promotion.

Clustering – similar to CHAID, but a general-purpose tool; it is the technique used by the developers of ACORN and MOSAIC.

- regression analysis – a statistical modelling technique used mainly for tactical mailings
- CHAID – an analysis tool that creates your own customer typology, often for a specific product or promotion
- clustering – similar to CHAID, but a general-purpose tool; it is the technique used by the developers of ACORN and MOSAIC
- neural networks – the newest technology, not yet fully proven in marketing.

All of these can be derived from standard statistical packages such as SPSS and SAS. The real skill is not in pressing the right buttons, but in understanding the data, interpreting the reports and applying the results. The results should be easily understood by third parties. You also need to be comfortable with the results, as you have to present them and sometimes defend them.

Development of customer relationships

Have you heard the story of the author who submitted a manuscript to his editor. The editor thought it would make a great book, but decided that David was not a good name for its hero. He felt that Arthur would be more appropriate. The author complained that this would entail lots of extra work, but the editor assured him that with word processing it was very easy to make a simple global change.

The author agreed to the change and the book was published. Too late, a reader pointed out that in one chapter the hero took his lady away for a romantic weekend and they gazed upon Michelangelo's statue of Arthur!

The point about this story is that technology can make some operations easy – sometimes too easy. As a marketer, you have to remember that your database is filled with people not just data.

The *Daily Telegraph* is an innovative newspaper that has started to sell subscriptions to consumers. It has done this via an Advanced Payment Programme (APP) where customers can pay in advance for several months' copies and receive a discount on the normal cover price.

Example

If you, as a customer, were thinking of buying something, would you be influenced by the fact that you had bought a product from the company before and you were happy with it? Of course you would. Therefore a company that has access to its customers can continue to sell to them and boost their loyalty. For the *Daily Telegraph* this future sale may be a renewal of the subscription or any other product that it offers in association with other suppliers.

Contented customers are more likely to recommend your product to their friends and colleagues. In fact, customers who have experienced problems that have subsequently been remedied are even more likely to recommend you. This shows the importance of continuing a dialogue with your customers and the marketing database offers you an excellent way of managing this process.

If you take out a subscription deal with the *Daily Telegraph*, you will have to decide at the end of your subscription period whether you wish to continue with the arrangement. The *Daily Telegraph* knows from its database records when this decision will have to be made and it will mail you beforehand. It will remind you what a great newspaper you read and restate the benefits of taking out a further subscription. The marketing database enables the newspaper to time these communications so they are highly relevant to the individual recipients.

The *Daily Telegraph* will not stop at simply sending you a simple reminder. It will also carry out anti-attrition studies. This is an important area. Having gone to the considerable time and expense of recruiting customers, one does not want to lose them as a result of not understanding their needs. Even worse, research show that dissatisfied customers tell up to 17 people to avoid the offending product.

With this in mind, the *Daily Telegraph* will ask lapsed customers why they failed to renew and will plot and analyse the reasons carefully. There may be some reasons linked to age, the length of subscription, address or household composition (number of adults, number and ages of children and so on). Whatever the factors involved, by knowing which customers are most likely to defect, the company can make a special effort to persuade them of the benefits of renewal.

Like many sectors, the newspaper industry is highly competitive. There have been price wars where rival newspapers have slashed their cover prices to increase sales. There have been expensive promotions, prize draws, bingo games and memberships schemes. Whenever a new initiative is planned, competitors will do their utmost to pre-empt it or at least spoil it.

Direct communication offers a way of talking directly with customers without telling all your competitors what you are planning. In real life, of course, your sharper competitors will be on your mailing list and will get to know what you are planning. Even so, direct communications can be used to make offers to the customer base; conduct market research or maybe just to say 'Thank you for your custom'.

Direct mail is clearly a private medium, enabling a continuing dialogue with customers. Of course, a newspaper is itself a private medium of sorts – communicating to its readers every day, but the difference is that the communication is one way. It also sends the same message to the entire audience whereas with direct communication we can vary the message for each segment or type of customer. The database is the tool that makes this possible.

This example shows that:

- all customers are different – they need differing messages
- it is easier to sell to existing customers than cold prospects
- the marketing database makes it easier to target and time communications correctly
- anti-attrition techniques help the *Daily Telegraph* to predict which customers are most likely to leave, and when
- direct communications are more discreet.

What data do you need?

Most businesses have more than enough data. The problem is not generally one of availability, but of centralization and management. One of the key questions will be 'What should be kept?'

If an item of data is to be used for communications, it must be kept up to date. Any data is better than none, but out-of-date information can be misleading, even harmful. Writing to the old address when customers have moved house may be difficult to avoid, but the impression left by your mailing would be very bad.

This is not to say that old data should be destroyed as it may still be very valuable for analysis and profiling. However, it makes sense to remove old records to an archive for occasional use, rather than have them taking up space and using data processing time on the main database.

A good start may be to:

- capture data essential for current requirements (names, addresses, products purchased and so on)
- collect key profile data (family size, number of cars, property type and so on)
- collect data which will aid future activity, such as cross-selling and repeat purchase stimulation (which offer they responded to, timing, ages of children and so on)
- collect data relating to the market place (peaks and troughs of demand, what other suppliers they buy from; as we saw in Chapter 1, this can be very productive).

A good rule is to define a use for each piece of data before you include it – if you cannot think of a reason to keep it, you probably do not need it. If you are really not sure, you can hold a separate file or table of such data which does not clog up the main database. Bear in mind that if you do not maintain it, it will eventually become out of date.

Where does the data come from?

Unless you are starting up a brand new company, there will be lots of data already available. For example:

- administration data – you will have details of existing and lapsed accounts, queries and special requests, invoices, reminders, demands and payments
- marketing data – names of enquirers from previous mailings, advertising responses and details of mailings and advertisements run and promotions organized.

On its own, departmental data is only of use for its original purpose. When different pieces of data are combined and co-ordinated, however, their true value can be much greater.

Example

An insurance company wants to select those clients who have some spare disposable income, to offer a premium priced but valuable additional service. Perhaps a new type of high-quality burglar alarm, linked directly to a local security firm 'flying squad'. The information it holds is either Segment 1 or Segment 2:

- Segment 1 is the amount of their buildings cover
- Segment 2 is the amount of motor cover and type of car.

From these data the company knows either the value of their house or the type and value of their car. Neither of these items of data, nor the two in combination, will tell you much about the clients' disposable income. Yet, supposing in the case of Segment 1, the company also knows the size of their mortgage, and for those in Segment 2 it knows their mortgage and their building value? Suddenly, the company has a lot of marketing information.

Table 6.1 Analysis of mortgage and building value

Type	A	B	C	D
Buildings cover	£55,000	£100,000	£350,000	£350,000
Mortgage	£55,000	£50,000	£300,000	£60,000

Just relating these two pieces of data gives us a much clearer picture of the available funds in these households. Types B and D are likely to be better prospects for a premium price service.

In Segment 2 there is an additional piece of data, namely the type and value of their car(s). This adds a further dimension to the assessment. If the client's car is a Ford Escort, he or she may not be especially likely to show an interest in the new service; ownership of a Jaguar indicates they are likely to be better prospects.

The continuing need for data

Although there may already be quite a lot of data in and around your business, additional data will probably be necessary and there is a continuing need to build and maintain your database.

Here is a reminder of some other sources of data.

- Customer and prospect questionnaires – these can attract quite large responses, such as 50% or more from established clients and 20% or more from prospects.
- Mailings to outside lists – there is a wide range of lists available for rent and any respondents can be added to the database, subject to the requirements of the Data Protection Act.
- Lifestyle database companies – provide a similar service for consumer records. These organizations have several million names and addresses on their databases.
- Responses from advertising, inserts and other promotions. Again, subject to the requirements of the Data Protection Act, these can be added to your database.

For information about businesses, Companies House is a good source of raw data. The information about companies is extracted from their annual returns. You can also buy the same information, but with additional 'narrative' and trend analysis, from information brokers such as Dun & Bradstreet, Market Location and Experian. These companies can provide not only names and addresses, but also additional data about size, performance and so on. They will also verify your own records and add any additional data they hold.

How can you capture the data?

However much data you already have, it will not all be in a computer, or at least the computer on which you wish to run your marketing database. Therefore, some data capture is inevitable. If you have the capacity to undertake data input in-house, this is the cheapest way.

It is important to avoid duplication of records so it is advisable to build some form of de-duplication process into the data-entry routine. (See the next page for more on de-duplication.) There are a number of software tools available, such as 'Quick-address', to help you check the accuracy of each address on entry. Most of these will also save a high percentage of the initial keystrokes.

As an alternative to in-house data capture, there are many bureaux offering this service and you will find these listed in the Yellow Pages under the heading 'Computer Services'.

How can data be kept up to date?

Data decays very rapidly – more than 10% of consumers move house every year; and up to 30% of business people move (desks at least) every year. It is vital that data is maintained correctly and some of the ways you can do this are:

- regular communication inviting response – questionnaires, offers of information and so on
- periodic comparisons with outside databases, for example the electoral register, lifestyle database companies, and for businesses with companies such as Dun & Bradstreet and Experian.

Every time a contact is made with a customer or prospect, by mail, telephone or in person, you should attempt to verify your data.

The importance of de-duplication

When you are adding names to your database, or perhaps planning to mail one or more outside lists together with your own, it is necessary to identify 'duplicates', that is people whose names appear more than once.

Lists from various sources, and your own names and addresses, can be run through a 'merge/purge' to highlight possible duplicates, which are then scrutinized and eliminated where necessary.

You should also include addresses you do not wish to mail (for example people who owe you money, who have asked not to be mailed, or those with whom you simply do not want to do business).

When adding new data, you can usually program your database to identify any duplicates. For a wider exercise, such as the one above, you should consider using a bureau.

There are numerous bureaux that can take your own and a selection of external lists and carry out the de-duplication process for you. Most bureaux have the latest hardware, highly sophisticated software and lots of experience. This is very valuable and, despite the charges, out-sourcing your de-duplication will frequently be very cost-effective.

The benefits of de-duplication are not purely financial – a merge/purge run can save much customer irritation and tell you something about the potential value of an external list.

For example, a prospective external list has greater potential:

- if it has no, or very few internal duplicates, that is addresses appearing twice on the same list (this problem is rare with rented lists, and if a list is very 'clean' it is likely to be well managed and, therefore, up to date)
- the higher the duplication with your own best customer list and the other candidate lists.

Names that are on all or several lists are often the best names of all and some mailers actually single these out for special treatment, such as more expensive products.

The addresses on different lists may well not be in the same format and some additional data processing may be necessary. However, most bureaux cope very efficiently with this problem and a merge/purge run will usually be cost-effective.

Note that de-duplication is important even if you are only planning to mail your own customers and prospects.

Duplication can be very common, even within internal lists unless you have been very careful in checking each new name as it is added.

Some companies keep records by account numbers or product type rather than customer names and addresses and this can lead to a high level of wastage and customer dissatisfaction.

For 10 years we lived in Normandy and worked in England, so my wife and I used the car ferry up to twenty times a year, ten or so with Brittany Ferries and the rest with P&O.

Example

We occasionally received a mailing from P&O, but Brittany Ferries really did it in style.

Brittany Ferries clearly did not believe in de-duplication as, whenever it sent out a mailing, we received twelve or more identical copies. The record was 19 copies of its annual timetable.

When I contacted Brittany Ferries to suggest some more careful database management, they dismissed my suggestions, pointing out that as 90% of all their customers travel only once a year, there was no need for such management (i.e. 90% of their customers didn't experience this problem)!

Apart from the frightening lack of concern for a good customer, this case illustrates the vital importance of de-duplication and good database management. Unless you check names as you add them to your database, or at the very least before you mail them, your best customers will receive the most copies of the same mailing.

How can the data be used?

Once you have collected this customer information, what can you do with it? The following section shows how and where the database can help you manage your business.

- Planning – the database helps you to define objectives, select customer segments, develop relevant offers and messages, and match costs to potential returns.

- Contact strategy – the process of deciding which medium or combination of media will be most appropriate for each task and each category of customer. Your database will also help you to identify individuals in order to send timely communications. There are many possible reasons for sending a mailing apart from soliciting orders.
- Data processing – the production of disks or labels for addressing your mailing; lists for follow-up activities; 'mail-merging' of letter copy and addresses; counts and reports to aid planning.
- Response handling – one of the key functions of your database is to record response to promotional mailings. This is easier if you use Unique Reference Numbers on your response forms.
- Lead processing – helping you keep to track of enquiries (leads) received, following these through the sales follow-up process and, where necessary, issuing reminders for future action.
- Campaign management and reporting – in addition to producing the necessary customer paperwork, your system should also produce periodic reports to help you manage promotional campaigns.
- Customer satisfaction surveys – information from questionnaires can be added to customer records helping to make the planning and selection processes more effective in future.
- Analysis – in addition to producing pre-determined reports, a good database system enables you to do ad hoc 'what if' analysis.
- Data maintenance – data, especially name and address details, decay rapidly. Frequent contact can overcome this providing you update records quickly and efficiently.

The marketing database is a series of tables. A table can be:

- a list of names and addresses
- a list of transactions
- a list of suppliers, delivery methods and so on
- a list of promotion codes
- a list of customers who have been mailed and their responses
- any logical collection of data.

The ways in which this data is assembled and manipulated are highly complex and beyond the scope of this book. However, as a marketer, you do need to be able to follow the logic of a database. For instance, it would not be logical to store details of every transaction against every customer in the same table. Some customers may have dozens of transactions, others only one. To avoid large areas of wasted space, transactions are stored in a separate table, with a link between the customer's name and address and the transaction.

Having assembled the data, records have to be selected for a particular mailing campaign. This is done by a process of raising queries. For instance, if we wished to mail customers who had spent more than £500 in the past 6 months we would:

- tell the computer to identify all transactions of £500 or more between the dates of XX and YY
- link these transactions to the name and address table
- get a count of how many names and addresses had been identified
- if and when required, extract the related names and addresses for use in the promotion.

Using queries in this way enables us to model campaigns and identify whether our selection parameters have been appropriate. If the count shows we have only 50 customers who fit the category (spent £500 within last 6 months) we may wish to broaden the parameters.

We could extend the period to 12 months and/or reduce the qualifying total to £250. This would produce a larger number of prospects.

The exact process used depends on the software being used. These days PC software is generally more user-friendly than in the past and allows the marketer direct access to the data. This makes modelling campaigns easier and quicker than was the case with mainframes and IT departments.

Mainframe and midsize computers require a separate team of technical people to become involved and this generally extends the process and makes it much less flexible. The process of changing query parameters described above would take 2 or 3 minutes on a PC; it may take 2 or 3 days with a mainframe. This is often because the IT people have many priorities and marketing tends not to be at the top of their list.

Also the mainframe may be busy running business management applications during the day and marketing queries may have to be scheduled for overnight runs.

Sometimes this problem can be overcome by using a hybrid system, such as the one used by a major European bank shown in Figure 6.2.

These people use the data to answer customer questions, but also to conduct data analyses using user-friendly Windows-based software (SAS or SPSS).

The IT people do not have to bother with marketing requests, which is a great relief for them. Marketing people do not have to think through the answers before they ask the questions.

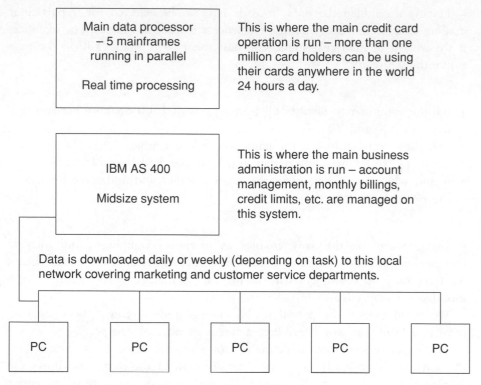

Figure 6.2 Hybrid computer systems for data management

Microcomputer hardware

Nowadays, with the exception of very large undertakings, it is possible for most organizations to run their business computer tasks on microcomputers (PCs or PC networks). The advantages of micro systems include the following.

- Cost – hardware is cheap and getting cheaper as it gets more powerful. PCs are manufactured in their thousands, using common or interchangeable components. This is not the case with mainframes and midsize equipment where components and background systems vary widely.
- Flexibility – micro systems are easily expandable. If your machine needs more disk space or memory, you can upgrade quite easily, often carrying out the task yourself. As a result of affordability, if your machine is no longer up to the tasks you are setting it you can buy another machine and hook it up to your current system.
- Data portability – nowadays it is possible to transfer data from one machine to another by a variety of means, including floppy disks; zip disks carrying up to 200 megabytes (Mb) of data; CDs holding more than 600 Mb; direct

cable connections; remotely through modems; and even via infra-red links requiring no physical connection at all.

- Development – much of the research and development taking place in the computer industry concerns microcomputers. By using micro hardware, you are remaining at the forefront of technology.
- Ease of use – today, with user-friendly graphical user interfaces (GUIs) such as Windows, sophisticated computing tasks are within the grasp of most people. Today's PCs come with pre-loaded software, modems and are often fully 'Internet ready'. You simply switch on and sign up.

The power and capacity of micros are expanding rapidly. It is unlikely that you will be managing a consumer database that will expand at a rate faster than the expansion of micro technology. In fact, it is likely that micro developments will far outstrip the advance of your marketing requirements.

Very few companies do not have at least one microcomputer; this is how universally popular they have become. This means that other users are easy to find, engineers are available in almost every town, your friends and colleagues can often help with queries and problems, and there are many easy-to-follow books and magazines covering all topics.

Most companies today accept the overwhelming arguments for the use of microcomputers for marketing applications. All mainframes and midsize computers provide interfaces with micros, although some are better than others. If your corporate culture does not allow for easy use of micros, investigate ways of downloading data to a micro environment. Even if you have to use some external expertise to make this happen, it will be worthwhile.

Chips, storage and memory

When choosing a microcomputer, the first consideration is the size and speed of the processor (chip). There are many chips available, but the best known is the Pentium series by Intel. Currently (late 2001), the fastest Intel processor is the Pentium IV running at around 2000 MHz. These machines are capable of running very large data processing operations at very high speeds. The faster the clock speed, the greater the cost. However, as costs are coming down almost daily, it pays to go for the fastest, most powerful system you can afford.

The next consideration is the amount of disk space you will require. Bear in mind that modern software requires lots of disk space and, as each development appears, more space is needed. A few years ago it was common to find PCs offering 50 or 100 Mb of hard disk space. Today, Windows XP requires more than 100 Mb before you have installed any applications such as word processing, spreadsheet, presentation, database and so on.

Anyone buying a new PC today should be looking for hard disk space in gigabytes rather than megabytes (1 Gb is 1000 Mb). Hard disk space is not very expensive, so order as much as you can.

The next point to consider is random access memory (RAM). RAM is a special kind of memory that is used to run current applications. So the more RAM you have, the more applications you can run at the same time, and the faster each will perform.

RAM is a special kind of memory that is used to run current applications. So the more RAM you have, the more applications you can run at the same time, and the faster each will perform.

Modern software requires lots of RAM to run at peak efficiency and manufacturers tend to ignore other applications that may be running at the same time. So a database product may quote minimum requirements of 8 Mb of RAM, but if you are running Windows and perhaps your word processor at the same time, 8 Mb will be nowhere near enough.

In the early 1990s, 8 or 16 Mb of RAM was considered adequate for most small business requirements. Nowadays, 128 Mb would be considered the minimum for a stand-alone business machine, with much more needed for a network of course. So, once again, the rule is, buy as much as you can afford.

Summary

- Microcomputer hardware is cost-effective.
- It is easily expandable or can be replaced cheaply.
- It is at the forefront of technology.
- Most micros are capable of large-scale high-speed number crunching.
- Check space and memory requirements (with data processing experts if possible), and allow for disk-hungry modern software and for contingencies. Make sure you buy plenty of hard disk space and RAM.
- Buy the most powerful processor you can afford.
- Get your data onto your micro whenever you can. It means you can model campaigns in your own time and make as many queries as you wish.

Microcomputer software

Having examined the arguments for microcomputer hardware, the discussion can now turn to the software you may need.

As the most popular packages sell in the hundreds of thousands and in some cases, millions, economies of scale mean that off-the-shelf software can be cheap. Its universal use means that:

- it is easy to recruit programmers and operators
- friends and colleagues can often help with advice

- files can easily be passed around, either physically through disks or cables, or remotely via the Internet
- training is cheap and readily available.

There is a vast range of packages from which you can choose. The market is currently dominated by Microsoft, of course, but there are a number of reasonable alternatives, for example Word Perfect for word processing and Lotus Organizer for your diary requirements. The two main statistical analysis packages are those mentioned earlier, namely SPSS and SAS.

The top-selling database packages, Access and FoxPro, are both from Microsoft. Both are excellent packages, although Access is easier for non-technical people to use.

Whatever your choice, today's micro software makes data very portable. It is easy to transport data from one package to another. This is an important factor as everyone has their own favourite package, and people are reluctant to train in another package. Consequently, the fact that data can be transferred easily from one package to another is a major benefit.

Micro software is generally designed for non-technical users, and its 'point and shoot' design and built-in help system makes it very user-friendly. This factor is often not appreciated by younger users who have never had to wrestle with the convoluted, non-friendly software written for mainframes.

Another feature of micro software is that it is relatively 'bug free'. Of course, everyone has a story about a piece of software that seems to have a mind of its own, but most people who complain have never experienced the trials and tribulations of working with a mainframe. First editions of a new package often do have bugs, but these are easily fixed and corrective patches can easily be downloaded from the Internet.

As stated earlier, there is a huge amount of research and development taking place in the PC area and it will always be at the forefront of technology, embracing all the latest advances.

A final important advantage of off-the-shelf PC software is the generally high quality of documentation and support. There is usually a comprehensive manual, on-screen help and additional online support in many cases. Such support is not always found with software written for larger machines.

Building your database on a PC

As we have seen, the starting point is to get your data into the PC domain. Next, you may need to engage experts (internal, external or perhaps both) to design the database you require. These experts should help you define the design you need, file layouts, disk space and data selection requirements and the reports you will need on a regular basis.

For database interrogation, it is a good idea to base your system on an off-the-shelf package such as Access or FoxPro. You will identify certain standard operations that you will need on a regular basis, for example:

- loading a certain set of data from a specific source on a given day of the week (this could be the number of advertisement replies received by the mail room last week)
- producing a set of reports on the status of various aspects of the business at the end of each month (number of new customers who have ordered, total value of new orders and so on).

These regular reports can be designed as 'push button' options whereby the operator has only to select a given 'hot key' to run these analyses. Such an approach minimizes error, makes operations more efficient and allows operators to concentrate on more important tasks, such as actually checking the contents of the reports. These reports can be written into your Access or FoxPro database by your developer.

When choosing a software supplier, choose an established company (as you would when choosing any other supplier). Talk to their clients and take up references. Any reputable supplier will be happy to volunteer these details.

The initial software is only part of the story, of course. You will need to strike up a partnership with this company, as there will be changes or upgrades required as new versions are developed. Suppliers should tell you about their testing and bug-logging procedures.

A good supplier will keep you informed at every stage of development. If you are simply presented with a completed system, you have had no chance to monitor or even steer the development. It can be very difficult to understand the workings of a system when you have not been party to its planning and evolution.

A final point is to ensure that your supplier caters for installation, training and ongoing support. You are bound to have problems, bugs, questions and comments and you need a supplier that will cater for this.

Summary

PC software:

- is cheap and available off the shelf
- is widely used
- is easy to use and train for
- can be obtained through a large number of suppliers and developers
- offers a wide range of options
- is easy to link with other packages
- is designed for non-technical people to use

- is at the forefront of technology
- is relatively bug free
- is well documented and well supported
- makes it easy to develop a relational database, using off-the-shelf packages, such as Access and FoxPro
- enables you to supplement the standard off-the-shelf features with bespoke additions written in the same language.

External data sources

It is worth considering what external data might be available to help you enhance your database. External data helps to improve your understanding of your customers, gives you alternative ways of selecting records, and provides a useful source of new prospects. External data can be related to demographics and lifestyle information.

Demographics

Demographics companies supply a system of categorizing the country into a number of different demographic types (such as 'High spending greys' or 'Pebble dash Subtopia'). Each postcode in the country is assigned one of these types. This means that each customer on your database can be matched to a demographic type. When this is done across all of your customer records, a demographic profile emerges.

As discussed earlier, popular demographic classification systems are ACORN, MOSAIC and Superprofiles. These are based on public domain data including the census, the electoral roll and County Court Judgement (CCJ) data. Key statistics such as car ownership (from the census), length of tenure (electoral roll), and any CCJs are put through cluster analysis to determine the classification system.

If you have a licence agreement with the demographics company, the codes can be used as a basis of selection. For instance, you could select all 'High spending greys' who have spent more than £500 with you.

It can be very useful to have such additional data, although external data will never be as powerful as your own customer data. When a demographic code is allocated to a customer record, it does not refer to that customer as an individual, it refers to the neighbourhood in which that customer lives. The advantage of demographics over your own customer data is that they cover the entire country.

Thus, if you know the profile of your current customers, you can apply this to find prospects who are likely to have similar needs and behaviour. You can profile your customer base and:

- order similar names from cold (rented) lists
- select advertising likely to be read or subscribed to by the sort of people who buy your products
- identify areas of the country where your prospects are likely to live.

This final point introduces a whole study in itself. Many retailers use demographics to measure market potential. Thus, if you know the sort of people who buy your products, you can evaluate areas on the ground to judge the likely demand for your products. This is one of the ways supermarket companies determine whether a site is worth developing.

Lifestyle data

Lifestyle companies collect information on customers' lifestyles. The data is assembled from various sources, such as guarantee cards filled in, in return for an extended warranty, questionnaires inserted in magazines or mailed to previous respondent, and competition entry forms.

Lifestyle companies collect information on customers' lifestyles. The data is assembled from various sources, such as guarantee cards filled in, in return for an extended warranty, questionnaires inserted in magazines or mailed to previous respondents, and competition entry forms.

Marketers can buy lists on the basis of lifestyle data. For example, you may wish to rent the names of 50,000 people in Northern England who earn more than £25,000 per year.

Lifestyle companies claim that Lifestyle questionnaires have been filled in by about 45% of adults (covering over 70% of UK households). This is well short of the 100% covered by the demographics systems but the data relates to individuals not simply to neighbourhoods. Thus, although the number of addresses will be smaller, you are selecting on the basis of actual individual data, so the 'fit' should be closer to your ideal requirements.

Another point to note is that the people who filled in the questionnaires are 'mail responsive' and, thus, untypical of the country as a whole. However, as you will often be using such data as the basis for selecting names for a direct mail offer, this bias can sometimes be a benefit rather than a penalty.

Another way of using the lifestyle databases is to send your customer file to them for profiling. The lifestyle company matches your file against their data bank and allocates additional data such as income, car ownership and other factors you request. Typically, only 30–35% of your file will be matched, but it is a much cheaper way of buying information than traditional market research.

After this exercise, you will have a good idea of income, car ownership, age, hobbies, readership habits and so on. If you set up a licence agreement with the company you can use these data for selection purposes. The lifestyle company can also supply you with names and addresses of prospects whose profile matches that of your customers. Such agreements have to be carefully negotiated with the data owners.

As a general rule, the hierarchy of data is:

- your own customer data – most powerful, as it relates to your customers and their existing relationship with you
- lifestyle data – relating to individuals by name and address
- demographic data – dealing with the characteristics of neighbourhoods rather than households.

Although customer data is the most powerful, it is only available for your own customer base. Lifestyle data is available of those people who have filled out a questionnaire (45% of UK adults, so about 70% of households). Demographic data is universal.

Summary

- Demographics companies allocate codes based on public domain data.
- Codes are allocated to postcodes and, thus, represent the characteristics of neighbourhoods rather than households.
- Data is not as powerful as lifestyle or individual data.
- All postcodes have been allocated a demographic code.
- It is used to profile existing customers on the assumption that prospects will be of the same profile.
- Demographic data is used for site location studies, general targeting, prospecting and measurement of market potential.
- Lifestyle companies collect data about individuals via questionnaires.
- About 45% of the adults are covered – although this 45% is the most mail-responsive segment of the population.
- If you send a file for profiling, 35% would be a good match rate (as opposed to almost 100% with demographic coding).
- Lifestyle data is more powerful, as it relates to individuals rather than areas.
- The company's own data is the most powerful of all (although clearly referring only to one's own customer base and thus having little roll-out potential).

Data warehousing and data mining

The amount of data collected by organizations today has been causing some difficulty. Tesco's Club Card scheme, which has been very successful, generates huge amounts of customer data. Dunn Humby, recently acquired by Tesco, manages this process very well, and Tesco is beginning to work very tight segmentation models from this data. However, it has taken some time to develop.

Data warehousing aggregates data from multiple locations and allows for quick interrogation on any variable. It should be available through the organization and is often accessed through a very user-friendly Web interface with the database via the company's intranet.

Data warehousing aggregates data from multiple locations and allows for quick interrogation on any variable. It should be available through the organization and is often accessed through a very user-friendly Web interface with the database via the company's Intranet.

The danger is that the information collected is not relevant and the ease with which enquiries can be made creates information overload. We are all aware of the amount of information we now have access to and the old maxim 'information is power' remains true, but information without intelligence is nothing!

The increased sophistication of software and hardware has allowed the process of data mining to emerge.

Data mining is the searching of databases for unseen connections between apparently unrelated data sets. This is facilitated through the use of neural nets. It can be objective driven or simply be a random process of exploring statistically valid and commercially relevant connections.

SUMMARY

This chapter began by looking at the move towards customer relationship management and the central role of the database to this idea. Despite the developments in IT, the database remains a problem area for many businesses.

We have seen that as for almost everything in direct marketing, the starting point for the design of the database is the customer. The information fuelling the database is often drawn from other areas of the business, including accounts, customer care, sales management and facilities management systems.

Data mining is the searching of databases for unseen connections between apparently unrelated data sets. This is facilitated through the use of neural nets. It can be objective driven or simply be a random process of exploring statistically valid and commercially relevant connections.

Through an analysis of Sodastream's use of its database, we looked in detail at the various uses of the database. These were:

- developing selective cost-efficient relationships
- providing reports on marketing activity
- segmenting customers into more manageable groups
- targeting groups with particular messages
- managing these groups for maximum profit.

Segmentation and targeting were seen as central applications of the database and the ability to target cost-effectively communications and products in order to improve our long-term marketing position was central to this.

We have looked at some of the techniques used to segment the customer base including:

- regression analysis
- CHAID
- cluster analysis
- neural networks.

We have seen that it is possible to carry out sophisticated analysis of the database using tools such as SPSS and SAS. However, at least a basic knowledge of statistics is required in order to understand and to communicate the results.

Using the *Daily Telegraph*'s customer relationship programme, we explored the value of developing customer relationships:

- customers are different
- they respond better to targeted messages
- we can acquire customers and retain customers more effectively
- the database helps manage this process discretely and efficiently.

In looking at the process involved in developing customer relationships, four questions were posed.

First, what data is needed?

- Data for current activity, including contact data.
- Profiling data, including family size and lifestyle.
- Data aiding future activity, including response history and timings.
- Data relating to the market, including competition and supply patterns.

Second, where does the data come from? A range of available internal and external sources was explored.

Third, how can it be captured? We saw that data capture can be handled in-house or through an external bureau and we looked at the software available to help the process.

Fourth, how is it kept up to date? We looked at the need for regular communication and cross-checks with external databases. To manage this process the need for de-duplication was stressed and the ways of managing this process were discussed in detail.

We have explored various uses of the database including:

- planning
- contact strategy
- data processing
- response handling
- lead processing
- campaign management and reporting

- satisfaction surveys
- analysis
- data maintenance.

We have seen how the database works to help us manage these activities and looked at the technical specification required to support the database.

The chapter has explored the advantages of desktop systems, which include:

- cost
- flexibility
- data portability
- that they are generally at the forefront of technology
- that they are becoming extremely fast
- ease of use and accessibility.

For most very large databases, a hybrid system of mainframes linked to local networks is used.

We saw that Moore's law and the pace of change in computing power means that system capability is improving constantly.

The chapter continued with an examination of the range of software supporting marketing activity and noted that the recording, storing, transferring and analysis of data is constantly being made easier. PC software allows the cheap construction of marketing databases that can be widely used and understood by non-technical staff.

We went on to explore the integration of external sources with our internal data looking at demographic and lifestyle lists.

Finally, we have looked at data warehousing and data mining and the use of analysis and processing.

REVIEW QUESTIONS

1   What are the benefits of using a marketing database and what are the difficulties?

2   Where do we obtain data to populate the database?

3   List five common uses of a marketing database.

4   What is the Pareto principle and what is its relevance in direct marketing?

5   Why do we segment the customer base?

6   List four techniques that help us segment the marketing base.

7   What is CHAID analysis?

8   What are the benefits of retaining customers?

9   What are the four types of data required to maintain customer relationships?

10   List five sources of external data.

11   What is de-duplication?

12   What are the characteristics of a marketing database that allow various applications to be supported?

13   What are the advantages of microcomputers in managing the customer database?

14   What is RAM?

15   What external data sources are available to help enhance internally generated data?

16   What is data mining?

EXERCISES

You are a local restaurant manager who has recently been on a training course run by the Institute of Direct Marketing on direct and database marketing. You have decided to set up your own marketing database on your business PC using Access.

• What information would you keep on the database?
• How would you acquire and maintain the data?
• What marketing applications would the database support?

Chapter 7

How to reach customers and prospects effectively

Introduction
- Brand versus response – the traditional conflict
- Brand response advertising works
- The start of the digital age
- Planning direct response versus brand awareness
- Integrated media planning – bringing it all together
  - The planning process
  - Identifying your audience – sources of media information
- Media selection
  - Press
  - Magazines
  - Loose and bound-in inserts
  - Buying and evaluating press advertising
  - Third-party distribution of leaflets
  - The telephone
  - Direct mail
  - Door-to-door distribution
  - Television
  - Radio
- Costs and responses
  - What does a direct mailing cost?
  - How much response do you need?
  - Should you try to make money immediately?
Summary
Review questions
Exercises

As we mentioned previously, what makes advertisements and mailings work is relevance. It is not easy to send a totally relevant message to a wide audience through broadscale advertising simply because the audience is made up of individuals who each have their own interests and needs. Consequently, what is relevant to one will not be relevant to another.

This is why, whatever our starting point, sooner or later we will find it more cost-effective to communicate selling propositions through direct communication methods such as face to face, Internet, mail and telephone, rather than broadscale options such as television, radio, newspapers and magazines.

However, even if we have the names and addresses of suspects, or even prospects, direct mail will not necessarily be the most cost-efficient place to start. With many products, especially those that are bought infrequently, it is not easy to establish the right time to communicate with an unknown prospect.

Under these circumstances, some form of broadscale prospecting may be a more cost-efficient starting point. When using this route, it is vital to find something relevant and interesting to say which will grab the attention of prospects and persuade them to contact us for more information. Once we have details of their precise requirements, we will often find that direct communications are much more cost-efficient.

Before we consider individual media, it is worth looking at the way a media planner would approach a direct communications campaign and comparing this with the method used by traditional advertisers.

Brand versus response – the traditional conflict

In many companies and agencies there is still the same old split between 'awareness' and 'direct response' with each side sure that its approach is correct. These conflicting opinions are usually felt to be totally opposed to each other and the debate continues.

However, there is another way, which is called integration. This is the way all advertisers will eventually go. Already more than one-third of all television commercials carry a telephone response number, as do more than half of all advertisements.

The challenge is to integrate brand and response messages in a way that does not simply avoid conflict, but positively enhances both awareness and response. On the face of it these two seem to be incompatible.

However, this is mainly because of the traditional attitudes associated with each type of advertising.

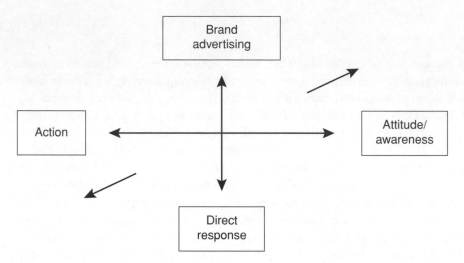

Figure 7.1 The traditional conflict between direct response and brand advertising

The awareness expert says, 'I don't want any nasty coupons or telephone numbers interfering with my nice creative work'. This was actually said to me by the creative director of a leading advertising agency.

The direct response expert says, 'Forget pretty pictures and tonal values, give me good old hard sell with large coupons and telephone numbers'.

So which way should we go? The answer is that well-designed attractive advertisements can change attitudes and generate response if the two sides will simply put aside their prejudices and work together.

The answer is that well-designed attractive advertisements can change attitudes and generate response if the two sides will simply put aside their prejudices and work together.

Figure 7.2 The impact of integration

Brand response advertising works

This new, or comparatively new, genre is proving effective for many advertisers targeting both consumers and business people. There are advantages for planners and designers, including the following.

- Greater choice of media – because of the dual-purpose objective, the campaign can be extended into media that would not quite satisfy the pure evaluation of either awareness or response planners.

- More response methods – today we can receive responses in at least five ways, namely mail, telephone, fax, e-mail or Web site. Most of these do not require a coupon so there can be less pressure on space. However, we must not forget that a newspaper survey showed that advertisements carrying coupons actually scored higher in awareness terms than those without coupons.

These advantages and the fact that many advertisers are experiencing great success means that brand response or 'dual purpose' advertising is here to stay.

The start of the digital age

Today's growth in digital technology is bringing about changes in all directions.

- New working practices – the virtual office is a reality, at least it is technically. There are still many people who will not willingly embrace, or perhaps do not have the self-discipline to accept, the freedom to work from home.
- New communications vehicles – now that we can send e-mail through our television set and mobile phone, we no longer need even a PC to stay in touch. Video links make office communication a possibility from anywhere in the world. The Internet also enables closed user groups to share bulletin boards and diaries across companies and countries.
- New channels of distribution – the Internet has also become a major distribution channel, enabling written and audio-visual material to be shared or sold around the world. Internet usage at home is now greater than that at work. (For more on this see Chapter 8.)
- Changes in social behaviour – although there are now more television channels than ever, overall viewing time is reducing. Consumers have greater choice, greater control and the opportunity for greater interactivity. Some analysts predict that by 2012 the digital console will be the only home communications channel in widespread use.

All of the above factors have to be considered when planning a communications campaign today.

Planning direct response versus brand awareness

First, we will consider the different objectives of the two types of media planner and then consider how these might be brought into alignment.

A traditional advertising planner aims to achieve maximum coverage of the market place in the shortest possible time. High frequency and repetition are considered desirable, maximizing 'opportunities to see'.

In Figure 7.3, we can see how coverage is built up week by week.

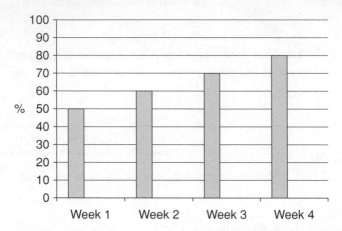

Figure 7.3 Traditional advertisers seek high frequency and repetition

However, experienced direct marketers know that this is not the most cost-effective use of the budget. When we are able to examine response data from each individual insertion, we find that the effectiveness of each subsequent advertisement declines rapidly if the insertions run too closely together.

So the direct marketing planner's chart, shown in Figure 7.4, looks very different.

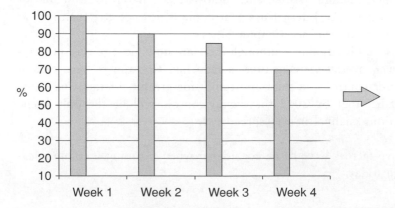

Figure 7.4 Direct marketers optimize response through careful phasing

This shows clearly how response declines as the campaign progresses and the direct marketing planner aims to minimize this decline in two ways.

1   By testing to find the ideal 'gap' between each insertion – broadly the longer the gap, the less the decline. There is, of course, a trade-off required as no advertiser can afford to wait too long between insertions. Careful testing enables the direct marketing planner to optimize the budget.
2   By developing two or more versions of the same offer, that is two different advertisement approaches. This enables frequency to be increased without the same level of decline in response. (This is discussed again in Chapter 11.)

Here is another way of comparing the differences between the two planning approaches. The traditional 'awareness' approach consists of four basic phases (Figure 7.5).

Figure 7.5   Planning awareness campaigns

The direct marketing approach is a continuous cycle of planning, testing, measuring and modifying as the campaign progresses (Figure 7.6).

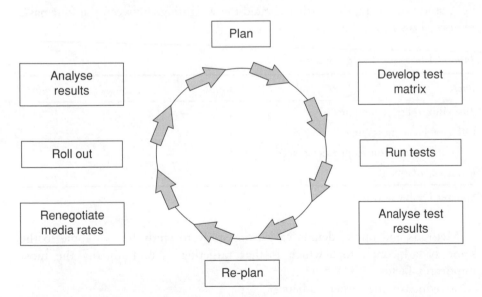

Figure 7.6   Planning direct marketing

Summarizing, the direct marketing approach sets out to identify prospect clusters that offer the greatest potential to deliver the required number of responses at the lowest cost per response. It is a continuing process of testing, measurement and refinement.

Integrated media planning – bringing it all together

The integrated media planner uses a mixture of media to achieve a variety of impacts which collectively add up to a successful campaign. The planner will use media for achieving positioning, understanding and to create 'noise'. Having this going on even in the background, enables response oriented advertisements to be more cost-effective. Using media in this way means that occasionally we need to accept a slightly higher cost per response than we would expect from a strict direct response campaign. However, we will have achieved a greater overall effect by adding the awareness elements to our campaign. This can have a beneficial effect on retention and repeat sales. It will also make future campaigns more cost-effective.

The planning process

We start with targeting, which is always the most important factor in the success or otherwise of any communications campaign. There have been many researches into the relative effectiveness of each factor in determining whether an advertisement or mailing will work well.

A study by Ogilvy & Mather elicited the weightings between the four basic factors shown in Table 7.1.

Table 7.1 Factors driving response

Factor	Value
Targeting – list or medium	6
Offer or basic message	3
Timing – in relation to prospects needs	2
Creative treatment	1.35

Source: Ogilvy and Mather

Methods and minor details vary from study to study but all come to the same broad conclusion, which is that targeting is undoubtedly the most important factor.

So which is the target audience?

- What are they like?
- Where do they live?
- What do they do?
- What do they think?
- What do they want, like and need?

When is the right time to approach them?

- What is the decision-making process for this audience/product?
- When are decisions made?
- When is the ideal time to influence them?
- When are they most likely to respond?

Where can they be found?

- Where do they live and work?

What media do they consume?

- Television – which channels and time slots?
- Cinema – what sort of films?
- What newspapers and magazines do they read?
- Are they receptive to direct mail?
- Do they listen to radio at home or in the car?
- Do they use trains or the underground?

How do they consume media?

- Where is their location?
- What are they doing?
- Involved/uninvolved?
- Active/passive?
- Interested/disinterested?

How much will it cost to reach them? The objective is to get the maximum for the minimum cost. So, build your ideal media plan by understanding the market forces and using flexibility and negotiation skills to achieve an acceptable compromise.

Next, we identify the available media, including:

- national commercial television contractors
- regional ITV companies
- satellite and cable channels
- commercial radio stations
- poster sites
- cinema screens
- national newspapers
- regional paid-for newspapers
- regional free newspapers
- consumer magazines
- trade publications.

Not to mention the telephone, sales force, sponsorship, promotions, interactive media, product placement and, of course, the Internet.

There are also thousands of 'ambient media' opportunities. You can advertise:

- in public toilets
- on petrol pumps
- in golf holes
- on supermarket floors
- in concert programmes
- on entertainment and travel tickets
- on escalators.

Media planning is about understanding your audience and where to find them, then using the appropriate medium intelligently so your message is seen as relevant and interesting. So how do you identify the right medium from the thousands of options? You start with research and profiling your existing customers if possible. This helps you to identify the characteristics of good prospects and of individuals likely to be low value/high risk and so on. Profiling characteristics may include:

- geographic factors – identifying people by region, town, ITV area, vicinity to stores and so on
- demographics – age, class, gender, household composition, marital status and so on; with businesses you may be looking at size, industry, number of company cars, sites, coffee machines and so on
- geodemographics – using some of the many property classification systems, such as ACORN and MOSAIC
- psychographics – here we are considering attitudes and lifestyle characteristics
- behavioural – purchasing patterns, frequency, value and so on
- media consumption – noting the media consumed by our customers is an ideal way of identifying the best source of good prospects.

The objective of profiling is to identify the best customers and then use research to locate similar people or companies with the highest propensity to become good customers.

The objective of profiling is to identify the best customers and then use research to locate similar people or companies with the highest propensity to become good customers.

Identifying your audience – sources of media information

Once we have defined our target, there are a number of media research sources to help us locate prospects:

- Target Group Index (TGI) – this is based on a sample of 24,000 UK residents aged over 15. The survey covers 200 publications across 500 product fields and 4000 brands. It can be used simply to identify the most appropriate publications for reaching a specified audience or in a much more complex way to identify attitudes, lifestyle characteristics and publications read by, say, Marks & Spencer shoppers.

- National Readership Survey (NRS) is a larger (38,000 people over the age of 15) but simpler study covering 287 publications. It is used primarily to identify the characteristics of, say, *Daily Mail* readers. These can then, of course, be compared to your own customer profile.

- British Business Survey (BBS), conducted by the Business Media Research Committee, is a bi-annual report that provides readership information on more than 3000 business people.

- Broadcasters Audience Research Board (BARB) reports on the size and viewing habits of the UK television audience. A sample of more than 4000 households is measured continuously using a combination of automatic and manual diarizing covering each individual member of each household.

- RAJAR is similar to BARB, but reports on radio audiences.

- POSTAR is similar, but for poster audiences.

- Cinema and Video Industry Audience Research (CAVIAR) maintains details of audiences by film and frequency of visit.

Rather than going into great detail about these studies, it is simply recommended that you contact each organization for their information pack – their addresses are listed in Chapter 14.

Most media are capable of carrying a direct marketing message. Their effectiveness varies according to:

- the size of audience you wish to reach
- how much you can afford to pay for a response
- the complexity of your message
- how appropriate a particular medium is for your message.

A good media plan:

- is built to deliver the number of responses your business needs
- considers branding as well as response requirements
- makes your communications stand out through innovation
- allows for constant testing and change where necessary.

Media selection

These are the various media options open to us.

Press

Press (newspaper) advertising can be used to initiate a relationship either through inviting a request for information or sometimes through a direct sale. The former is called two-stage or two-step advertising and the objective is to generate a 'lead' or enquiry. Direct sales are referred to as one-stage, one-step or 'off-the-page'.

Press advertising can also be used in a dual purpose (or 'double-duty') role, where we can achieve awareness and generate leads at the same time. Some critics say that dual-purpose advertising does not work, but my experience with Ogilvy & Mather and Stan Rapp's experience with Rapp & Collins prove otherwise.

As a support medium, a well-timed press campaign can increase response to a concurrent activity such as a mailing, door drop or even a television or radio campaign. It can also make sales force activity more productive and it can be highly effective in driving traffic into a Web site. In business to business, it can reach decision-makers that we may never know about. However well targeted a direct mailing is, it may not get the order if the budget-holder has not heard of the company. Thus, press advertising can be the deciding factor in achieving an order in a business-to-business campaign.

Press has the following advantages.

• Large audiences – some press audiences run into millions, so press can be an effective way of reaching large numbers of people quickly.
• High response volumes – although response percentages are low, perhaps as low as 0.01%, the actual number of responses can be large.
• Fast results – a daily newspaper has a very short 'life', consequently 80% or more of your responses will come in within a week. This shortens the process of testing and re-planning media.
• Flexible rates – advertisers with reasonably sized budgets will find many publications are ready to negotiate on price. The best discounts are obtained through short-term buying and especially distress buying.

Distress buying is when the newspaper has a space it cannot sell in tomorrow's edition and, by having artwork ready to go, you may be in a position to negotiate a good space for well below half price.

You cannot depend on this for an entire campaign of course – many professional space buyers avidly seek such spaces, so there are not many opportunities that hit the open market.

- Testing opportunities – many newspapers offer A/B split run facilities enabling direct response advertisers to test alternate copy or offers. A/B splits are explained in Chapter 11.
- Reader relationships – many regular readers tend to trust their paper and, therefore, the advertisements appearing therein. Some advertisers have discovered that writing advertisements for specific papers, that is with copy in the style of the editorial, increases responses.
- Low-entry cost – although artwork can be expensive, entry cost is much lower than for television. It is often possible to test a region of a paper before 'rolling out' nationally, thus minimizing the cost until the publication is proven to work.
- Cost-efficiency – press responses can be surprisingly cheap. Some advertisers can actually make a profit 'off-the-page', although this will not always be the most important factor.
- Short lead times – if you have a piece of artwork ready, you can book a space this afternoon and see your advertisement appear nationally tomorrow morning.
- Creative versatility – the range of sizes, shapes and special positions available in most newspapers enables a high level of creativity to be applied.
- Regional opportunities – several national publications print separate regional editions and this is ideal if your business is centred in one region only.

The perceived weaknesses of the press are as follows.

- Competitive clutter – unless you buy large spaces or pay a premium for a solus position, your advertisement is likely to be accompanied on the page by at least one other. If it is competitive, as are so many in, say, the financial pages of a paper, your advertisement will lose some of its impact.
- Cost – in a national newspaper, even a very small space can cost hundreds of pounds.
- Short 'life' – today's paper is 'dead' tomorrow.
- High wastage – however carefully we target, there will be high wastage in newspaper advertising.
- Low quality of response – short copy and broad audiences tend to produce unqualified replies, so in two-stage advertising conversion to sale can be quite low.
- Low readership of any individual advertisement – research shows that as little as 5% of 'readers' will actually notice any individual advertisement.
- Lack of environmental selectivity – again, unless you pay a premium (or are a very good negotiator), your advertisement will be placed 'run-of-paper'. 'Run-of-paper' means it could go anywhere in the newspaper from city pages

'Run-of-paper' means it could go anywhere in the newspaper from city pages to the sports section.

to the sports section. The surroundings may not be appropriate for your offer and, therefore, not attract the right sort of readers.

- Direct response 'ghettos' – some publications tend to group direct response advertisements and place them all together in the back of the paper (this is particularly prevalent in newspaper magazine supplements). The publishers argue that this creates a 'department' and this can be true. However, unless actively seeking a direct response opportunity, your prospect may not even enter the department and, thus, will not even see your offer.

What size of advertisement will be most cost-effective?

Traditional advertisers, with their requirements for 'coverage' and 'opportunities to see', prefer to take large dominant spaces and these may often be highly effective, of course. Direct marketers, however, know that the smaller the space, the more cost-efficient it will be (assuming that the smaller space contains the same wording and offer as the larger one).

There have been a number of research studies into the relationship between size and cost-effectiveness.

Philip Sainsbury analysed the results of several studies when developing his 'square root principle'. Sainsbury noted that, although doubling the size of an advertisement might be expected to double the response, in fact it only increases response by around 41%. The square root of 2 is 1.41 and, as multiplying size by 2 gives a response of 1.41 times, he called this Sainsbury's square root principle.

The principle works in both directions as Figure 7.7 shows.

Philip Sainsbury analysed the results of several studies when developing his 'square root principle'. Sainsbury noted that, although doubling the size of an advertisement might be expected to double the response, in fact it only increases response by around 41%. The square root of 2 is 1.41 and, as multiplying size by 2 gives a response of 1.41 times, he called this Sainsbury's square root principle.

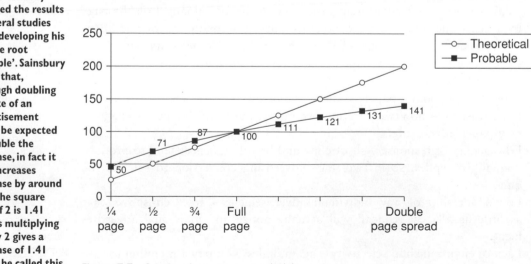

Figure 7.7 Sainsbury's square root principle

What Sainsbury showed is that, if a full page produces 100 replies, a half page will produce around 70 replies and a quarter page around 50.

Now, if your advertising objective is to impress your distributors with the amount of money you are putting behind this launch, then small spaces are not likely to be successful. Equally, if the main objective of your campaign is awareness building, small spaces may not be so effective in the short term. However, if your main priority is cost-effective direct response, you should plan to use the smallest space into which you can comfortably fit your message.

Magazines

Magazines are frequently used by direct marketers for both one-stage and two-stage campaigns. They are useful when you want to target specific groups, whether based on demographics (such as 'UK women') or lifestyle character-istics (such as 'anglers').

Many advertisers have had great success in magazines with highly targeted offers such as:

- a collectible cat plate – hugely successful when run in *Cat World*
- a children's book club run in titles targeted at parents.

Major strengths of magazines include:

- high reader interest – so if your offer is well targeted, your advertisement is likely to be read by more people than the same copy run in a general newspaper
- long life – many magazines are in circulation for months or even years; some advertisers in the *Reader's Digest* receive replies years after running their offers
- pass-on readership – some magazines have a very high 'secondary' reader-ship, which can increase the exposure to your advertisement
- prestige – some titles are considered to be the authority on a subject, so an advertisement in one of these can gain additional prestige.

However, there are also some weaknesses and these include the following.

- Long copy dates – whereas a newspaper advertisement can be booked and run in a few days, colour magazines quite often require artwork several weeks before the publication is distributed. This can make testing and roll-out a lengthy process.
- Cost of testing – producing colour artwork can be expensive, so small tests are often uneconomical.

- Limited testing capabilities – although some magazines offer split-run facilities, these can be withdrawn at short notice when the volume of advertising exceeds a certain limit. With the exception of television programme journals, there are few regional testing opportunities.
- Graveyards – some publishers group direct response advertisers into 'graveyards' at the back of the magazine.

Loose and bound-in inserts

There are several types of inserts.

- Loose inserts (the most common) are the leaflets that fall out of a newspaper or magazine.

- Bound-in inserts are usually made of card and this in itself can increase readership, as the magazine tends to fall open where the card appears – this is called a 'hot-spot'.

- Outserts is the name given to a leaflet bound onto the outside of a magazine. This can be expensive to arrange, but is of course very responsive as no-one can look at the magazine without seeing the advertisement.

- Tip-on cards are typically the same size as a postcard and are glued onto the page on which an advertisement appears. They are fairly expensive as you have to pay for production and print of the card, a colour advertisement in the magazine and an additional charge for gluing ('tipping on') the card. People use them because they generally produce lots of response.

A word about design and printing: most leaflets are inserted by machine, so there are some restrictions regarding size, shape and positions of folds and perforations. It is important to discuss your plans with the publication before finalizing print.

Many of the limitations of magazines and newspapers discussed can be overcome by the use of loose or bound-in inserts. These leaflets arouse criticism from many people but they are a highly effective advertising medium. Recent studies have shown response increases of 500% by using a loose insert rather than a full-page colour advertisement in the same publication.

Table 7.2 shows the results of two noting studies comparing readers noting magazine advertisements with those noting loose inserts.

As we can see, the noting scores are much higher with inserts than with advertisements.

The use of inserts has grown rapidly over the last 10 years and there are several reasons for this.

Table 7.2 Readers noting studies – inserts to magazine advertising

Space Advertising

Size/Position	Mean noting	Max. noting
DPS Colour	39	59
Page colour	33	57
Page Mono	27	42

Loose inserts

Advertiser	Size of insert	Noting %
Toys 'R' Us	48 pages	87
Royal Life	4 pages	83
Littlewoods	4 pages	79

- High responsiveness – in the final analysis, the only reason for a medium to grow is that it produces the results advertisers require. As most loose inserts carry direct response advertising, they are highly measurable. They have obviously been producing consistently more cost-effective replies than page advertising.
- More media opportunities – 15 years ago very few newspapers would accept loose inserts. Today many newspapers, including major national titles, carry inserts. Most local paid-for and free newspapers also carry them.
- Ease of response – prospects can tear off a reply card or post or fax back the entire piece.
- Creative flexibility – there is almost no limit on space (but see the note 'A word about design and printing' on the previous page about enclosing machinery). It is quite common to see A5 catalogues of up to 64 pages used as loose inserts.
- Use of existing leaflets – if you have some spare leaflets, inserting can be a very cost-effective method of distribution. This again is subject to compatibility with the inserting process.
- Test opportunities – inserts offer much greater flexibility for test programmes. There are several benefits. Part circulations can be bought, whereas with a newspaper advertisement you have to buy the whole circulation, or at least an entire region, so it is difficult to test to a small percentage of readers. With a loose insert you can specify the quantity you want to test and in many cases the region too. It is economical in that you can place, say, 500,000 inserts in *The Sunday Times*, and then supply several different leaflets each carrying a unique offer or copy approach. In this way, you can answer many questions with quite a modest test budget. You have the ability to vary copy by type of reader or region. For example, you might want to

run an offer to all European readers of *The Economist*. If you run an advertisement, you will be limited to a single language, but if you use loose inserts you can vary the language for each batch of magazines – ensuring that readers in each country can read your offer in their own language.

- Localized use of a national medium – some national newspapers now permit selective loose inserting down to the level of a local wholesaler. So a business in, say, Worcester can advertise locally using a national Sunday paper such as the *Mail on Sunday*.
- Quality control – with some magazines, the colour reproduction of your product may not be as good as you would like. With inserts you control the print quality yourself.

Among the stated weaknesses of inserts are the following:

- Cost – they are quite expensive, as you have to produce the leaflet and then pay for insertion. A full distribution of inserts may cost four or five times as much as a full-page advertisement. However, response will often at least compensate for this, so this is not necessarily a weakness.
- Timing – because of the leaflet production time, it can take a lot longer to set up an insert campaign than an advertisement campaign.
- Quality of response – it has often been reported that the quality of insert responses (measured by percentage conversion to sales) can be slightly lower than advertisement responses. This is I think largely a historical judgement, based on a period when most responses came by post. Under those circumstances, the existence of a convenient tear-off reply paid card did tend to stimulate a greater number of casual replies. Nowadays, however, when more than half of the responses come by telephone, this factor is not so relevant. In 1999 one multi-million pound advertiser reported that conversion to sale from insert responses was actually higher than from those received through the mail.

Buying and evaluating press advertising

Most publishers have a 'rate card', which sets out charges according to a variety of circumstances. The main factors affecting cost are date and position.

If your advertisement must appear on a fixed date, you will be expected to pay a premium on top of the basic charge for the size of space you require. You can avoid this extra charge by specifying 'run of week'. 'Run of week' means that the publication can place your advertisement when it is most convenient to it. There is a mid-point when you may specify a 3-day period (such as Tuesday to Thursday), when the additional charge will be less.

There is also the seasonal factor – advertisements in early December may carry a premium simply because all traders are advertising their Christmas

'Run of week' means that the publication can place your advertisement when it is most convenient to it. There is a mid-point when you may specify a 3-day period (such as Tuesday to Thursday), when the additional charge will be less.

offers so space is literally 'at a premium'. If your business does not require your advertisements to be so precisely timed, you may be able to negotiate very good discounted rates in off-peak times.

Position is the second factor. Not all pages attract the same level of readership. Publications will either research their audiences or often simply go with the accepted 'wisdom' that says that the following positions attract more readers and, thus, are worth a higher charge:

- cover positions (front cover, back cover and to a lesser extent inside front and inside back cover)
- television programmes page (generally accepted to attract a high readership)
- readers' letters page; early pages (especially right-hand pages)
- 'solus' and 'semi-solus' positions (a solus position is where you are the only advertiser on a page, semi-solus is where you share the page with only one other advertiser)
- facing matter (if your advertisement is placed on a page that faces editorial rather than more advertising it is considered to be worth a premium – of course, this may depend on what the editorial is about)
- within a feature (an obvious one if your product will appeal to those interested in such a feature)
- front of section (a financial advertiser would pay extra to be on the first page or perhaps the contents page of a financial section, such as *Money Mail*)
- size (obviously the larger the advertisement, the greater the cost; spaces of less than full or half pages are usually charged by the single column centimetre)
- colour (obviously a colour advertisement will cost more than a mono space, that is a black and white space)
- market demand (this can be seasonal, but there are also times when through general economic booms and recessions space is more or less freely available; in 2000 it was very hard to get into some media at all because of the proliferation of dot com companies, now that this bubble has burst the buyer's market has returned).

The first thing to do if you have a sizeable budget is to appoint a good media buying agency. They can often save you lots of money through their experience, knowledge and sheer buying power. They will advise you, but the things you can do to help them buy economically are:

- keep your plans flexible and do not specify a fixed day if you will be happy with a 2 or 3 day option
- specify the front third of the paper, say, rather than the first right-hand page

- do not use unusual sizes – they are very difficult to buy at discount rates
- allow for short-term or distress buying – all publications have problems occasionally – an advertiser has been forced to cancel at short notice and they need to sell that space in tomorrow's paper now. If you have a piece of artwork ready to run you may find you (or your agency) can buy a space at less than half of the rate card cost.

Third-party distribution of leaflets

In addition to inserting leaflets in newspapers and magazine there are numerous opportunities for enclosure in mailings, invoices and parcels despatched by non-competing 'host' companies.

For example, some consumer mail order companies will enclose your leaflets in their parcels. Your product must not be competing with theirs, of course, but with that restriction this is often an excellent way of targeting good prospects.

This is an expanding medium with a current annual capacity of more than 1 billion leaflets. Among the many such opportunities are enclosures in:

- customer mailings
- catalogues and statement mailings
- product despatches
- directory distributions
- sample packs
- shared envelopes
- subscription magazines and newsletters.

Among the benefits of such distributions are:

- implied endorsement from the host
- leaflets are highly targeted at mail-responsive audiences
- low cost – a fraction of the cost of a mailing
- it is difficult for competitors to monitor your campaign.

There are a number of companies, for example, Royal Mail that organize these leaflet distributions and circular distributors and you will find their addresses in Chapter 14.

The telephone

The growth of the call centre or contact centre, as it is becoming known, has been extraordinary. Some commentators have put the value growth of call centre activity at 40% per year since 1994. In 2001 more than 1% of the UK's working population is employed in call centres, more than in agriculture, manufacturing and mining combined. The largest like the Sky Subscriber Centre or First Direct, employ thousands of call handlers in their centres.

The telephone is ubiquitous and the mobile telephone revolution has added to the power of the telephone. Forty million mobile phones are owned in the UK. The use of WAP technology was not as successful as it might have been; however, the new third generation mobile devices promise a truly integrated experience. Watch this space.

The telephone can be used and is most effective as a support medium, but it is also used as a stand-alone direct marketing medium. The use of the telephone for cold calling is not recommended, although it is often used in this way. It tends to give the industry a bad name, but the fact that it is still used shows that it does work. My advice is not to use the telephone in this way and if you do choose to make sure you are familiar with the requirements of the telephone preference service (see Chapter 14 for contact details).

The telephone is a very powerful adjunct to direct mail – not only as a response device, but also as a follow-up tool. Many advertisers have found they can treble or quadruple their response by adding a telephone follow-up call.

For in-bound and out-bound work to existing customers the telephone is unparalleled as a medium as:

- it is immediate and interactive
- it can personalize the brand
- it is highly personable and targetable
- it is extremely flexible so cross-sell and up-sell opportunities can be exploited immediately
- it is superb for customer care, complaint handling and information gathering
- in combination with other media it can significantly boost response.

Against this, the telephone is expensive and its immediacy means that even existing customers can find calls intrusive. It demands skilled, well-trained and motivated staff.

Direct mail

Direct mail and the telephone are the two first choice communications options when contacting existing customers and prospects. There is very little wastage, provided the databases have been built and used properly.

The information gathered is used to select only those for whom a particular offer will be relevant. The same information base also enables us to identify those for whom it will not be relevant and, thus, reduce annoyance whilst avoiding wasteful expenditure.

Direct mail is immensely flexible – the message can be varied according to what we know about this customer or 'cluster' of customers. We can also vary the timing, increasing relevance even more.

Direct mail messages are retained far longer than those sent by other media. A study for an international airline found that 74% of those mailed remembered the key messages 3 months after the mailings were received.

Although there is a lot of talk and press comment about junk mail, the majority of business people and consumers say that they like receiving direct mail 'providing it is relevant and interesting'.

Making direct mail interesting

Direct mail offers greater creative freedom than any other medium as a whole range of enclosures can be used to attract the attention of the recipient, for example some companies have mailed bricks, shoes and footballs. In a postal research study conducted a few years ago senior business people were asked, 'Which of the mailings you receive do you open first?' The most frequently ticked answer was 'Those that are bulky or look most interesting'.

Mailings can offer sound and movement (using tapes and videos), enabling demonstration of almost any product.

Direct mail is a perfect testing medium, allowing valid comparisons of lists, offers, timing, creative themes and response devices.

The high cost of mailings

Critics of mailings often cite their high cost compared to broadscale advertising. A mailing can cost £500 per thousand or more, whereas a television audience can be bought for less than £10 per thousand.

However, the much tighter targeting inherent in direct mailings can reduce wastage to such an extent that this differential is often more than compensated for, enabling mailings to deliver a lower cost per response than television, radio or press. This depends on the precision of your targeting, of course, so direct mail will not always be the best choice for initial prospecting.

| Example |

If we wanted to sell decorating materials such as wallpaper or paint by direct marketing, the first requirement would be to identify people who are thinking of decorating. There may be some broad targeting factors such as 'People who have just moved house may want to decorate' and 'People tend to decorate in the spring', but it is almost impossible to isolate these from the broad mass market.

So a sensible first approach may be to run a series of press advertisements offering advice for those about to decorate – people who respond are identifying themselves as good prospects. Once they have responded it is possible to use direct mail in a cost-effective way.

Do-it-yourself?

Most advertising media require highly skilled professionals to produce copy, layouts, print and so on. Whilst professionals will generally produce a better mailing and thus a higher response rate, this may not always be the most cost-efficient method. When writing to your own customers if you can place the right message in front of the right person at the right time, you will be sure of receiving attention. This does not mean to say that you should always produce your own customer mailings, but that it is a genuine option for you.

Door-to-door distribution

DTD is a medium that has grown dramatically in the last 10 years. Many millions of leaflets and 'mailing packs' are delivered to UK homes in this way every year. Response rates, whilst not so high as for addressed mailings, are generally quite good.

Time of delivery is quite important and items delivered by Royal Mail tend to generate higher responses – this is not because alternative suppliers fail to deliver, but mainly because the Royal Mail packs are delivered with the morning post and, thus, are given greater attention. There is a cost penalty, of course. Royal Mail door-to-door (DTD) costs quite a lot more than that delivered by other suppliers. However, the difference in cost is often recovered in the higher response.

Television

Direct response television was very popular with many mail order advertisers in the 1970s and 1980s, largely because of the availability of the per inquiry deal. First seen in the United States, the per inquiry (PI) deal is where a television or radio station is prepared to run a commercial for a nominal charge – plus an agreed amount for each enquiry it generates. This can be varied to be based on orders rather than enquiries and is also offered by some newspapers and magazines.

Originally, such deals became available in UK mainly for television, and they were very attractive to mail order advertisers. They were dropped after some large FMCG advertisers threatened to withdraw their advertising if the stations did not cease offering 'free' airtime to these companies.

The recession in the early 1990s saw the reappearance of some of these

First seen in the United States, the per inquiry (PI) deal is where a television or radio station is prepared to run a commercial for a nominal charge – plus an agreed amount for each enquiry it generates. This can be varied to be based on orders rather than enquiries and is also offered by some newspapers and magazines.

offers and they can still be found on certain radio stations, in local newspapers and so on. It is always worth enquiring about these and similar arrangements, as they reduce the risk for small or first-time advertisers.

After the demise of the PI deal, direct response television went through a period when it was seen as prohibitively expensive, but since the end of the 1990s recession it has been growing rapidly.

Currently, it is estimated that more than one-third of all television advertisements carry a response mechanism, and this growth has taken place for several reasons. The first reason is the number of channels now available to direct marketers, which in turn means greater opportunity for targeting. However, in certain sectors (notably financial services and insurance) it is far higher. Also the development of digital interactive channels, whilst in their infancy as yet, has extended the capability of brand-building awareness television into the potential to create a very rich one-to-one direct marketing experience. Most important, however, is the change in consumer behaviour and the acceptance of the telephone as a means of doing business.

Another major reason for response devices appearing in commercials is the growth of the Internet. Many companies now offer a wide range of services via their Web sites and 'drive to Web' is rapidly becoming one of the main response mechanisms for all forms of advertising.

Television offers advertisers a number of advantages:

- low cost per thousand – television still delivers large audiences cheaply at around £5–10 per thousand, although this is changing due to the proliferation of channels
- off-peak time is cost-efficient – direct response television commercials run off-peak can be extremely cost-effective (this may be due to the tendency of the audience to use breaks in top programmes to put the kettle on or go to the bathroom)
- targeting – television is increasingly capable of reaching narrow audiences due to the increase in the number of specialized channels (however, this sometimes reduces the cost-efficiency as cost-per-thousand viewers can be less attractive)
- credibility – in the eyes of the consumer, television carries significant weight
- it offers a content-rich experience – it can communicate a range of brand values and demand response.

That said, television has several disadvantages, including the following.

- It is complex to buy and manage.
- It generally offers low response percentages.
- Response handling can be a problem – the majority of responses will occur directly after the commercial has aired, and contact or call centres must be adequately resourced to cope with this sudden influx. A good commer-

cial, aired in a top programme such as 'Coronation Street' can generate many thousands of calls from a single showing.

- Messages are limited due to regulation and airtime – you cannot develop a lengthy description of your product in 40 seconds.
- Production costs can be very high. Although it is possible to make commercials relatively cheaply, it is important to remember that, in many instances, they are competing with expensively produced programmes. A certain level of professionalism and, thus, high cost is necessary and in reality there is no such thing as a low-cost television campaign.

The keys to the successful use of direct response television are to:

- be clear about the objectives and the audience
- use a good creative team (you have 30 or 40 seconds to get the message across)
- remember that the key objective is response (always give them time to write down the number or address)
- use a simple, memorable response number (good examples of memorable telephone numbers are 0800 40 40 40 for Trust House Forte or 0800 28 28 20 for Guardian Direct)
- demonstrate the benefits of the product (use the advantages of the medium).

Radio

Radio has always been an important option for direct marketing media planners. The number of local stations offers cost-effective targeting opportunities. There are hundreds of radio stations in the UK and the reach of commercial stations is well over 28 million adults each week.

The Radio Advertising Bureau produces some excellent research on the effectiveness of radio as an advertising medium. Its strengths include:

- creative flexibility – words can create very persuasive images in the mind
- intrusiveness – although a strength, this can also be a weakness
- relationship with the audience – even more than with television, consumers describe the radio as 'a friend'; this makes it very powerful as both a stand-alone medium and as a support medium in an integrated campaign
- cost-efficiency – radio audiences can be reached quite cheaply; the cost per thousand is amongst the lowest; however, response rates can also be low
- local identity – many stations have a strong local identity making them ideal for local campaigns
- production costs – whilst it is possible to spend a lot of money on producing a radio commercial, it is largely down to the fees of the presenters; most radio stations have the facilities to produce commercials using their own

presenters and these can be a lot cheaper than using national stars
* testing – the relatively low costs make radio an excellent testing medium
* targeting – audience research is comprehensive and it is possible to target specific audiences well.

The weaknesses of radio include that:

* there is no visual element – this can reduce memorability and, thus, requires frequent repeats to achieve memorability
* repetition can lead to channel switching – if the same commercial is repeated several times during the same hour of 'drive time', listeners tend to switch channels; the best campaigns rotate several different commercials to avoid this problem.

Costs and responses

Having reviewed the numerous media options, let us now look at some typical costs and responses. These are for guidance only, as actual costs will vary according to the individual publication or medium you choose, how negotiable their rates are this month and so on. Nevertheless, they can be taken as a rough guide to normal differentials between media. Table 7.3 is an evaluation of cost per thousand.

As we can see, there is a 'trade-off' of cost versus communications capability. Where the message is a simple one with appeal to a broad audience, we can consider the use of broadscale media (such as newspapers or even radio). Costs quoted are generally rate card (that is those quoted by the publication). It will usually be possible to buy at better rates than these, but this depends on the state of the market at the time and the skill of the negotiator.

Example

Table 7.4 takes these costings and applies them to an imaginary campaign for lead generation for a sales force.

This table shows that the most cost-efficient source will be mailings to targeted segments of our own database, producing a cost per lead (CPL) of £25.

Table 7.3 Media, audience type, cost per thousand and message

Medium	Audience type and size	Cost per thousand (£)	Volume/complexity of message
Television	Mass market regional/national	Lowest: 5–10	Limited
Radio	Mass market – local/national	Lowest: 5–10	Limited
National press (Half page mono)	Mass market – national/some segmentation	Low: 5 Quality title: 25	Increasing
Specialist press (Page colour)	Niche market Identified groups	Medium: 50+	Increasing
Local press (Full page)	Local – some papers have strong readership	Low: 5 – 15	Increasing
Inserts	Identified groups – by magazine content Better targeting – can be good in local freesheets	Medium: 55+ including print	Higher
Direct mail	Highly targeted	High: 500+	Unlimited
Door to door	Good targeting by property type	Low: 55 including print	Unlimited
Telephone	Highly targeted and personal	Highest: inbound 2000+ outbound 2500+	Less information, but interactive

Table 7.4 Analysis of a typical multi-media campaign

Media type	Volume reached	Cost per thousand (£)	Total (£)	Possible response (%)	No. of responses	Cost per lead (£)	Rank
Television	2,000,000	8	16,000	0.010	200	80	10
National press	1,000,000	15	15,000	0.025	250	60	7
Local newspaper (Half page)	20,000	15	300	0.020	4	75	9
Loose inserts (Local freesheet)	20,000	55	1100	0.2	40	27.50	=2
Telephone (Outbound)	500	3000	1500	5.0	25	60	8
Door to door	15,000	55	825	0.1	15	55	6
Direct mail:							
Own database	5000	500	2500	2.0	100	25	1
Rented lists	5000	620	3100	1.0	63	49.20	4
Direct mail + telephone follow-up:							
Own database	500	5500	2750	20.0	100	27.50	=2
Rented lists	500	5620	2810	10.5	53	53.01	5

Next will be mailings to the same source, but followed up by telephone within 3 days of mail receipt – this works out at £27.50 per lead, an increase in cost per lead (CPL) but producing a greater volume of leads. We would expect these leads to convert at a lower rate than those from the non-telephoned sample. Loose inserts come in at the same CPL as database mailings and telephone, but conversion to sale would be lower from inserts.

Loose inserts are often cost-efficient in both local and national newspapers – it is now possible to take small sections of a national circulation, even as small as the area covered by a single wholesaler, namely part of a town.

Newspaper advertising is rarely as cost-efficient as more direct media, however, this is only true where we take advantage of the main benefit of direct media, which is the power of precise targeting.

We must also be aware that advertisements in the larger circulation papers carry a certain amount of prestige and such advertising can be beneficial, particularly in generating awareness of your organization.

Note that although these costings are hypothetical, they are typical of what has been achieved recently by advertisers in the UK.

Costings will vary from market to market, but the comparisons between the media types are likely to remain fairly constant.

What does a direct mailing cost?

This will depend on whether you produce it internally, or whether you use external services and expertise.

Table 7.5 looks at the costs of producing a direct mailing by doing the whole job yourself, by using local resources and using a professional specialist direct marketing agency.

* Column 1 Do It Yourself – you do the whole job yourself, finding addresses from your database or local sources/directories and so on. Note that no allowance has been made for the cost of your time. The £65 cost against artwork and print in this column is a nominal allowance for stationery, laser toner, envelopes and so on.
* Column 2 Local resources – you may pay a part-time worker to collect names and addresses for you. Alternatively, you could place small advertisements in local newsagents and supermarket noticeboards. The £50 allowance would cover the cost of these plus perhaps the cost of your part-timer entering the names onto your PC. Under 'Copy and design' and 'Artwork and print' we have included allowances for you to pay your local printer who may be able to offer a simple copy and design service. In this

costing, we have assumed that you will use the commercial printer rather than your own desktop printer. It is assumed that you will assemble and 'fill' (enclose) the mailing yourself.

- Column 3 Professional agency – here, in addition to costing out the 1000 quantity, we also show the costs for mailings of 10,000 and 50,000. There are two reasons for showing these figures. First, it is to demonstrate that, with small quantities, the use of fully fledged agencies will rarely be cost-effective. Second, it shows how, as your business builds and your mailing quantities increase, the cost of professional expertise can be spread and, thus, become more cost-effective.

As Table 7.5 shows, the most cost-effective way of organizing a small mailing is to do it yourself. Using professional direct marketing agencies will rarely be cost-efficient for very small mailings, although once mailing quantities go over 10,000 the costs of professional design and artwork are more easily absorbed into the overall cost.

Note that it is not intended to suggest that you should *never* use a professional agency for very low volume mailings, simply that to do so will rarely be the most cost-effective option. You may well have other objectives.

Table 7.5   Cost comparisons in mailing – in-house v. outsourcing

Item	DIY	Local resources	Professional agency		
Quantity mailed	1000	1000	1000	10,000	50,000
List rental	–	£50	£100*	£1000*	£5000*
Copy and design	–	£250	£5000**	£5000**	£5000**
Artwork and print	£65	£500	£4000**	£8500**	£23,500**
Lasering & enclosing, etc.	–	£65	£265	£465	£1250
Postage***	£210	£210	£210	£1785 (15%)	£7875 (25%)
Total cost	£275	£1075	£9575	£16,750	£42,625
Cost per thousand	£275	£1075	£9575	£1675	£853

* List rental charges will vary according to the quality of the list and the number of additional selections you wish to make. We have used a typical cost of £100 per thousand for demonstration purposes. You would normally be faced with the list owner/broker's 'minimum order' charge and have to rent, say, 5000 names. You do not have to mail them all, of course.

** These costs are not intended to be definitive, but are included to show the sort of money with which you may be faced. Design charges from direct marketing agencies can be very much higher than this (few will charge less). A good alternative is to seek out local freelance copywriters and designers, many of whom are former employees of agencies in any case.

The 'Artwork and print' cost is made up of £3500 for artwork and £500 per thousand for printing the smaller quantities. The 50,000 mailing is estimated at £400 per thousand for print.

*** Postal costs will vary according to the class and type of service you use. For demonstration purposes, we have used the normal second-class rate for the smaller mailings and assumed discounts of 15% and 25% off this rate for the larger quantities.

For example, if you are writing to your 1000 best prospects to interest them in a premium-priced, high-quality service, a cheap DIY mailing may not be so effective as a professional, more costly alternative. Having said that, you may find it even more effective to send each prospect a 'real' letter, individually produced and personally signed.

Like the media comparisons, these costings are not intended to be fixed rules, but simply to be used as guidelines. You do not need to follow any set route, but costing your mailing in such detail will enable you to make better-informed decisions.

How much response do you need?

This depends on whether your objective is to 'break even', that is to get your money back without making any profit, or to make a profit on your first transaction.

The simple calculation of break even is: Number of sales needed to break even = Total costs/Profit per sale

The simple calculation of break even is:

$$\frac{\text{Total costs}}{\text{Profit per sale}} = \text{Number of sales needed to break even}$$

In Table 7.6 we have taken the typical costs from Table 7.5 above, which listed the costs of producing a direct mailing, and have calculated the percentage of response needed from each of the mailings to break even, at two different levels of profit (£25 and £50 per order).

This is a common form of costing in direct marketing, on the basis that if you can achieve break-even on a prospecting activity (mailing new names), you are building up a valuable resource for future sales and profits. As mentioned earlier, this will depend on your funding and your profit targets.

The figures in this table have been calculated on the basis that:

- one in every three replies results in an order (thirty replies = ten orders)
- profit per sale is calculated after allowing for reply costs (postage and/or telephone charges, response packs, brochures, catalogues and so on).

This comparison shows that simple DIY direct mail can be produced economically and that, with such a cost structure, the responses needed for break-even are quite modest. These calculations also show that, depending on the profit and conversion levels, using some additional 'local' help could be cost-effective for small mailings.

Clearly, using a professional agency would not be so cost-effective for a mailing of 1000 pieces, but the examples at 10,000 and 50,000 show how, once your agency costs are spread over a larger quantity, response required to break even can be quite achievable.

Table 7.6 Breakdown response rates on mailing costs in-house *v.* outsourcing

	DIY	Local resources	Professional agency		
Quantity mailed	1000	1000	1000	10,000	50,000
Cost per thousand	£275	£1075	£9575	£1675	£853
Profit @ £25					
Orders	11	43	383	67	34
Replies	33	129	1149	201	102
Response %	3.3	12.9	Not viable	20.1	10.2
Profit @ £50					
Orders	5.5	21.5	191.5	33.5	17
Replies	16.5	64.5	574.5	100.5	51
Response %	1.65	6.45	57.45	10.05	5.1

Note: in the final column some numbers have been rounded, so are not exact.

Should you try to make money immediately?

The calculations in the two tables above are based on 'break-even' – the costing method you might use if you have sufficient funding to allow you to develop new customers over a period of time.

In these circumstances, the objective for your prospecting activities will not be to make a profit. Indeed, the reverse may be true. You may even be prepared to lose money on the initial transaction with a new customer in order to generate the maximum response.

Note that neither approach is 'correct' – the decision on which approach to take will be made according to the situation in the individual business. (See the calculations in Chapter 12, pp. 257–63.)

SUMMARY

This chapter has looked at the process of communicating with our customers. We started from the perspective of the media planner. The relevance of communications material has been seen as central to the effectiveness of marketing communications and it is this that is driving the growth of direct marketing. We have seen that the traditional approach of awareness advertising is giving way to dual-purpose advertising where direct communications and awareness are integrated and work more effectively together. The reasons for the growth in this area included:

- a greater choice of media
- more creative flexibility
- more response methods.

We have seen the need to take into account the growth in digital media when planning a campaign. However, the need to plan for response remains constant. This varies from the traditional approach to media planning in which awareness is built over time. In direct marketing terms, response reduces over time. The direct marketer's objective was shown to be to try to reduce the rate of decline. Finally, we have looked at the planning cycle for direct marketing communications and have seen that it was a constant cycle of planning, testing, measuring and modifying as the campaign progresses.

The process of direct marketing has been described as identifying clusters that provide the greatest potential to deliver the required response at the lowest cost.

The chapter continued with an examination of the importance of integration in media planning and looked in detail at the planning process. The process starts with targeting and its six key questions.

1 Who are the potential customers/audience?
2 When is the right time to approach them?
3 Where are they?
4 What media do they use?
5 How do they use media?
6 How much will it cost to reach them?

These questions were then dealt with in detail, looking at the role of research in identifying audience and their patterns of media consumption. These included geodemographics, psychographics and behavioural research.

We saw also that studies such as the Target Group Index could help significantly in the task of media selection.

When choosing media, it depends on:

- the size of the audience we wish to talk to
- the budget
- the complexity of the message
- how appropriate the medium is to carry the message.

We have looked in turn at the strengths and weaknesses of the following media:

- press
- magazines

- inserts
- third-party distribution
- direct mail
- door-to-door distribution
- telephone
- television
- radio
- outdoor/posters.

The costs and response rates of various media have been considered and a chart comparing the various attributes of media was presented. Crucially, it is clear that the lowest cost per thousand does not always deliver the most effective response.

The chapter has finished with the typical cost of putting together a direct mail campaign, looking at the differences between a DIY approach, the use of local resources and the use of a professional agency. Agencies appear suitable for large-volume campaigns, but for smaller quantities it is possible to manage the work very effectively in-house. The final section also considered response rates and break-even from a hypothetical campaign. We saw that in some cases the response rate needed to break even can be quite modest.

REVIEW QUESTIONS

1   Explain why relevance is vital in the process of delivering marketing. Why is this leading to an increase in the use of direct marketing media?

2   What are the advantages of media integration?

3   What is the main difference between awareness and response advertising?

4   Explain the direct marketing planning process. How does it differ from the awareness approach?

5   What is the most important factor in the planning process?

6   What are the six questions the direct marketing media planner should answer when planning a campaign?

7   What is TGI? How can it help the direct marketer?

8   What makes a good media plan?

9   List the strengths and weaknesses of at least three direct marketing media.

10   Explain Sainsbury's square root principle.

11   What is the role of a media-buying agency?

12   List three ways of reducing costs in magazine advertising.

13   Why are the lowest cost direct marketing media not always the most effective?

14   How do we calculate break-even on a direct marketing campaign?

15   When should we use a direct marketing agency?

EXERCISES

Your company is a provider of financial services in the UK. You have been asked to launch a new flexible mortgage product. The target market is affluent 35–45 year olds with an outstanding mortgage balance of over £100,000. You need to acquire 25,000 customers to reach the financial targets for this product. Of these customers, 10,000 will come from your existing customer base.

- How will you communicate with your existing customers?
- What media choices are open to you when you look to acquire new customers?
- Which media would you choose to test?

Chapter 8

Direct marketing and the Internet

Introduction
- – European e-commerce
- – What are the opportunities for direct marketers?
- The Internet as a marketing tool
  - – Building relationships with customers/prospects
  - – Public relations
  - – Low-cost, immediate publishing
  - – Disintermediation
  - – New business models
- The Internet as a selling tool
  - – Virtual retailers
  - – Selling on a smaller scale
- Using Internet technology to improve business processes
  - – Supply chain management
  - – Intranets
- Barriers to using the Internet
  - – The solutions
- How to go about planning an Internet strategy
  - – Site promotion

Summary

Review questions

Exercises

INTRODUCTION

This chapter begins with a few statistics about the Internet, although it is difficult to be precise as estimates vary wildly from source to source.

Two of the best sites for information on the Internet are www.nua.com and www.forrester.com. However, there are many others. Nielsen has recently launched a new service called 'Net ratings', which is a panel assessing Internet usage. Whatever the true picture there is no doubt that the take-up of the Internet has been extremely rapid compared with other technologies. It took radio 37 years to achieve 50 million listeners, television took 13 years to reach a 50 million audience, it has taken the Internet 3.5 years.

In 1999 there was a 50% increase in UK direct marketing expenditure on the Internet (although in 2000 this rate of growth slowed) and 40% of 0345 call traffic was attributed to Internet. It was established that:

- 33% of press advertisements feature a Web address
- 17% of television commercials carry a Web address.

Of those marketers already online, 7% of the marketing budget was spent online in 1999 and this is forecast to rise to 14% in 2002.

NUA estimated that worldwide, in 1999, there were 412 million home and business users of the Web, shown in Table 8.1 broken down as:

Table 8.1 Breakdown of Web users worldwide

Region	Users (millions)
United States and Canada	109
Latin America	15
Asia	90
Japan	90
Europe	105
Africa	3

Source: www.nua.com

Dataquest predicts that by 2002 the number of Europeans on the Web at home will exceed 69 million.

This growth is happening despite major telecommunications barriers, greater techno-phobia than in the United States, and Web content that is largely in the English language only. Like the United States, however, European users are making the Internet a part of their lives. More than half of the 1.4 million Belgian users claim to surf the Web at least once every week.

In the business-to-business (B2B) market, things are still hot despite the burst of the dot com bubble. In the United States in 2000, the business-to-business market was worth US$114 billion according to Goldman Sachs and is forecast to reach US$1.5 trillion in 2004. Forrester Research predicts that this figure will be US$3.2 trillion worldwide in 2003. It also forecast that the Internet would account for 18–43% of all B2B sales. In 2000, the Internet accounted for just 9% of sales value.

European e-commerce

From bacon to PCs, just about everything is now being sold online in Europe. E-commerce revenues in Western Europe were expected to increase from US$30 billion in 1999 to more than US$200 billion by 2001, according to IDC. If this is the case, business managers will need to wake up to the opportunities fast.

For the four major consumer categories alone (air travel, books, music and software), Jupiter Communications predicts online shopping revenues in Germany, France and the UK will reach US$3.3 billion by 2002. Only 9% of users in France, 11% in Germany and 14% in the UK shopped online in 1997. These numbers are forecast to reach 35%, 40% and 40% by 2002. Among European regional markets, Germany is considered to have the greatest growth potential.

Selling across countries presents its challenges due to factors such as the differences in credit card penetration and efficiency of postal services.

What are the opportunities for direct marketers?

Over the next 10 years, the Internet will change the business landscape. According to Metcalfe's law, 'the value of a network increases with the square of the number of users'. As the Internet continues to grow at an exponential rate, so the benefits of the medium will increase and customers will become more powerful. As Patricia Seybold writes:

> In the electronic commerce world, knowing who your customers are and making sure you have the products and services they want becomes even more imperative than it is in the 'real' world ... The corner grocery needs only to approximate what customers really want because the convenience factor brings in the business. But when you eliminate this advantage – when customers can go anywhere to get what they want – you'd better know what they're looking for.

Many believe that access to the Internet via mobile telephones or handheld devices will overtake the number of people accessing the Internet via

According to Metcalfe's law, 'the value of a network increases with the square of the number of users'.

the PC in the near future. It is predicted that by 2005 the world will have 1 billion mobile phones.

Those wishing to take advantage of the opportunities on the Web will need to harness what the Internet is good at now, by identifying the right sectors of the Internet economy to target. It is also important to recognize what the Internet is currently not good at and to ensure that your strategy stays in line with market developments.

The Internet is not the panacea to all the business problems that the hype would have you believe, but it is not just another advertising or marketing channel either. Some of the possibilities are outlined in this chapter.

Marketers should not underestimate the threat from their competitors who are already using the Internet to their advantage (see the details of Amazon.com at p. 161 and Pedigree, below). Companies are finding new business models to eat into the market shares of their competitors, which previously would not have been possible.

To compete effectively the new dot com companies and traditional companies with a clicks and bricks approach, i.e. an online and offline strategy, will need to realign themselves quickly to become more customer-focused. Customer relationship management strategies will need to be adjusted to integrate multi-channel information. The main obstacle in the way of achieving the single view of the customer for many companies is the sheer cost of bringing together all their internal databases and systems.

After analysing where Internet technology could support business objectives, ensure that you prioritize. It may not be a Web site that is needed as a first priority. Some companies may benefit instead from an Intranet to improve internal communications or an Extranet system to link key partners to improve the efficiency of the supply chain.

It is vital that managers start understanding and planning integrated strategies to take advantage of emerging digital technology (e-business, mobile communications, digital printing and so on), as the growth of these markets gathers tremendous pace.

There will be many opportunities for astute marketers, but the examples in this chapter fit broadly into three categories:

1 using the Internet as a marketing tool (building customer and prospect relationships, lead generation, growing your customer database and so on)
2 how the Internet works as a selling tool (e-commerce – where transactions are actually conducted online)
3 using Internet technology to improve business processes (Intranets for improving internal knowledge management and Extranets for more efficient supply chain management, customer service, technical support and e-mail communications).

The Internet as a marketing tool

Building relationships with customers/prospects

There are two key tools that no company should be without today: a customer-oriented Web site and a well-designed and well-maintained database. As we have explored in Chapter 6, a database is invaluable for determining who your customers are, and for managing your relationships with them. The Internet is a dynamic way to interact with existing clients and new prospects as well as to deliver information and sell products. Combining these two technologies allows companies to create very powerful and productive relationships with their customers.

The following are some examples of the power of combining database and Web technology to help build customer relationships.

Example

AIR MILES (www.airmiles.co.uk) has built a highly personalized Extranet site for online relationship management. Due to the high volume of calls processed by its call centre, AIR MILES has used its site to help reduce customer service costs while still delivering a high level of customer service. When moving its relationship management online, AIR MILES also wanted customers to enjoy the benefits of self-service, ultimately being able to spend their air miles more conveniently. AIR MILES has achieved this by integrating its huge customer database, and partner databases, with the Web site. As a result, the company is able to target specific groups of customers with personalized promotions, incentives and travel programmes, based on their profiles, mileage balance and purchase preferences.

The Petcat Web site (www.petcat.com) is aimed at cat lovers and is published by Pedigree Foods. It is designed to capitalize on the strong relationships between cat owners and their pets. Site visitors are asked to enter their own details and their cat's profile on entering the home page. The result of this approach benefits both parties:

- Pedigree Foods is able to collect valuable market research data and build a database of highly targeted consumers to whom new product or promotional information can be mailed
- personalized information is served to cat lovers ranging from what diet their particular cat should be on to the personality traits of particular breeds (the site has a very high level of repeat visits as users return to their personalized articles, diaries, games and community events).

Public relations

Online, anyone has a voice and size is not necessarily an advantage. Regular Internet surfers expect honest and open dialogue and can spot flaws or obvious omissions in a company's Web site very easily. Moreover, your competitors are only a click away if they suspect that you are trying to cover something up.

Example

Shell (www.shell.com) has used its Web site, amongst other things, to strengthen its public relations efforts. Instead of hiding from the controversial environmental debates in its industry, it met them head on by setting up various discussion forums and 'speakers' corners' to encourage debate with environmentalists. The forum is well managed and negative postings are responded to quickly and constructively.

Low-cost, immediate publishing

The Internet is a very cost-effective place to store filing cabinets of information for downloading.

Example

The Inland Revenue (www.inlandrevenue.gov.uk) now publish all of its leaflets and guides on its Web site. This is very useful if you have left your tax return until the last minute and you want a particular leaflet quickly in order to complete it. The latest tax returns have been encouraging people to make their submission electronically. Over time, the Inland Revenue will be able to reduce their print and data entry costs – perhaps this will bring tax bills down, but do not hold your breath!

Another example is in catalogue marketing. The Great Universal Stores site (www.shoppersuniverse.com), which contains 40,000 products, is updated daily with new products and special offers. This would not be possible with the printed versions of its catalogues.

Some companies are gathering customer information online, which can then be written directly into a database. A personalized brochure can then be created using pre-defined templates and either delivered immediately online or sent out in the post after being printed digitally. Companies are also using services such as Agfa PrintCast, where a brochure is developed and then delivered over the Web for digital printing in local markets – offering major savings on shipping costs and often more economical local printing too.

Disintermediation

Disintermediation means removing the middleman. The number of 'virtual' travel shops, recruitment sites and banks that target customers directly and, thus, cut out the middlemen is growing on the Web. Some are already eating into traditional intermediaries' market share.

In industries where the product is digital, that is information, music, video, images and so on, the threat of disintermediation is greatest.

Disintermediation means removing the middleman.

> **Example**
>
> The site www.expedia.co.uk allows you to compare and book flights (from any airline), a hotel room or a rental car, search for the latest special deals, register to receive e-mail notifications of low fares as soon as they are available, and find out detailed information about the place to which you are travelling, including recommendations for books and more. Some people rarely visit travel agents anymore and this has serious implications for the travel industry. However, of course, there will always be people who want to talk to a travel agent before booking their holiday.

The list broking market is currently the subject of fierce debate in the direct marketing industry about the potential for disintermediation. The debate focuses on the amount of added value a list broker adds to the buying process. It is usually larger companies that benefit from consultation and advice, whilst the costs may be prohibitive for small and medium enterprises (SMEs). Perhaps the Internet will offer a way to service both SMEs (via a direct service over the Web), whilst still retaining the current business model for those with larger budgets.

> **Example**
>
> Wise and Loveys Information Services operates www.MarketingFile.com which is a Web site that enables direct mailers and direct sales organizations to buy and download lists immediately. There is no minimum order level and there is no charge for counts and interrogation of files.
>
> This site offers a wide range of business and consumer lists and also a data cleaning service that again has no minimum order. This is ideal for small to medium-sized businesses.
>
> Charles Schwab (www.schwab-europe.com) and E*Trade (www.etrade.co.uk) launched online share trading systems in the UK in 1998 and these are currently doing large volumes of business at a fraction of the cost of traditional share transactions.

Web-based dealing has already moved to the mainstream in the United States, as investors have rushed to take advantage of its low cost. Online brokerages have driven down commissions aggressively. Investors can now trade stocks for less than US$10 (£6.20) per deal – one-third, or less, of what a traditional British stockbroker would charge. Internet trading is intrinsically cheaper than conventional trading because it bypasses highly paid stockbrokers, instead routing investors' trade instructions automatically to the relevant exchange.

Schwab, which moved into conventional brokerage in the UK 3 years ago by buying Sharelink, is offering UK investors automated electronic trading of UK stocks. UK investors get access to US stock markets too. Both Schwab and E*Trade offer real-time market data, such as share price information, trading execution and clearing, as well as online account information and portfolio valuation.

New business models

The Web has enabled new businesses to emerge that previously would not have been possible. Amongst these are 'portals', such as Excite and Lycos, which started out life as search engines, helping people navigate the Web. As the value of being *the* gateway to the Internet was realized, these companies have included all sorts of useful added-value content and services, such as the weather, shopping guides and personalized calendars, in the race to increase their market share.

Example

UpMyStreet.com (www.upmystreet.com) shows how innovative an Internet solution can be. If you want to move house and are considering different areas, UpMyStreet.com lets you check house prices for a variety of different types of dwellings in a specific postcode. It will also plot a graph for you showing how prices have risen and fallen over time and what the national average is.

It will tell you how many homes have been sold in the area, what the most popular and successful schools are (by exam pass rate), and other ancillary information such as crime clear-up rates, ambulance response times and council tax bands. All this on a single page. A search function enables you to find local plumbers and electricians from the same page, without having to trawl through online directory sites such as Thomson and the Yellow Pages.

Data, previously not easily available in one place, has been gathered from freely available government sources (such as the Land Registry) and assembled in a useful way.

This site was set up to demonstrate how the Web can really be put to work but the potential for this to become a commercially viable site is huge.

The Internet as a selling tool

Online retailing is in its infancy, but as digital certificates and signatures emerge (see the details on security on p. 167-9), more and more Web sites are offering online sales. There are successes and plenty of failures too.

Argos sold very little over its site as it tried to target its usual broad market, instead of focusing on the profile of the typical Internet user. Great Universal Stores is also continuously re-focusing its Web site (www.shoppersuniverse. com) to match the Internet profile much more closely (young males, sports gear, software and so on).

It is difficult to quote companies that are making a profit from online sales, but there are many companies generating serious revenue:

- Dell.com now claims to sell more than US$30 million of computers per day from its Web site
- Tesco.com generated £125 million (12% of its total sales) in 1999
- Cisco sold US$21 million of product per day from its Web site in one quarter.

All expect that a significant proportion of their revenue will come from their Web sites over the next few years.

Virtual retailers

These are companies that have set up specifically to sell online. They have low overheads, no shops and hardly any inventory as they have special arrangements with wholesalers.

Amazon.com (www.amazon.co.uk) is synonymous with book retailing on the Web. Its Web site offers every book imaginable (which you can search for by title, author or ISBN), reviews (from critics and from other customers who have read the book) and discussion groups. You can ask Amazon to notify you when a new book is available. You can purchase online, securely. Delivery is fast and you can keep track of your shipments at any time.

Although not yet profitable, in only 5 years Amazon.com has become a trusted and well-established brand – over 70% of total customer orders are repeat orders.

Example

Companies in the same business as virtual retailers are under threat. In an attempt to combat the threat, Waterstone's has set up online retailing, but this could cannibalize revenue from their existing shops.

Selling on a smaller scale

One of the strengths of the Web is that it is opening up new wider markets for smaller companies which previously could not afford to market on a global scale.

Example

In 1997, Jack Scaife, a Yorkshire butcher, set up a small Web site costing less than £1000 (www.classicengland.co.uk/scaife.html) and orders have poured in. The site explains the bacon-curing process and invites potential customers to place an order. After 1 year, 25% of all orders came via the site, from all over the world, with a high level of repeat orders. In December 1999, Jack Scaife's site beat Harrods in online consumer shopping tests. In 2000, the traditional family shop in Yorkshire closed and the company now only trades virtually. Turnover has increased from around £70,000 in 1997 to almost £750,000 in 2000.

The Web is particularly good for marketers wishing to open up niche markets, for example where the total audience is limited to a small number of people scattered around the globe. There are thousands of niche sites on the Web.

Example

A university student in Jakarta noted that a lot of Indonesians live abroad either working or studying and he reasoned that they would be missing their national food.

He set up a Web site offering typical Indonesian food items, such as shrimp crackers, hot sauces and spices, traditional medicines and any other products specially requested. His Web site attracts orders from Indonesians living in Australia, the United States and Europe. He receives payment in US dollars and, although he is still finishing his degree, he now has a thriving business run from his own warehouse in Jakarta.

Using Internet technology to improve business processes

Supply chain management

Michael Dell is pursuing his direct business model one step further with his 'virtual integration' model. Dell is using Web technology to blur the traditional boundaries in the value chain between suppliers, manufacturers and customers.

Direct relationships with customers create valuable information, allowing the company to communicate back up the value chain through manufacturing to product design. Dell reaps the advantages of being vertically integrated via Internet technology, without incurring all the usual costs associated with vertical integration. Therefore, Dell is kept focused, agile and can react much more quickly to market forces than competitors. In conjunction with advanced manufacturing techniques, inventory is kept to a minimum, allowing the company to introduce new models and technologies very quickly.

- Dell claims to generate more than US$30 million per day of revenue from its global Web sites
- it intends to make 50% of its total sales over the Internet by 2001
- it intends to move every aspect of its business onto the Web
- Dell uses encryption technology for secure transactions.

Visitors to the Dell UK site are logged and reported daily to senior management, along with daily revenues by product and customer type. Marketing expenses are measured against the increasing number of visits and sales.

Intranets

An Intranet is a private company network based on Internet technology. It can also be connected to the Internet with the appropriate use of a firewall (a security system that monitors and filters the traffic in and out of a corporate network).

An Intranet can unlock new business opportunities. Using Internet technology an Intranet can:

- unify people, business processes and corporate knowledge, helping to speed up time to market
- provide a collaborative technology and communication infrastructure that permits the organization to behave as a whole entity, with everyone sharing a common knowledge base

An Intranet is a private company network based on Internet technology. It can also be connected to the Internet with the appropriate use of a firewall (a security system that monitors and filters the traffic in and out of a corporate network).

- help build a learning organization
- help reduce operating costs.

The use of Intranets is growing rapidly. Indeed, many experts predict that this will become the major use of the Internet in the future. Microsoft stated in 1997: 'The most important new computing platform since computers were introduced into the business environment.' Microsoft and Netscape estimate the eventually 80% of Web technology will be used by corporate, closed-user groups.

Already many UK County Councils have them, but they need careful planning and implementation to be successful. Intranets can have massive cultural implications, so it is essential that requirements analysis and management of expectations are considered carefully.

Example	At Sun Microsystems, the Intranet is a fundamental part of everyone's work. All human resources forms, quality guidelines and sales figures are on it. Worldwide Chief Executive Officer Scott McNealy sends out regular voice and video bulletins about how the company is doing and what visions he has for the company. It is very motivational.

On a smaller scale, UK e-business consultancy Chord9 has a simple Intranet which lets all employees access a common set of files, calendars, phone directory, client database, portfolio and market research – all through browser technology.

Managing Director Helen Trim can dial into the network (via a mobile phone or a PC), check on her colleagues' diaries and book meetings from wherever she is in the world. As Chord9 grows, all employees are encouraged to share ideas and knowledge on this system. They still have face-to-face meetings of course, but the Intranet means that no idea, however small, is allowed to get lost through pressure of work.

Barriers to using the Internet

Common reasons quoted for not taking the Internet seriously are:

- it is not a large enough market
- what is the return on investment?

With figures as low as they are for the UK market, in terms of the number of people actually making purchases online, many managers think that the market place just is not big enough to warrant the investment. It is also difficult to put a value in terms of pounds sterling on a company Web site if it is not being used for direct selling.

However, given the involvement of many companies already and the predicted growth rates, companies simply cannot afford to ignore the opportunities the Internet presents. Any company seriously planning for the future should be prioritizing its Internet strategy now. Of course, for some companies their assessment may result in the conclusion that the Internet is not the right tool for them yet.

The technology can be slow and unreliable. Speed is a realistic concern. Modems are becoming more powerful to make connection faster, but until the Internet is linked up by a fibre optic network (that is a network that can transmit data at the speed of light), speed will remain an issue. This is because although the main telecommunications networks now consist of optical fibre, data will only move across the system at the speed of its slowest part – much of the Internet is still accessed via the copper phone wires that link homes and offices to the main systems.

Once a high-speed network is available in all homes and offices, we will see the convergence of the visual and sound quality of television with the interactivity of the Internet.

In the meantime, compression techniques are improving all the time, speeding up data transfer. BT is currently introducing a service called the Asymmetric Digital Subscriber Line, which will make accessing the Web from home over existing copper phone wires up to ten times faster than the current 56 Kbs modem speeds.

A further problem is that consumers find the interface difficult to use. This is an area that will need to be improved to overcome techno-phobia. One of the problems is that many Web sites and associated systems are written by highly computer-literate people, who just cannot appreciate why people have difficulty understanding what they see as simple instructions. For example, some online shopping services are not that easy for the uninitiated and each purchase can be a hit and miss affair. I once spent more than an hour trying to buy a book and received a message from the technical support team apologizing that their server 'was down'. As a regular online shopper I understand the problems, but it is not very impressive from the point of view of customer satisfaction. It is fine if, like me, you are prepared to persevere but most customers simply would not come back.

Consumers also worry about protection of personal data. The trend towards personalization on many Web sites does have its downside. Consumers are becoming more resentful about the amount of information they are required to give up before entering a site, and how that company uses that information.

There are various ways that data is collected ranging from normal enquiry forms, through 'cookies' (see p. 327 for an explanation) to sophisticated tracking software from companies such as Broadvision and Vignette.

In the future, there may be explicit agreements between consumer and marketer. Visitors will 'pay' for access to a site, for personalized content or special information, by giving up personal details. In return, marketers will 'pay' for personal details by offering this content. In effect, this happens already, but making it explicit will make both sides think hard about the contract into which they are entering.

Companies that build Web sites where information is gathered should have a 'privacy policy' which states how customer information is to be used. In the UK the new Data Protection Act will force companies to do this. Companies crossing international borders will have to be aware of the privacy legislation (and other legal issues) in different countries. It is not easy, but it is an essential part of planning.

There are security issues. Internet crime is difficult to quantify – the e-commerce companies talk down the risks, whilst security software companies talk up the risks. It does exist, however, and comes in many forms, including the following.

Hacking is breaking into a company's computer network.

- The shop front or investment scam – a Web site can be set up as a legitimate-looking front for bogus shops or investment scams.
- Fraudulent use of credit cards to attempt to place orders on a Web site – in the United States, criminals have used programs that randomly generate credit card numbers to make fraudulent online transactions. If the site does not use online verification of a card, the merchant or bank can lose money.
- Spoofing – this is using special software to falsify the sender identity on an e-mail, in order fraudulently to obtain information.
- Hacking is breaking into a company's computer network. In one famous incident, the German-based Chaos computer club demonstrated on live television how money could be transferred from one bank account to another, without anyone knowing. Various US research programmes, however, show that most (75%) danger comes from internal hackers within the company.

Whatever the size of the risk, companies should be aware that Internet crime exists and put the appropriate measures in place to protect them against it.

The solutions

Encryption

Secure Socket Layer (SSL) is the most commonly used encryption and is built into all recent Web browsers. SSL and most encoding systems use public/private key encryption. A credit card number is encrypted by the public key, available on the Web site, and can only be decrypted using the private key, which is held securely by the merchant. The two keys are generated from a complex mathematical algorithm that makes it impossible to guess the one by seeing the other.

Put simply, I send you a box with a key. You put some confidential data inside the box, lock it and send it back to me. I can then unlock it using a key that I have kept safely with me.

The main drawback with SSL, which is addressed by digital certificates and signatures (see below), is that it cannot authenticate the parties involved in the transaction.

Digital certificates and signatures

There are risks to e-commerce for sellers because of the remoteness of the transaction. A supplier is dealing with an unknown person and this makes it difficult to check whether they are honest, or whether they are in fact who they say they are. Although it is extremely difficult (particularly with the new 128 bit systems), it is also theoretically possible to crack an encrypted message. For these reasons, there is still need for major development in security systems for the Internet.

Part of the problem is that the credit card system itself is fundamentally insecure, requiring you to keep a 13 digit number secret except when you wander into a shop or pick up the telephone and give it to a complete stranger. However, there are now ways to solve this problem when you are buying online.

Secure Electronic Transactions (SET) is a credit card security software that has been developed by MasterCard, Visa and others. It lets you use a credit or debit card, or even a store card, to pay for goods and services online. The SET user has an electronic 'wallet' which is available from vendors such as Microsoft and IBM. The wallet contains the card details (not digital cash, just the numbers). It also has a certificate for you, holding a copy of your public key signed by a recognized Certification Authority (CA) and other identification information.

When you buy something from a SET-based site, your wallet communicates with the shop's payment software. It encrypts your credit card details using the public key of the card issuer and sends it to the shop. The shop does not know your card number and, therefore, cannot store it insecurely or re-use it without your knowledge. The shop then forwards your payment details to the card issuer, along with details of the amount you want to spend.

The card issuer can then decrypt your card number using its private key. Providing you have enough credit, the card issuer then generates a payment authorization, encrypting it using the shop's public key and sends it to the shop. Once the shop receives this, it can confirm the sale as it knows that it will be paid for the goods.

Finally, there is the issue of non-repudiation. If someone pays for something over the Internet and then the seller denies receiving the payment, SET resolves the problem by creating an audit trail, with proof of a transaction residing with the CA.

There are only a few SET sites currently on the Web and it has taken much longer to take off than expected. The transaction is quite complex and digital certificates need to be issued to banks, card issuers, shops and users.

As SET has lost momentum, less complex forms of digital certificates, with stronger encryption are predicted to provide the answer to many of the security issues that SSL does not solve. Numerous companies (including Verisign, Royal Mail and BT) have become CAs and have a legal responsibility for the digital certificates they issue. Signing up for a digital certificate means that individuals can digitally 'sign' transactions on the Internet whether buying goods or sending an e-mail message.

For the latest information and developments about digital certificates look at SET (www.setco.org), Verisign (www.verisign.com) and BT (www.trustwise.com).

Smart cards

A new generation of chip-enabled, multi-application smart cards is at the forefront of the fight to eliminate Internet fraud. These cards are considered an integral requirement for the opening up of the Internet to the mass market, particularly with respect to their use with mobile phones.

The main Internet-related use of smart cards is to provide a secure place to store the cryptographic keys needed to produce digital signatures, instead of on the computer hard disk which is at risk to hackers.

When the smart card is connected to a PC, security can still be ensured. The user reloads his or her card with digital cash by entering a personal code on an external card reader connected to a PC. When the consumer makes a payment over the Internet the amount is confirmed on the reader, not on the PC. Strong cryptography and digital signatures ensure that the electronic money does not fall into the wrong hands.

How to further reduce the risks

Even the highest levels of Internet security cannot absolutely guarantee against attack and, as e-commerce continues to grow, Internet crime will undoubtedly become more professional.

Companies and shoppers can reduce the risks by taking the following measures.

- Making sure transactions are conducted over an encrypted Internet connection and by not keeping information such as credit card numbers on a computer connected to the Internet.
- Using software that can look for signs of a 'spoofed' mail, such as the absence of the sender's return e-mail address. It can also control the content of e-mails and Web sites going in and out of a computer network.
- By using one of the 'non-repudiation' systems available, such as BT Trustwise, where the system sends an 'evidence token' to a third party. If the transaction needs to be examined later, the token can be opened up.
- When purchasing investments over the Internet, the UK's Financial Services Authority recommends that you first answer three basic questions. Where is the company based? Is it regulated? Which country's laws apply in the event of a dispute? All companies dealing in investment business with investors in the UK must, legally, be authorized.
- To protect your corporate network from hackers, use firewalls, encryption software and virus checking programs.

How to go about planning an Internet strategy

In many companies there is confusion over who owns the Web strategy. Of course, the technical implementation will require IT specialists, but the brief and control should be in the hands of marketing people, who understand what their customers need. Historically, it has been the IT department or an enthusiast within the company who has set up a Web site. This is why you see so many awful sites which cause great damage to well-established brands.

Business objectives must be identified – cost savings, increased sales and so on – and benefits should be quantified if possible. As mentioned earlier, this may reveal that the first priority may not be a Web site for customers – it may be an Intranet or Extranet to achieve operational efficiency and cost savings. There can be huge cultural barriers to overcome and there are often issues relating to the re-engineering of the business process to be addressed.

This all needs to be sold to the board, the members of which are often Web unaware and need to be educated. Do not underestimate the need to assess carefully the business processes involved in setting up an e-commerce site or Intranet. It may require a change in the way you currently do business.

Questions such as how a transactional Web site might have an impact on other departments (accounts, customer service and distribution), or how an Intranet might actually add to information overload, are not always addressed.

A strategy that is well thought through may cover an analysis of all departments, which makes choosing a project owner difficult.

One solution may be to pick a tried and tested application, such as e-mail, a stock catalogue or an electronic telephone directory, to create interest in, and familiarity with, the technology. Running a pilot system with a few people in the organization before rolling it out full scale is a sensible way to proceed.

Critical success factors are:

- Get the right people from the right disciplines together to form a team.
- Harness the knowledge of any 'enthusiasts' in your organization.
- Talk to lots of people about the project (suppliers, partner companies and so on) to understand more about the opportunities and threats.
- Prioritize objectives and features according to how well they support business goals.
- Do not try to target all your customer groups at once. Be clear about which groups you are going to prioritize and what their needs are.
- Make sure that the project is integrated with existing business processes and marketing communications strategies.
- Start with a pilot and build confidence.
- Recognize that a Web site is a long-term project, not just something to be developed and left to run on its own. Significant resource will be required to maintain it and keep it current and evolving. Without constant updating your site traffic will simply fade away – to your competitors!
- Keep up to date with the latest e-business trends and adjust your strategy as required.

Site promotion

How do you go about getting people to visit your site? There are two broad areas to consider – online and offline (using external media).

Online options

Search engines
One of the main ways people find relevant Web sites is by use of Internet search engines and key directories. Some surveys have shown that 70% of Internet users reach Web sites via search engines. Undoubtedly, search engines are *one* of the primary ways that people find Web sites, particularly consumer sites. So if your site has a good search engine listing, you should increase the traffic to your site significantly.

Everyone wants high rankings and in the past, if you knew all the techniques, this was highly achievable. Since the Web has grown up and become more complex, getting indexed and more importantly high rankings has become more difficult. In addition, many sites are high on graphical images (these hinder search engines, which prefer good old-fashioned text) and competition for the top spots has intensified. Getting listed in Yahoo! used to be routine, but now the sites listed there are fortunate as the editors are overwhelmed with submissions.

To be successful, the first step is to understand which are the major search engines and directories and how each one works. Then you need to ensure that your site is designed to maximize the probability of (a) getting indexed and (b) getting high rankings.

Remember that there are no secrets that will guarantee a top ranking – despite what some companies claim. There are, however, a number of techniques that you can employ that can sometimes produce good results.

The main search engines are Alta Vista, Excite, HotBot, Go/Infoseek, Google, Lycos, MSN Search, Netscape Search and WebCrawler. The best-known directory is Yahoo!

Search engines work by identifying strategic keywords that are embedded in the computer code behind your page or on the page itself. It is necessary to monitor the words people are using to make sure that your site has these included. Thus, when a potential site visitor is looking for details of say a Conference on Business Law, he or she would perhaps ask the search engine to find sites dealing with 'Business Law', 'Business Conferences', 'Law Conferences' and so on.

The search engine would then list a number of sites that include these words or phrases. Search engines tend to favour sites with few images, so good design is important to success here.

There are some important trends emerging in the world of search engines that will change the way you approach promoting your site. Since 1999, three out of the top six search engines moved to human-compiled directories, in addition to the more usual crawler-based results. Directories make searching for information much easier and you often get 'editors' choices', which really help users narrow down their choices.

There is also a rise of a greater reliance on 'off-the-page' ranking, such as 'link popularity' or pay-for-placement models. The construction of the site with the right 'words on the page' will always be important for more obscure searches, but it is rapidly becoming an outdated method for finding the most popular pages for the more popular queries.

The best promotional activity you can use for your site is to build a quality Web site to impress editors when you submit your site for review. They are looking for fast-loading sites that are easy to navigate and that offer added value to their target audiences. To do this, focus on building relevant content and functionality, build reciprocal links with other sites that are likely to bring you relevant traffic and put other promotional activities in place that will benefit you in the future.

Reciprocal linking with relevant industry Web sites

This is potentially a very good source of visits – perhaps even better than search engines for a B2B site. You need to identify sites that attract the same profile of people, but are generally not competitive (although in the United States competitors are more willing to be linked together). You should not agree to link to another site unless they agree to be linked to yours.

Newsgroups

There are more than 25,000 newsgroups (discussion areas) accessible via the Internet. These are an excellent way to spread the word about your Web site, but you must be careful to avoid giving the impression of blatant advertising. So this is an area for 'infomercials', rather than obvious commercials.

E-mail advertising

This is a useful technique to let existing customers know about your Web site and any new information you have posted on it. Customers could opt to receive a regular free e-mail newsletter. Main points in the newsletter can be 'hyperlinked' to the main site. This enables you to keep the newsletter short whilst giving interested readers the opportunity to instantly call up from the Web site the additional details in which they are interested. This is an excellent way to generate repeat traffic for your Web site.

This method would obviously need to be used carefully with prospects, as they might see it as an intrusion. It might be best to give all customers and prospects the opportunity of opting in or out of receiving e-mail bulletins.

Banners and buttons

Site traffic can be built up by using banner advertising. There are many possible deals ranging from 'swaps' (where you and another organization simply carry each other's advertisements) to paid-for advertising through search engines (where you pay a set rate per thousand 'impressions').

A banner advertisement typically appears at the top of a page of a Web site that the advertiser has decided is likely to have relevant traffic. They can be advertisements in their own right (non-clickable or just a box for you to enter your e-mail address), but tend to be animated and clickable to take people through to a Web site. It is easy to target and measure the success of a banner advertising campaign. The big search engines, for example, offer 'keyword' purchase. You buy a series of keywords that visitors might type into the search engine such as 'business law' or 'legal practice' and when anyone enters those keywords, your banner advertisement will appear on the results page. Click-through rates can be measured easily.

Banner advertisements are under debate in the industry as their effectiveness is questioned. There is a concern that people are becoming less tolerant of banner advertisements that take up valuable download time and are often irritated by them. This aspect needs close scrutiny in the future.

For this reason, other techniques such as superstitial campaigns are currently being tested.

'Interstitial' refers to a thing that comes between something else. In the case of online advertising, this is a message that pops up between two pages of editorial content. This can be extremely irritating for the user (particularly as getting to relevant information is difficult enough as it is) and can get in the way of the content you really want.

The problem with the delivery of most interstitial advertising has been that the message begins loading at the same time as the next piece of editorial content is also trying to load, delaying access to the new page. To minimize this delay, interstitials were normally small in size, which limited their impact.

This is changing with the introduction of the 'superstitial' from Unicast (www.unicast.com). They have basically redefined the interstitial format by combining, in their words 'the power of rich media with a seamless, non-intrusive delivery mechanism'.

With a superstitial the advertisement is downloaded in the background, but *only* when no other editorial content is downloading. In other words, it never interferes with the surfing experience by causing a delay to the editorial content.

When it does pop up (when you move to a new page), all manner of rich media technologies can be used to create the advertisement. According to British Airways, which has recently tested its first superstitial campaign, click-through rates increased significantly in comparison to its banner campaigns.

Viral techniques

These have proved very successful in driving traffic to the Web. E-mail is sent with either something of interest or of value attached or promised. The marketer relies on the recipient to use the forward button to spread the message. A 2000-2001 John West salmon advertisement was very successful as an e-mail attachment and a number of subscription-based services have used viral techniques to spread their offer (for example www.virginwines.com and www.netprofit.com). The problem with viral techniques is that they are very hard to test and although it is possible to track the progress of the e-mail, it is not easy to monitor or measure.

'Interstitial' refers to a thing that comes between something else. In the case of online advertising, this is a message that pops up between two pages of editorial content.

With a superstitial the advertisement is downloaded in the background, but *only* when no other editorial content is downloading. In other words, it never interferes with the surfing experience by causing a delay to the editorial content.

Offline options

This is as wide as your current communications programme. Your Web site should be mentioned in all forms of communication – advertising, public relations, direct mail and all stationery.

The most important thing is to ensure integration, so that your advertising does not mention something that is not clearly signposted on your home page. This is a surprisingly common occurrence on many Web sites.

How to measure success

On a regular basis, all site statistics should be reviewed to track traffic and usage patterns over specific sections, pages and downloads. Most aspects can be measured, although the name of the person visiting will only be available if they choose to tell you (you may still be able to identify their company via the host name).

As with all direct marketing activities, tracking of response is vital – without careful monitoring, you cannot evaluate the success of your investment or know which areas require adjustment or greater development.

SUMMARY

This chapter has looked at the recent growth of the Internet and e-commerce in general. It started by giving some statistics on the Internet and its commercial applications. We have looked at the sources of information and recommended two sites to find up-to-date information on trends in the market.

We have considered the impact of the Internet in both consumer and business-to-business marketing and have seen the value of Internet transactions increasing rapidly.

We then went on to explore the implications for direct marketing. Whilst it is clear that Metcalfe's law on networks relating to the Internet will have significant impact on the direct marketing profession, it is ever more important to be customer focused and to implement digital strategies that reinforce the bond between the customer and the organization.

The chapter then explored three applications of the Internet:

1 the Internet as a marketing tool
2 the Internet as a selling tool
3 the Internet as a means to improve business processes.

As a marketing tool, the Internet has several benefits:

• it allows us to build better relationships with customers
• it is very good for public relations

- we can provide a vast amount of information to our customers very cheaply
- it allows for new approaches to customers through new business models, such as the development of portals and disintermediation.

As a selling tool, we have seen that the Internet allows direct transactions with customers and considered a range of examples, including Amazon.

As a way of improving the business process, the Internet allows a more effective supply chain and the creation of Intranets. Intranets were shown to have four key benefits:

1 they unified the organization
2 they created a collaborative atmosphere across a range of applications
3 they created and fostered the development of the learning organization
4 they reduced costs.

Microsoft anticipates 80% of Web-based traffic will eventually be generated through Intranet systems.

We then looked at the barriers to the use of the Internet. These are:

- a concern over the levels of return on investment
- the speed and unreliability of old systems
- data protection
- security
- the difficulty customers have using it.

We have seen that there were several ways of ensuring the security of online transactions including:

- encryption
- digital certificates and signatures
- secure electronic transactions
- smart cards.

The chapter moved on to examine how to manage an Internet strategy. The need to set firm and quantified objectives was clear as was the need to sell the project at board level. We then considered the critical success factors in implementing a Web site.

Finally, we have looked at ways of promoting a Web site online and offline and the use of:
- reciprocal links
- search engines and directories
- newsgroups
- e-mail

- banner buttons and superstitials
- viral marketing
- advertising, public relations and other marketing communication tools.

The chapter concluded with the need to ensure the correct measurement and evaluation of the strategy.

REVIEW QUESTIONS

1   List two sources of information on the use of the Internet.

2   What are the differences between a search engine and a directory?

3   What is viral marketing? What are its strengths and weaknesses?

4   Explain why encryption is important in Internet commerce.

5   What is Metcalfe's law?

6   What are the three main applications of the Internet in business?

7   Explain why there is reluctance to get involved in the Internet.

8   What is a banner advertisement and how does it compare to a button or superstitial?

9   How should we measure the impact of Internet business?

10   What is an Intranet? List the ways that an Intranet can help a business.

11   List three ways of promoting your Web site online.

12   Why is it important to develop an offline strategy for promotion?

13   List three critical success factors in Web site implementation.

14   What is the underlying factor for success for any business?

15   List and describe three ways of attempting to ensure secure transactions over the Web.

16   What is a newsgroup and how can newsgroups be used to develop an online presence?

Select an advertisement with links to a Web site. Using the address, follow the link to the sites.

- Answer the following questions.
- How does the online brand compare to the offline execution?
- How user friendly is the site?
- Does the site offer online transactions?
- If so, how comfortable are you in using this service?
- What are the reasons for these feelings?
- Try ordering a brochure. How easy is this?
- Make a request for further information. How soon is this provided?
- Would you recommend this site to a friend? If so why, if not why not?
- How would you improve the site?

Chapter 9

The importance of having an offer

Introduction
- What exactly is an offer?
  - The promise of a solution to a problem
  - A specific promotional device
  - Quality – the best available
  - Value – best at this price
  - Availability – 'only from ourselves'
  - Reassurance
  - Added value
  - Better performance or technical superiority
- Positioning
- Promotional offers
  - Using prize draws and competitions
  - Competitions
  - Using incentives in marketing
- Balancing response, conversion and long-term positioning
- The trade-off from hard sell
Summary
Review questions
Exercises

What exactly is an offer?

Your offer is basically the end user benefit, that is what your prospect will get in return for doing what you ask. This may be something highly tangible such as a consumable (a case of wine, a book or an item of clothing for example). On the other hand, your customer may not be buying a tangible product at all, but something that gives a feeling of security (such as an insurance policy).

Whatever you are selling, you have to find a way of presenting the end user benefits in a clear and persuasive way.

Sometimes it is not possible to make a direct 'one-stage' offer because of the complexity of the product, or perhaps the breadth of your range. In such cases, you need to develop an offer which will generate a 'lead' or enquiry.

Let us suppose you sell energy-saving systems for large companies – automatic light switches which turn off after a period of time with no movement in the room; insulated windows and walls to preserve heat and thus reduce power consumption and so on.

It would be quite difficult for you to sell such a product through a one-stage approach, even if you were able to quote lots of happy customers. In this case, you may decide to advertise or mail prospects the offer of a free energy audit.

This would be attractive to prospects as the audit would tell them the various ways they could save money and precisely what this would cost to achieve. It would also be attractive to the vendor, as it would identify, from a wide 'suspect' audience, those likely to be good prospects.

Although price and 'free gift' offers are very common, an offer does not have to include a discount and is it not even necessary to be 'promotional'.

Your offer can comprise of any combination of the following elements.

Your offer is basically the end user benefit, that is what your prospect will get in return for doing what you ask. This may be something highly tangible such as a consumable (a case of wine, a book or an item of clothing for example). On the other hand, your customer may not be buying a tangible product at all, but something that gives a feeling of security (such as an insurance policy).

The promise of a solution to a problem

If you have the solution to a specific problem, and you do not have lots of competitors offering similar solutions, you may merely need to tell people they can buy this from you.

Example

Take the example of a company offering a will-writing service. A high percentage of people do not make a will, although many realize that they should. The company research shows that the most common obstacle is apathy. People just cannot be bothered to get started with their will, especially because of the apparent size of the task. There seems to be a huge amount of work involved in listing and valuing one's assets.

What if the company were to offer a trouble-free service, where it visits the prospects in their homes, and which includes a free valuation of assets, saving the prospect the trouble? That offer would clearly solve the problem and could be quite successful, without the need for discounting.

A specific promotional device

Such a device might be timed and include incentives or discounts. For example, some companies make 'early bird' offers where the prospect is offered a discount or free gift if they order by a certain date.

A variation on this might be a quantity-based offer, such as 'buy one get one free' (a BOGOF) or a typical magazine subscription offer where a publisher offers a special discount if the subscriber signs up for 2 or even 3 years.

This sort of offer can be attractive to customers and it is very attractive to the publisher, who gains in three ways:

1 cash flow is improved
2 the margin available for discount is higher, as there is no marketing cost for the second (and perhaps third) year's subscription
3 the extended commitment from the customer makes longer-term planning easier.

Another way of retaining subscribers longer is to take advantage of the apathy of the average person. Most people signing up with a standing order such as a Variable Direct Debit Mandate (VDD) or a Continuous Credit Card Authority (CCA), just cannot be bothered to take the necessary action to cancel their arrangements, even where they are no longer interested in taking the magazine.

This is why many publishers and membership organizations offer an added incentive for a signed standing order form. Even a deferred standing order works well for many companies. You may well have seen an offer that is phrased in the following way:

15 months issues for the price of 12 – simply complete and return the attached direct debit form and we will send you your first 3 months' issues absolutely free. In this 3-month period you are free to cancel your subscription without having to pay anything at all. After three months, we will process your standing instruction and commence deducting the agreed amounts from your account (or 'charging them to your credit card').

This offer clearly puts the customer in control, but very few actually bother to cancel the standing order and thus carry on paying for months or even years after the initial interest in the product has worn off.

Quality – the best available

If you use this claim, make sure that quality is important to your prospects. It would not be worth making such an offer to a group of prospects that buy solely on price. Therefore, it may be worth segmenting your customers and varying your offers according to their buying behaviour.

Value – best at this price

This works well for many marketers – just make sure you can sustain your price or even reduce it further when the competition reacts.

Availability – 'only from ourselves'

If you have exclusivity on a product which is in demand, you may not need to make any more detailed offer than 'Now available from . . .'.

Reassurance

Every advertiser tries to persuade you that theirs is the best product on the market. As a result, advertisers' claims are devalued by prospects. However, if you can quote a credible third party endorsing your claims, it is much more believable.

You should always make the strongest guarantee you can. A small number of people may take advantage of you, but many more will be reassured and thus encouraged to make a purchase decision.

Example
In the mid 1970s a company selling duvets 'off-the-page' was seeking a way of increasing response to their Sunday supplement advertisements.

Peter Donoghue, who was then chairman of the company's advertising agency, suggested that it should offer a 10-year, unconditional, replacement or full-money-back guarantee on every duvet it sold. The company chairman was appalled, saying, 'A duvet is only expected to last for about 10 years – your guarantee will make us bankrupt'.

Peter explained that, whilst the guarantee must be honoured, most customers would be very happy with the reassurance that they could return it if they wished. Of course, a small number of customers may be sufficiently zealous to take advantage of the guarantee if their duvet started to wear out after 9 years, but the majority would not.

Eventually, Peter persuaded the company to test this new offer and sales doubled.

The company realized a fortune due to Peter's suggestion and a careful study over the 14 years since the offer started had showed no measurable increase in guarantee claims.

Added value

Customers also respond well to offers of help. So telephone helplines and free advisory booklets can be very successful.

Better performance or technical superiority

This is another area where testimonials help you achieve greater credibility. Every one expects you to say that your product is the best, and to a certain extent your statements are discounted. However, if the Chairman of ICI says it is the best, it is a more powerful and believable testimony. Such statements are especially persuasive if they quote some sort of performance improvement, for example: 'Since we changed to XYZ, we have noted a 15% reduction in machine downtime.'

If you have not got any testimonials, do not despair. Assuming your product is as good as you say it is, testimonials are not difficult to get.

Do not do what a well-known consultant advises on a public platform 'Write your own!' Not only is this highly unethical, it is also foolish – there is no need to resort to such practices.

The best way to get testimonials is to ask for them. Not in so many words perhaps, but in the following way. When you send a satisfaction survey questionnaire to your customers ask a final question with an open response. You might say something like 'Is there anything else you would like to say about our products or services? Please tell us whether they are good or bad'. Some will say you are absolutely useless and you must respond to these immediately with remedial action. However, some will say yours is the most wonderful product they have ever encountered. These you respond to with a request that they let you use their statement in promotional material. Occasionally this will be refused, but most people will give their permission. Some will offer to say something even nicer if you wish. This technique never fails to produce powerful, believable testimonials.

Many seminar delegates ask why business-to-business advertisers quote names and companies of people who give testimonials, whilst consumer advertisers rarely do. 'Is this because many consumer testimonials are false?' they ask. The truth is reassuring and depressing at the same time.

When a company quotes the name and address of someone who recommends its product, the subject often receives 'hate' mail from cranks. This does not often happen with business addresses – it is a sad comment on modern life!

Remember that an offer does not always have to be a hard 'promotional' gimmick. Simply telling the right story in the right way to the right person will often be sufficient.

Whatever you decide about your own offer, bear in mind that it must also link to your longer-term positioning.

Positioning

For many people, positioning can be a difficult concept to grasp. Positioning is not something you do to your product, although it may well require you to make changes to your services.

Positioning is the overall impression you wish to leave in the mind of your prospect once they have read your advertisement or mailing. Your copy will describe the benefits which your product will bring to the prospect, but something more is needed – what is there you can say which states very succinctly what this product *means to the prospect*?

Moving away from the theoretical approach, we can consider some examples.

Example

Rolls Royce is positioned as the top-quality car marque. Mercedes are probably engineered just as well, if not better, as are Lexus cars. However, they are still not Rolls and the difference is positioning. Rolls has pre-empted the top-quality position to the extent that the name 'Rolls Royce' has become a colloquial description of quality for all sorts of products and services.

American Express is positioned as *the* prestigious financial instrument. It makes sure its communications reflect this positioning. Rolls Royce's positioning is largely to do with the excellence of the product, American Express is primarily selling a service. Its product is quite similar to other charge cards, but the way it describes it gives it a cachet of better quality.

Rolls Royce would clearly need to be particularly careful about any incentives they offered to prospective buyers. A cheap free gift would be out of context with their positioning. So would a special weekend sale. On the other hand, free membership of a motoring organization such as the RAC or AA would be quite appropriate. I once saw a free gift offer related to a Rolls Royce sale which was very interesting. A dealer in Scotland offered: 'Buy this Rolls Royce and we will give you a free Mini for a member of your family.'

Similarly, a free baby safety seat would be appropriate to the positioning of a Ford or Volvo, but less so for a high-powered sports car.

What can you do to sustain a positioning? Perhaps you could offer a telephone advice line as mentioned above, or provide a series of leaflets explaining changes in legislation as they happen. Perhaps you simply need to make a promise of availability whenever your customer has a problem.

Some agency copywriters ask clients the question 'What impression do we want to leave in the mind of the reader?' The copywriter is looking for a positioning statement and, in answering this question, it can be helpful to use an analogy. The following are the two most popular in the advertising agency business.

- 'If this product were an animal, what would it be?'
- 'If it were a motor car, what would it be?'

Such a simple analogy enables the copywriter to get a good feeling for what is required in terms of image, reliability and efficiency.

Whatever positioning you choose must be appropriate for your product. It is easy to say, for example 'I will offer the Rolls Royce of home catering services', but if your customers perceive your service as a Lada you leave yourself open to criticism.

Your offer will vary according to what you want the customer to do. It may be quite acceptable to offer a helpful free leaflet to business people in return for an enquiry about your product, but a free leaflet will not in itself persuade a prospect to order a £5000 product. A free technical helpline may, on the other hand, be enough to give your product the edge over a competitor.

You can vary your offer to pre-select the quality of enquiries you attract. The way you phrase your offer in your initial advertisement will have a major bearing on the quality of enquiries you receive. The less specific you are, the 'looser' your leads will be.

For example, you could simply say, 'Return this coupon to rid your house of flies forever.' This may attract thousands of 'loose' leads (enquiries), but when the prospects discover they have to spend £1500 having screens fitted to all doors and windows, your conversion to sale ratio would be very small.

On the other hand, an advertisement that said 'A single investment of £1500 would rid your home of flying insects forever' would attract very few leads, but the conversion rate would be much higher. These would be 'tight' leads.

As we can see, loose leads do not convert as well as tight leads but you get more of them. When deciding which type to use, take into account the cost of servicing a lead, the amount of sales or telemarketing resource you have available and the competitive situation.

You may well have to carry out a series of tests to determine the ideal method for your business. (See Chapter 11 for details of testing procedures.)

You must make sure that your offer is *relevant* to your prospects. People rarely buy products because of their technical superiority. They buy the product because of what it delivers in terms of user benefits. They do not buy a lubricating oil because it is a technological marvel. They buy it because it stops a door squeaking. They do not buy features, but benefits. A lecturer's pocket pointer is a nicely engineered telescopic device, but the end user benefit is that it fits in the pocket.

Promotional offers

When discussing offers, many people think only of discounts and 'buy one get one free' approaches. These are certainly offers, but, as we have seen, not the only ones.

There is no doubt that price and volume offers attract increased response, but we must also consider the effect on our conversion ratios and long-term sales potential. Generating a high volume of low-grade enquiries may not be the ideal way to build your business.

Also a 'buy one get one free' offer will not be appropriate for all products or audiences. Consider the relevance for your own market. There are many products that do not lend themselves to a 'two for the price of one' approach either.

However, if you have enough information about your prospects, you may be able to make highly selective offers of this sort. For example, your customer may have a daughter who will be 18 next month – that could be an opportunity for a 'two for one' offer on a variety of products.

Offers do not have to be the same for all prospects – they can be varied by segments. If you hold detailed information about prospects, you can communicate with them directly varying your offer according to your knowledge of their circumstances.

| Example |

A company that sold bulk supplies of foods to people in the catering industry, built up a sizeable database by offering free product samples through press and direct mail.

It did not specify the amount of free product a respondent would get and on the sample request card it asked 'How many meals do you serve each day?' This information enabled it to deal with each enquiry according to potential.

An establishment serving 500 lunches every day would receive a 1000 portion sample. One serving 25 lunches would receive a 50 portion sample. The buying incentives would also vary. The 500 lunch prospect would be offered, for example, an electric food mixer in return for an order for a 10,000 portion pack. This would be a totally unrealistic offer for the smaller prospect, so it would be offered perhaps a set of ladles as an incentive to order a 500 portion pack. This incentive would have had no stimulating effect on the larger prospect. Indeed, the company would simply have been giving away free gifts without attracting any additional orders.

The information on the enquiry form also enabled the company to determine the ideal contact strategy for each type of prospect. The larger prospects would have their samples delivered in person by a member of the sales force. Smaller prospects could have their samples mailed to them.

There is often scope for selective marketing of such offers, once you have the information to enable you to segment your prospects.

Using prize draws and competitions

Prize draws have been working well for many years. Many people like the chance of winning something, especially when all they have to do is send you their name and address.

The popularity of the National Lottery has tended to reduce the effectiveness of some of the larger prize draws, but they are still worth testing – especially with smaller prizes.

Some prize draws have been known to double response – even when the only prize was a free meal for two or a case of wine.

Note that it is illegal to place a condition on entry to a prize draw. So you cannot say 'Only open to anyone who buys this product.' However, although a prize draw must be open to everyone, not just the people who buy your product, many respondents feel that they will have a greater chance of success if they do buy, so prize draws tend to increase order levels as well as response.

Competitions

There are two major differences between a prize draw and a competition.

A competition requires the entrant to satisfy some test of skill, although this often requires minimal intelligence. Unlike the prize draw entry, a competition entry can be tied to a purchase, for example: 'Only open to customers placing an order of more than £50.'

Competitions can be used to ensure that a customer pays close attention to a catalogue or leaflet. A typical example would be where a mail order company asks entrants to match silhouettes with photographs in the various sections of their catalogue. This could be an effective 'traffic builder' ensuring that customers look through the catalogue with some care.

Another popular method is to ask customers to answer questions about the major benefits of a product. These benefits would be included in the promotional copy on the pack. Thus, entrants have to read the pack copy in order to be able to answer the questions.

A competition requires the entrant to satisfy some test of skill, although this often requires minimal intelligence. Unlike the prize draw entry, a competition entry can be tied to a purchase, for example: 'Only open to customers placing an order of more than £50.'

Using incentives in marketing

There are two main ways of using incentives – in return for a purchase and in return for a trial. The former works quite well in consumer marketing, but less well in marketing to large businesses.

Many businesses and all public offices and government departments will flatly refuse to accept any form of consideration in return for placing orders, but, whilst this can be understood, a sensible seller can often find a way of offering an inducement which does not contravene the regulations in force.

You could try offering an incentive for a free trial – perhaps a free gift that might benefit the business as a whole, such as a day's free consultancy. Although this would not compromise the company executive, the free gift technique is still frowned upon by many large corporations.

Alternatively, you could offer an incentive in the form of free merchandise. Assuming they are interested in the product, some additional supplies could be quite acceptable. A laser printer could be supplied with some spare toner or several reams of paper. This would be more acceptable to many organizations.

You must decide what is right and permissible in your market place. Remember that your promotional strategy will affect what customers and prospects think of you. As we said earlier, cheap free gifts are not advisable when you are selling top-quality products.

Balancing response, conversion and long-term positioning

Every business would like to improve the cost-efficiency of its marketing budget, and, as we shall see in Chapter 10, there are numerous devices that will increase response.

In your quest for more cost-efficiency, be aware that although making powerful offers will increase the response you attract:

- generating response is only the first step, even if you sell direct and a response is an order
- the eventual profitability of a direct marketing business depends on total customer satisfaction with your product and your promises – repeat sales are generally a highly important factor given the cost of acquiring new business
- it is therefore highly dangerous to over-stimulate prospects and indeed to over-promise regarding the quality and benefits of your product
- unless your product lives up to the claims, you will suffer in three ways – you will have a higher than expected level of returned orders; you will not be able to sell additional products to disappointed customers in the future; and dissatisfied customers will each tell several people, losing you an unknown amount of future business.

As mentioned earlier, offering incentives in return for enquiries will increase your enquiry levels and reduce your conversion ratio. There is no set rule about this. You need to test in your own market place and find an offer that produces the best balance for your own business.

The trade-off from hard sell

You can usually increase your response by using aggressive techniques, but remember that your response is likely to be simply the tip of the iceberg. If

2% of people mailed, or 0.2% of those who read a newspaper, respond to your offer, it is probable that around five or ten times as many actually noticed and read at least part of your message.

What do they now think of you? Some will not change their attitudes, but some will find your aggressive approach off-putting and may even think less of your company as a result.

One of the most powerful selling weapons is door-to-door selling, but this also attracts the most disfavour.

Next on the list comes the telephone salesperson – the more powerful the technique, the more people resent it being used on them.

This same principle applies in advertising and direct mail. Some of the world's most successful marketing organizations use very hard sell mailings, attracting huge responses but also much criticism.

To achieve the correct balance requires careful judgement. You have a duty to both your customers and your company. If a hard sell works, it is generally because your offer meets your customers' needs better than your competitors'. As long as companies abide by the industry codes of conduct and use the mailing preference service (MPS) and related services, there should not be a problem. The key is trust and this is what brands ultimately promise. Fail to deliver on this promise and you will ultimately fail in business.

SUMMARY

This chapter has explored the use of offers in direct marketing. We have seen that an offer is the end user benefit. This may be a promotional device or simply the promise of a solution to a problem. In using promotional devices, the underpinning principle is relevance – the offer must be relevant to the target market.

Where the offer is one of better quality or better value it is often necessary to support your claim with third-party endorsements. Providing you really do deliver on your promises, good testimonials can be obtained quite easily.

Offers should always support the positioning of the product and we examined positioning through a definition and the use of examples.

We have seen that positioning happens in the mind of consumers through a range of inputs, including advertising. The key question is 'What impression do we wish to leave in the minds of our consumers?'

We have seen that offers will vary in terms of what we would like our customers to do and the nature of the offer will pre-select the quality of the enquiries gained.

The chapter has discussed the use of promotional offers and the key area of relevance to diverse segments. We have looked at the types of promotional offers available to direct marketers, including:

- prize draws and competitions
- free trial
- free products.

These need to be used in an appropriate way – in certain markets, the use of incentives to purchase may compromise our relationships.

We have seen that powerful offers may attract customers who are more interested in the offer than the product. There is a need is to balance response conversion and longer-term retention of customers to maximize value to the organization.

REVIEW QUESTIONS

1   What is an offer?

2   What is the key factor in deciding an offer?

3   What is a BOGOF?

4   Why is direct debit and continuous card authority so useful to direct marketing?

5   What is the value of testimonials?

6   Define positioning. How is positioning used in direct marketing?

7   How can we pre-select the quality of enquiries?

8   What are the differences between a prize draw and a competition?

9   What types of incentives are available to direct marketers?

10   What is the role of testing in the use of offers?

EXERCISES

For a company of your choice, select an advertisement that offers an incentive to respond.

- How does the offer reinforce the positioning of the product?
- Would the offer cause you to respond?
- Is the offer appropriate to the target market?
- What other incentives could have been used?
- How would you improve the advertisement?

Chapter 10

How to increase responses through more effective creative work

Introduction
- Define your objective
- Developing a creative outline
- Managing response
  - Planning your communication
- The essential elements of a direct response advertisement
  - Awareness advertising
  - Direct response advertising
  - Targeting
  - Timing and frequency
  - Creative
  - Rules for successful direct response advertising
- Direct mailings
  - The letter
  - Additional enclosures
  - Newspaper and magazine reprints
  - The essentials of a good response device
  - Checklist
  - Direct mail follow-ups
  - Following up by telephone

Summary

Review questions

Exercises

INTRODUCTION

The chapter begins with an apology to anyone who has read my previous book (*The Royal Mail Guide to Direct Mail for Small Businesses*). There are only a few ways of developing consistently sound creative work and they are all variations on the same general theme. So, the approach to planning, especially of direct mailings, is very similar to that given in the earlier book.

A number of delegates ask, 'Why don't my ads and mailings work?' Many advertisements and mailings do seem to fail to achieve their targets, even though the advertiser thought they were very well written and designed.

It is clear that, despite numerous disclaimers by many very experienced practitioners, many people still think that if you produce a good 'creative', you are bound to succeed. In fact, creative is probably the least important of the various elements in a promotion.

Earlier chapters have stressed that the three most important factors in the success of an advertisement or mailing are targeting the right person (by selecting the right medium or list); saying the right thing (developing an attractive and relevant offer); and delivering your message at the right time.

If you target the wrong person, or if he or she is not in the market this month, your promotion is likely to fail because, no matter how well you have sold your proposition, it is simply not relevant to the reader.

On the other hand, if you get the three major factors right, you have a chance of achieving great things. If you achieve the three objectives, your results are likely to be acceptable, '*almost*' regardless of the quality of your creative work. I say 'almost' because many good, well-targeted messages have been destroyed by poor design and typography.

The purpose of this chapter is to show you how to turn an acceptable response into a good or even exceptional response, by using the right creative techniques.

Define your objective

The first step is to be quite clear about what you want to achieve. Do you want to:

- sell your product or service direct, that is ask for an order now
- persuade prospects to send for more information
- ask for a salesperson to visit
- encourage prospects to visit your shop or office
- invite them to a demonstration or other event?

Defining a clear objective at the start will help you to decide how much information you need to convey.

A one-stage proposition usually requires lots of detail, because you are intending to move the prospect through all the stages of buying in a single communication. They have to be given everything they need to know in order to make a purchase decision.

With two-stage promotions, you can usually use less copy – all your advertisement must do is persuade prospects to call or send for more information.

Another factor governing the amount of information necessary is the knowledge already held by your prospect. Your product may be one that everyone will know about (such as 80 gsm white copier paper) or one that requires lots of detailed explanation (such as a laser printer). You will need to say more about the printer than the paper.

Another consideration is whether your prospects have bought from you before. Regular buyers need less information about your products and your company.

The issue of whether copy should be long or short will be dealt with later in this chapter, but we can start here by addressing those critics of long copy whose objection is simply 'No one will read long copy.' This is absolutely untrue. People read for as long as they are interested and no longer. Thus, long copy is appropriate for some circumstances and not for others. In a one-stage situation, long copy will often be needed if:

- you are addressing a new prospect – who may never have heard of your company or your product
- your product is a complex one – so there are many factors which must be explained to the prospect
- your product is totally new – therefore unknown, even to established customers
- your audience likes to read long copy – this may sound unlikely, but in the 1990s the World Wildlife Fund addressed some letters to established donors who wanted to know what was being done with their money; the letters were invariably three or four pages long and, far from being unacceptable to recipients, they actually generated a sizeable response from people saying how much they appreciated hearing all the news.

Generally, established customers will not need very long copy, even in a one-stage situation, because they already know something about you and your products.

In a two-stage situation, you are even less likely to need long copy because the prospect has a second chance of getting the information he or she needs. Bear in mind, however, that the more you tell them up-front, the fewer wasted enquiries you will receive.

The key difference between 'mail-shots' and effective targeted communications is that the former assume that all prospects are exactly the same, whereas the latter address the information needs of each individual.

The key to writing effective copy is to think about your prospects and imagine you are face to face with them. What do you need to tell them to persuade them to buy your product? What questions will they ask? If you can list the key questions, your copy will almost write itself because it is simply a series of answers to these questions.

It is clear that copy length and complexity will vary according to several factors. The natural corollary to this is that we should not write the same copy to everyone.

The key difference between 'mail-shots' and effective targeted communications is that the former assume that all prospects are exactly the same, whereas the latter address the information needs of each individual.

Example

A publisher is writing to persuade an existing subscriber to renew. In this case the copy may be quite short. The subscriber will want to know the price, and any new or special features that the publisher is planning to introduce which may enhance their opinion of its magazine.

The publisher may be planning a new telephone helpline for subscribers and will, of course, need to explain the benefits to them. However, the publisher will not need to explain what its magazine is about. To do so would simply underline the fact that it is treating all prospects in the same way.

If, instead, the publisher is writing to a rented list of people who match its subscriber profile but have, as far as it knows, never read its publication, it will need to tell them more. It may tell them what regular features they will find and perhaps even send them details of contents over the past 6 months. In this situation, longer copy will be required.

Developing a creative outline

Once you have established your objective, you can develop your creative outline as follows.

- Objective – confirming what you have decided above.
- Target audience – a clear definition of your audience is needed here.
- Offer – what will make the audience respond in the way you wish? Should you use one-stage or two?
- Timing – when are they likely to be interested?
- Medium – this will depend on who they are. Existing customers will generally be approached using mail, e-mail, telephone or the sales force; new

prospects using one or more of broadcast, press advertising, door-to-door leaflets, loose or bound-in inserts, direct mailings, e-mail and the Internet.

- Creative approach – your message and how this can be delivered. For example, your approach to copy length (long or short) will vary according to your objective, target audience, offer, existing relationships and the complexity of the product. It will also depend on your chosen medium – broadcast dictates shorter copy; direct mail longer copy. Consider the components of any mailing, such as envelopes (colour and message if any), letters (length), leaflet 1 (purpose), leaflet 2 (purpose and if required) and methods of reply (mail, telephone, fax, e-mail or Web site).
- Implementation – production of copy, artwork, films and so on, selection of suppliers, including printers and computer bureaux.
- Response forecasts – your estimates of volume and plans for efficient handling and despatch of material and orders.
- Follow-up – to stimulate response or perhaps to acknowledge enquiries and orders.

We can work through this outline for the publishing example mentioned above.

Situation 1

Target: Existing subscribers due for renewal.

Offer: Renew within 30 days and receive a free appointments planner. Details of telephone helpline and of new monthly European Update feature.

Example

Timing: Mailed to arrive approximately one month before existing subscription expires – mailed in batches according to renewal dates.

Medium: Direct mail.

Creative: Message – renewal offer, details of free gift and new helpline.

Envelope – message about free appointments planner.

Letter – laser printed with name and personalized salutation, fairly short, leading on free gift for renewal, but mentioning new helpline and key new features.

Leaflet 1 – explaining new helpline, including a testimonial from prominent person.

Leaflet 2 – free gift details.

Reply form – laser addressed, attached to the letter by perforation.

Reply methods – reply paid envelope (freepost), freefone telephone and fax numbers.

Implementation: Computer department (or external supplier) to deliver counts and address tapes/disks each week for batches to be mailed. Artwork and bulk printed items produced. Personalized items produced by computer department or laser print bureau. Mailing house/department briefed to receive, assemble and despatch mailing batches.

Response handling: Estimates of responses to receiving department. Plans for response handling (data capture and updating of database subscription records, despatch of free gift).

Follow-up: Plans for further action to remind people who have been mailed and who have not responded.

Situation 2

Target: Rented names – people who match the profile of our existing subscribers, such as business people (generally managers and above, aged 30–45). Possibly some more sophisticated customer typology, for example 'global thinkers' and 'computer literates'. This depends on how much profiling work has been done on the publisher's own customers and how much data is available about those on the rented lists.

Offer: Special introductory discount offer of 30% off the full price, 40% discount for 2-year subscription. A special free gift for an annual direct debit mandate or continuous credit card authority – this tends to increase retention/renewal dramatically.

Timing: No specific timing constraints – mail as soon as possible.

Creative: Message – subscribe now. It will enable you to do your job better and enhance your career prospects. Details of introductory offers and free gifts. Sample contents and testimonials.

Envelope – message relating to free gifts.

Letter – laser printed with name and personalized salutation. At least two pages long and using a testimonial as a headline. Referring to other enclosures.

Leaflet – descriptive leaflet about magazine, plus testimonial comments of eminent readers.

Reply form – laser personalized, attached to the letter by perforation.

Reply methods – reply paid envelope (freepost) and freefone telephone and fax numbers, e-mail and Web site addresses.

Implementation: List brokers to deliver counts and address tapes to addressing bureau. Artwork and printed items produced. Personalized items produced by laser bureau. Mailing house briefed to receive, assemble and despatch mailing.

Response handling: Estimates of responses to receiving department. Plans for response handling (data capture and updating of database subscription records, and despatch of free gift).

Follow-up: Plans for a follow-up mailing to non-respondents.

Note that these examples are not intended as creative briefs, but are simply to help you devise a brief without forgetting any major feature. (Briefing is dealt with in detail in Chapter 13, on page 300.)

Managing response

Businesses need a constant supply of new leads, but with limited resources it is important not to generate enquiries you cannot handle quickly and efficiently. Therefore, you need to estimate response very carefully and, if necessary, phase your mailing or advertising programme so that the flow of leads is easily manageable, without you having to resort to expensive overtime or external resources.

By sending out a controlled number of mailings each week, a business gains two advantages:

1 the quantity of leads received is manageable
2 each lead can be followed up quickly, ensuring maximum conversion.

A badly handled enquiry can do more than lose you a single sale – it may have been your first contact with a potentially huge customer.

Planning your communication

Many people find it useful to devise a checklist when planning the design of a communication. We can consider the desired sequence of events. The first task is to attract attention. In an advertisement, apart from any considerations of size, timing and position, you will do this through a combination of: headline (size and wording) and pictures.

When writing headlines and designing advertisements, it can be useful to ask someone to look at your work and tell you what they 'take out' of it. It is all too easy to attract attention with a 'stopper', whilst leaving totally the wrong impression in the mind of your reader, as the following example shows.

The Australian Government planned to run a campaign aimed at young drivers to try to reduce the incidence of drunk driving in this group.

The advertiser had some striking photographs of youngsters blowing into breathalysers, and asked two agencies to present ideas using one of these. One was a traditional advertising agency, the other a direct marketing agency.

Example

The traditional agency, exponents of short, snappy copy, wrote the headline 'Don't blow it!' above a picture of a young man blowing into the bag.

The client liked this headline, but fortunately it was subjected to comprehension research before being run. Only 4% of the people shown this advertisement understood it. Many thought it was a protest advertisement from a civil liberties group!

The direct marketing agency came up with 'Don't blow your licence', which was used with the same photograph as above. All the people shown this version understood it clearly.

David Ogilvy discovered many years ago that long explicit headlines containing news always out-pull short, snappy, non-specific headlines.

With a mailing there are two opportunities for headlines – one on the outer envelope and the other at the top of the letter. There is considerable resistance to envelope messages from those not experienced in direct response, but more often than not such a message increases response.

The second task is to establish the relevance of your offer. Where possible you should try to vary this for individual customer segments – given the necessary personal information, this will be fairly easy to achieve with a mailing or telephone campaign. It is, of course, more difficult in broadscale advertising. It is possible to vary copy in different publications but not to various segments of the same readership (unless, of course, you use loose inserts – see Chapter 11, p. 237).

Next you must convince the prospect of the benefits.

Again, you should vary this where possible. It will be more convincing if you back it up with credible testimonial statements.

You can then close the sale. With a powerful 'call to action' and, in a letter, a postscript reminding readers of the major benefits of replying, or perhaps the penalties for not doing so.

The next task is to confirm the action required and take the order. A clear statement of 'How to take advantage of this offer' will generally increase the number of responses. This is probably because it makes things easier for the reader. A well-designed coupon or reply form, pre-printed where possible with the prospect's name and address, will make sure you maximize your response.

Make sure you give all the possible response options – freepost, freefone, fax, e-mail or Web site (whatever is appropriate to your audience). A high percentage of UK households have a fax and every month more and more homes are becoming equipped with computers and modems.

Having looked at the process of developing a sales argument by mail or advertisement, we can take a closer look at direct response press advertising.

The essential elements of a direct response advertisement

First, we need to define direct response advertising. There are broadly three types of advertising.

1 Awareness advertising – the objective here is to increase awareness or influence opinions. This form of advertising does not invite a response and will often not even carry a response address.
2 Direct response advertising – the objective is to generate a response or lead by use of an offer. Direct response advertisements include response addresses, telephone and fax numbers and e-mail addresses. Those carrying a coupon tend to attract more attention (see p. 202).
3 Dual purpose advertising – where there is a primary and a secondary objective, for example an awareness advertisement which carries a telephone number or address will often attract large numbers of responses, requests for further information and so on. Equally, an advertisement whose principal objective is to generate enquiries can have a measurable effect on attitudes and awareness of a product or service.

Awareness advertising

This type of advertising is still widely used although companies who have tested and researched the third type (dual purpose advertising) have found that their brand and image objectives can be achieved whilst their advertisements simultaneously produce valuable responses from interested readers.

More than this, however, some studies have shown that response advertisements with reply coupons actually achieve higher awareness scores than their mainstream equivalents.

Therefore, it is recommended that, where awareness is required, you consider the use of dual purpose advertising as a first option. The resulting enquiry data can be very useful for research purposes in satisfaction surveys, customer profiles and so on.

As in most cases direct marketers are primarily seeking response, we will now concentrate on the second type (direct response advertising).

Direct response advertising

The critical success factors for direct response advertising are largely the same as for direct mail, but the way they interact and the precise emphasis of each varies slightly.

Awareness advertising – the objective here is to increase awareness or influence opinions. This form of advertising does not invite a response and will often not even carry a response address.

Direct response advertising – the objective is to generate a response or lead by use of an offer. Direct response advertisements include response addresses, telephone and fax numbers and e-mail addresses.

Dual purpose advertising – where there is a primary and a secondary objective, for example an awareness advertisement which carries a telephone number or address will often attract large numbers of responses, requests for further information and so on.

Offer – the main product message, terms and promotional factors, for example discounts.

- Targeting – as with all forms of advertising, the message can only work if it reaches the right person. Therefore, the first step is to select the right publication.
- Offer – the main product message, terms and promotional factors, for example discounts.
- Timing and frequency – this is an issue which is very different for advertisements as opposed to mailings, mainly because we cannot vary the exposure of the message according to our prospect's ideal timing. Therefore, we tend to time our insertions to fit times of peak interest or demand.
- Creative – although creative is correctly placed in relationship to the other factors, such a simple listing is not totally appropriate for press advertising. In a newspaper or magazine, the creative treatment may be a crucial factor in targeting the reader. Without an attractive headline, displayed in the correct manner, the prospect may not even see the advertisement.
- Response mechanics – the main purpose of response devices is to make it easy for the prospect to reply. In this case, we cannot fill in the name and address of the prospect, but we must do all we can to facilitate the process. We must also give the postal address, telephone and fax numbers, e-mail and Web site addresses where possible.

Let's look more closely at some of these factors.

Targeting

Selection of the right publication is vital and there are several ways you can approach this.

1 You should know which publications are read by your existing customers (from questionnaire research and so on). You can then match prospect segments against your customer profile and identify the most appropriate media.
2 Where customer data is not available or not clear, you may have to undertake some telephone or postal questionnaire research to find the information you need.
3 Newspapers and magazines will generally have some research of their own. This will tell you the type and quantity of prospects you can reach through their publication.
4 If none of these gives you a good enough answer, you will probably have to test one or more publications to see which produces the most response, or perhaps the best conversion rate.

In fact, you will probably use a combination of all the above methods. If you do decide to test several publications, remember that where loose inserts are available they can be the most cost-effective test method. (See Chapter 7 for more information about loose inserts.)

Timing and frequency

Timing is very important, but unlike in direct communications, we cannot vary this for individual segments of the audience. This means that we may need to run the same advertisement several times to be sure that a large proportion of our prospects have an opportunity to see the advertisement at a time appropriate to them.

Alternatively, we may try to deal with this problem by breaking down the communications process into stages. With a targeted and appropriately timed mailing we may attempt to move the reader in one stage to taking action. With an advertisement, we cannot be confident of getting the timing exactly right. So, unless our offer is one which is likely to appeal to a sizeable proportion of the audience at any time, we may well consider a two-stage approach.

Here we will ask readers to send for more details and, at the same time, try to discover when the timing will be ideal for each respondent. In these circumstances we need some sort of attractive but inexpensive offer – perhaps a free booklet that those in the market will find appealing. For example, a company that produces household security systems (which are expensive and may be bought at any time of year) could produce a booklet entitled '20 things every householder should know about security'. People who sent for this booklet would be singling themselves out as prospects for the product.

An alternative to this approach is that used by direct insurance companies whose message in broadscale media is 'Do you want cheaper insurance? Call this number now'. This can be more economical, but it requires a very simple proposition for success.

Creative

As mentioned above, the creative aspects of a direct response advertisement interact with each of the other issues, and creative is in some ways the most vital consideration.

Rules for successful direct response advertising

A direct response advertisement is an 'action-oriented' communication calling for a response from the prospect. To be successful, it must conform to certain 'rules', which should only be broken after careful testing.

1 As readers generally scan an advertisement in the order of picture, head-line and then copy, the layout should be arranged in the same sequence. In tests of headline position, there have been response increases of more than 100% simply by placing the line below the picture. See Chapter 11 for more information about testing.

2 The picture should be striking and 'action oriented'. You might think that this is easier said than done, but simply showing a pair of hands on a computer keyboard can produce more response than if the keyboard is shown on its own. On one occasion, a company tested a leaflet where the addition of a hand filling in a form caused a dramatic increase in response to a subscription offer. So, where possible, show your product in use.

3 Photographs usually work better than drawings. Here, as in all forms of direct communication, you must think about your audience. Are you advertising to surgeons or engineers? If the latter, drawings may create more attention.

4 As 80–90% of 'readers' will not read further than the headline, the head-line and main illustration must put across the entire proposition in clear simple terms. Only very rarely do people buy a publication to read the advertisements and, even then, they generally scan the headlines first. Thus, the headline must be informative. Remember David Ogilvy's research showing that long, informative headlines usually out-pull short, witty ones.

5 Body copy length is not critical, so long as the picture and headline attract interested prospects. However, clear layout is essential. It must not look difficult to read. Some advertisers have had huge success with very long copy in direct response newspaper and magazine advertisements. Length of copy will depend on the objective – longer copy for direct orders, shorter to generate enquiries for more information.

6 Turn features into benefits. Features and attributes of the product must be expressed as 'end-user' benefits – customers are only interested in the relevance of this product to their own needs.

7 Include a coupon. The inclusion of a clear, obvious coupon not only increases response, but also awareness scores. This was noted in a study completed by a UK national newspaper in the 1990s.

8 Include a prominent, easy-to-understand 'call to action' directing readers to the coupon and/or telephone, fax, Web site and e-mail addresses. Ask someone not directly involved to read the advertisement and then to tell you if they understand what is required.

9 Repeat the main points near the coupon. If your picture and headline have done their job properly, some readers will skip directly to the coupon bypassing the body copy. Therefore, it pays to restate your proposition near the coupon.

10 Include a second address. A second address should be featured outside the coupon. This will ensure that any 'pass on' readers can respond even

if the coupon has been clipped. In practice, this will be a very small number. Some publishers insist on this to avoid problems in case of complaints from readers.

11 The smaller the space, the more cost-effective the result. If a cost-effective response is your main objective, the smaller the space you use the better. However, there are three caveats. First, make sure you use enough space to tell the whole story in readable typeface and size. Second, small spaces will not impress your sales force or retail distributors. Third, it is not as easy to negotiate large discounts on small spaces.

12 Avoid sans serif type for body copy, as reader comprehension is dramatically reduced. See the research data on pp. 212–14.

This sentence is set in sans serif type and several researches have shown that adults reading several lines of copy in this sort of face cannot answer as many questions about what they have just read as those reading the same text in a serif face.

This sentence is set in serif type and research has shown that adults reading copy in this sort of face achieve much higher comprehension scores than those reading the same text in a sans serif face.

This does not look obvious, in fact the sentence in sans serif actually looks clearer. This is why we must read the research rather than use our instinct.

13 Do not reverse out body copy. The same research tells us that we must never use 'reversed out' type for body copy. In this case the decline in comprehension is even more dramatic. See the following example, then read the comprehension statistics on p. 214.

This sentence is set in serif type, but is 'reversed out', that is printed in white on a dark background. Research shows that adults reading copy in this sort of face score very badly in comprehension tests compared to those reading the same text and type style printed black on a white background.

Designers like reversed-out type because it looks dramatic and stylish. Unfortunately, far fewer people read it so it does not get your message across effectively. Do not permit inexperienced designers to reduce your responses in this way.

14 Use right-hand pages where possible. An advertisement on a right-hand page often produces more response than one on a left-hand page at the

same point in the publication. However, the difference in response will not always justify paying a premium for the position.

15 Buy early positions if you can. Advertisements early in a publication often out-pull those on later pages (this depends, of course, on whether there is any specific section or editorial feature which will attract the people we are aiming for).

Note that, as with all 'rules', there are many exceptions. Some advertisements which 'do everything right' fail to work and others which break all rules work well.

Direct mailings

The crucial difference between a mailing and an advertisement is targeting. If you have done your research carefully, you should be able to vary your mailing copy for different segments of your audience. So in planning a mailing give some thought as to how you may be able to make these variations cost-efficiently.

It may be useful to run through the elements in a typical pack and consider at the same time which could be varied without excessive cost.

With the outer envelope, you might opt to use a plain envelope or even to have a generalized message or a simple logo. As many advertisers have discovered that printing messages on envelopes can increase responses, we should consider how we might print relevant envelope messages to each prospect segment.

If we are planning a very large mailing with segments in excess of 50,000, the economics are such that we could consider making printing plate changes to give a different envelope message to each audience segment. Whatever the print quantity, it will generally be more economical to restrict message changes to a single colour.

With smaller lists (and smaller budgets) there are still the following options.

1 A second window – print a large batch of envelopes (perhaps a full year's supply) with, say, your company logo, and with a second window like the example shown in Figure 10.1.

You can then plan your letter to carry a headline which will show through the lower window. In theory, you can change this as often as you wish. Note that you will need to shop around for such envelopes, as they can be quite expensive. The second window could easily add £10 to £15 per thousand to your envelope costs.

2 Stickers – one company had great success by buying small stickers and affixing these to the appropriate batches of envelopes. This can be quite

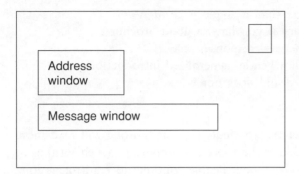

Figure 10.1 Adding a second window enables low budget marketers to use relevant envelope messages

an inexpensive option. The company, through excellent negotiation, paid only £7 per thousand for the stickers.

3 Print them yourself – most desk-top printers can address envelopes, although this is usually a very slow process. It is, however, very cheap and you can vary the message as often as you like.

4 See-through envelopes – plastic envelopes can be used to show all or part of your enclosures. With care you could show a letter headline in the same way as in a second window. This type of envelope is also appropriate when you have an attractive brochure or catalogue.

Remember that your envelope is the first thing your prospect sees, so be sure you make a good impression.

Ask yourself if your message is truly relevant to your prospect. Put yourself in the place of your prospect, sifting through a pile of mail deciding which envelopes are worth opening. An envelope that indicates, through a very general message, that it is a mailing but which does not say anything of interest to the reader, may be the first into the bin. So, a message that is too general may well be worse than no message at all. Some recipients like envelope messages because they save time. The message helps them decide whether they will be interested in the contents.

Now, having ensured that the prospect will look at and open the envelope, we want them to read our letter.

The letter

The letter is the key to success in direct mail. If you draw your reader in by an interesting envelope message, it is only logical to start your letter with the same thought. We should start by tackling the following common misconceptions about direct mail letters.

1 They should never be longer than a single page of A4.
2 They are not really necessary if you have a good brochure.
3 Personalization does not increase response.
4 The letter should start with a gentle, generalized introduction.
5 Using a P.S. is old fashioned and does not work.

Popular myth number 1

A letter should never be longer than a single page as 'no one will read more than a single page'. This is held to be especially important when writing to business people and it is entirely wrong. People continue to read for as long as they are interested. Marketers have had great success with mailing letters of three, four and even five pages to business people, often directors and chief executive officers.

Of course, there is the odd fanatic who will not read anything longer than a single page 'on principle', but people who are so dedicated to learning nothing can be considered in the same category as that person so beautifully described in *The Economist* posters: " 'I never read *The Economist*'. Management Trainee, Aged 42."

Popular myth number 2

A letter is not necessary in a mailing – 'if you have a colourful brochure you do not need a letter in a mailing'. This is another fallacy. In more than 30 years of producing direct mail, I have only once seen a test where the absence of a letter increased response. I have many times seen a letter increase response.

The brochure should demonstrate the product; the letter should explain what it would do for the prospect. This is another important point because if we are trying to increase the relevance of our mailings, we will want to vary our copy for different segments. This is easy to do in a lasered letter, but is quite expensive in a colour brochure.

Popular myth number 3

Personalization does not work – many people think it is not important to personalize letters, but tests indicate this is not true. However, we must define personalization carefully. Simply saying 'Dear Mrs Smith', although a good way to start a letter, will not increase the response dramatically. Referring to some recent event, transaction or query often does increase response.

Take care not to overdo personalization – especially with dubious data. I received a letter, airmailed from Gibraltar, which started with the headline 'Were you born on 3rd March 1936? Then I have some very important news for you. In exactly 7 weeks and 2 days you are going to be very lucky!' Unfortunately for this advertiser, I was not born on that date and, thus, the entire basis of the mailing was destroyed.

The more you use personalization, the more important it is to have totally accurate information. Ideally, you will be mailing a list that you know is up to date and you can then proceed with confidence. If you are not sure, it is wiser to be safe by avoiding such closely personalized factors as birth date, and adopting a general salutation such as 'Dear Manager', rather than addressing someone by the wrong name, gender or even title.

Popular myth number 4
You should start with a little gentle introduction such as:

> Dear Mr Thomas,
>
> You as a Marketing Consultant will know that relationship marketing is becoming a concern for every senior marketing executive.
> We at M & M Direct Marketing have been helping customers build relationships with their customers since 1988.

This is another common error in direct mail. Readers cannot be bored into accepting your proposition, yet this opening tells them one thing they already know ('You, as a Marketing Consultant') and another that they do not need to know at this stage ('we have been doing it since 1988'). Neither of these sentences is relevant to the prospect. Siegfried Vogele's research (see p. 209) shows that many readers will not read further than the first couple of sentences unless they encounter something of true relevance.

The third paragraph of this notional letter contains the first item of interest.

> You may be interested to know that an entirely new customer relationship management event, CRM 2001, is about to be launched. In the words of George Johnson, Chief Executive of the UK CRM Association, this will be 'The definitive CRM event – covering every aspect of customer management from computer systems to staff training; sales to call centre administration'.

Now, although this may be an interesting paragraph, if it is run after those two opening paragraphs, this section may never be read. If the copy had been displayed differently, the advertiser may have been able to hold attention and get the reader through to the gist of the message, which starts with this paragraph:

> Visit our stand at CRM 2001 and you will have the opportunity of gaining a FREE 2-hour customer relationship management consultancy with one of our senior partners.

If you have got them through to this point, they may well be thinking 'What is a 2-hour consultation with this company worth to me?' At this point, you can start to tell them about your long and varied experience in this field – now the second sentence in the original letter becomes relevant to the reader.

This letter could have been made more interesting and compelling in the following way.

> *Envelope message:*
> 'Customer relationship management is the future for British business'
> George Johnson, Chairman, UK CRM Association
>
> *Letter headline:*
> 'Customer relationship management is the future for British business. No professional manager can afford to miss CRM 2001.'
>
>   George Johnson, Chairman, UK CRM Association
>
> Dear Mr Thomas,
>
> Recent research by the CRM Association shows that more than 80% of senior marketers now feel that customer relationship management is critical to their future success. CRM 2001 has been developed to answer all their questions. George Johnson went on to say: 'CRM 2001 is the only event which focuses on the integration of an entire company, from sales to customer services, in order to develop strategies for establishing profitable relationships.'
>
> Put these dates in your diary now [details of dates and venue].
>
> **Make sure you do not miss the M & M stand**
> Visit our stand at CRM 2001 and you will have the opportunity of gaining a FREE 2-hour customer relationship management consultancy with one of our senior partners.
>
> **13 years of relationship building**
> We at M & M Direct Marketing have been helping clients develop powerful, profitable relationships with their customers since 1988 – who better to help your organization?
>
> [Remainder of letter follows here . . .].

When the letter is displayed in this sequence, it exposes the elements in the correct order for easy assimilation by the prospect.

Popular myth number 5

The P.S. is old fashioned and does not work. However, many experienced mailers always use a P.S. Siegfried Vogele, the German marketing researcher, carried out a 20-year study into the way people read mailing letters. In his book *Handbook of Direct Mail* (see the bibliography in Chapter 14), Vogele reported that nine out of every ten people he studied read the P.S. first and that they read it more slowly and carefully than the rest of the letter.

Why should this be so? Perhaps people are starting to recognize that the P.S. is a quick reference to the gist of the offer contained in the letter. Whatever the reason, you should experiment with the P.S. – it might make the crucial difference to your letter.

Incidentally, Professor Vogele says that the P.S. is less important in very short or in original (i.e. truly individual) letters.

So Vogele tells us that readers 'scan' letters before they read them. This starts to explain why longer copy letters tend to generate more response – the scanning process 'burns off' the casual reader very quickly, but real prospects will read as much as is relevant to their needs.

Your prospects are reading your letter to see whether it contains any news or other information pertinent to their needs. They wish to spend the least amount of time possible in establishing this. You must get to the point very quickly.

So, whilst short copy is not important, rapid explanation is. People do not generally select reading material according to how long it is – they are more concerned with how interesting it is.

Techniques to make your letters more effective

Long copy often works because it answers all the questions that a real prospect might raise in a face-to-face discussion. It will be too long for the casual scanner, and of course for the long-established customer who knows all about you and your products.

Some of the most successful letters start with a strong headline or statement of benefits. These are sometimes run above the salutation in bold face like this:

> **'80% of UK businesses are spending too much money on acquiring new customers and not enough on developing existing customers'**
>
> 2001 Research Survey by IMDA
>
> Dear Mr Jones . . .

Headlines sometimes stand out better in a box like this one.

Free Energy Audit of your business

Telephone 0800 24 24 24 ☎

No charge and no obligation.

Dear Mr Jones,

Figure 10.2 A headline in a "Johnson Box"

This is called a Johnson box, named after a US direct marketer.

Starting a letter with a heading works because this immediately tells prospects whether the letter is relevant to them.

Sub-headings help to get the gist of your message across. If you do use long copy, you must make sure that it is broken up into short paragraphs with a liberal use of sub-headings. Remember Vogele's findings that prospects scan before they read – sub-headings enable scanners to see the key points quickly.

Other successful letter techniques include:

- indented paragraphs – these give long copy an 'easy-to-read' appearance. The indentation does not need to be great, as a single 'tab' position is sufficient to make a paragraph stand out and lighten the whole appearance
- displayed selling points – where you have a lot of points to get across, it can be easier for the reader if these are displayed as numbered or bulleted points like this.

Three good reasons why you should choose James's 1999 Directory of Engineering Products

1 James's is more comprehensive – it carries 50% more references than any comparable directory.
2 It uses high-quality illustrations to demonstrate key products – most comparable publications are in text only.
3 It is also available in an interactive CD-Rom version – this costs only £15 extra.

Note how, where necessary, each point can be extended to qualify the stated benefit.

Using the right style of type

In letter-writing seminars one of the things most delegates find hardest to accept is that letters which look as though they come from a typewriter often produce more response.

Delegates say that this is old-fashioned and contravenes their house style (which is usually Univers or Helvetica – of which more later).

> This is the face which many highly experienced marketing companies use for their letters. It is called Courier and, for some reason, it seems to increase response to many mailings.

Perhaps it is because it is large and clear; or maybe because it looks like a typewriter face, it is subconsciously regarded as more like a letter.

If you study the mailings of many major direct marketers, who test their responses regularly, you will find that they continue to use Courier. This must be because it still works better for them than serif faces, such as Times New Roman, or sans serif faces, such as Univers.

There have been numerous studies into the efficiency of typefaces over the past 50 years, the most recent being a lengthy study carried out by Australian journalist Colin Wheildon between 1984 and 1991. Wheildon set out to test how well panels of readers comprehended text printed in a variety of type styles, faces and colours.

Wheildon asked people to read an article and then to answer ten questions about what they had just read. Before we show the results, we can look again at a demonstration of what each typeface looks like.

> This sentence is printed in Times New Roman, a popular serif face.

Serif is the short terminal stroke at the end of the main stroke of a typographical character. Many advertisements and newspapers are printed in serif typefaces, although some magazines tend to ignore the rules, and print in 'fashion' type styles. Experienced direct response designers use serif faces for all body copy, except where they use Courier for letter text.

Serif is the short terminal stroke at the end of the main stroke of a typographical character

> This sentence is printed in Univers, a popular sans serif face, used by many designers in the advertising industry.

It is interesting to note that sans serif faces are used much more frequently by designers of traditional (non-response) advertisements. Most experienced direct marketing designers know that using sans serif faces can reduce their response, despite the fact that they actually look clearer than the serif type.

The next example shows another style popular with designers, but not with experienced direct marketers – reversed-out type.

> Another form of display to avoid for body copy is this, which is 'reversed out'. We can reverse out any typeface. This is Times New Roman, whereas the next sentence is in Univers. Some people feel that when reversing out, sans serif faces work better than serif, but there is very little evidence to support this.

Let's look at Wheildon's statistics. Groups of adults and high school students were each given a magazine article to read.

The tests were repeated at intervals, with groups being switched from serif to sans serif type, and articles varying from those of general interest to those of direct interest to the reader.

Participants were supervised whilst reading and were then given a printed questionnaire asking ten questions about what they had read. In the tests mentioned here one group was given the articles set in Corona (8 point on 9 point body), a serif face similar to Times New Roman; the other group read the same article set in Helvetica (8 point on 9 point body), a sans serif face similar to Univers.

Comprehension was judged on the following basis:

- 7 to 10 questions answered correctly = good comprehension
- 4 to 6 correct answers = fair comprehension
- 0 to 3 correct answers = poor comprehension.

Table 10.1 shows the results of this section of the test.

Table 10.1 Comprehension data – serif v. san serif type

Type style	Comprehension level (%)		
	Good	Fair	Poor
Serif type for body copy	67	19	14
Sans serif type for body copy	12	23	65

After the tests and questionnaires were completed, readers were asked if they had any comments on what they had just experienced. These too are very interesting. Here is an extract from Colin Wheildon's report:

Comments made by the readers who showed poor comprehension of articles set in sans serif type had a common theme – the difficulty in holding concentration.

An analysis of the comments offered by one group of 112 readers who had read an article of direct interest to them, set in sans serif type revealed:

Of the 112 readers, 67 showed poor comprehension, and of these:

- 53 complained strongly about the difficulty of reading the type
- 11 said the task caused them physical discomfort (eye tiredness)
- 10 said they had to backtrack continually to try to maintain concentration
- 5 said when they had to backtrack to recall points made in the article they gave up trying to concentrate
- 22 said they had difficulty in focusing on the type after having read a dozen or so lines.

Some readers made two or more of the above comments.

Yet when this same group was asked immediately afterwards to read another article with a domestic theme, but set in Corona, they reported no physical difficulties, and no necessity to recapitulate to maintain concentration.

The conclusion must be that body type must be set in serif type if the designer intends it to be read and understood.

In another series of tests, Wheildon examined the effect of reversing out the text people were asked to read. The format of the tests was the same – one group read the article printed in black on white background; other groups were asked to read the same article in white on a black background, white on a purple background and white on a deep blue background. In all cases, the typeface was a serif face. The comprehension scores are shown in Table 10.2.

To complete this series and to test the school of thought which contends that reversed-out type is only a problem with serif faces, a final set of groups was tested on reversed-out type but this time set in Univers (Table 10.3).

Note that it is not suggested that you avoid sans serif or reversed-out type for short headings or occasional emphasis. This can make things stand out well against the rest of the text. The above tests and the comments (mine and Colin Wheildon's) relate to body copy only.

Table 10.2 Comprehension data – black on white text v. white 'reversed-out'

Type style	Comprehension levels (%)		
	Good	Fair	Poor
Text printed black on white *	70	19	11
Text printed white on black	0	12	88
Text printed white on purple	2	16	82
Text printed white on deep blue	0	4	96

* Very similar to the serif scores in the previous tests (same type style).

Table 10.3 Comprehension data – reversed-out text using sans serif type

Type style	Comprehension level (%)		
	Good	Fair	Poor
Black on white **	14	25	61
White on black	4	13	83

** Very similar to the sans-serif scores in the earlier tests (same type style).

Additional enclosures

Leaflets and brochures

As stated earlier, the aim of the letter is to sell the proposition, whereas the brochure's role is to demonstrate it. Pictures, showing the product in use, with captions emphasizing the benefits can ensure that the brochure is a valuable addition to the pack.

Do not ignore the value of captions. Most people read them, so make sure they state the benefits and are not just throwaway lines. A major charity once

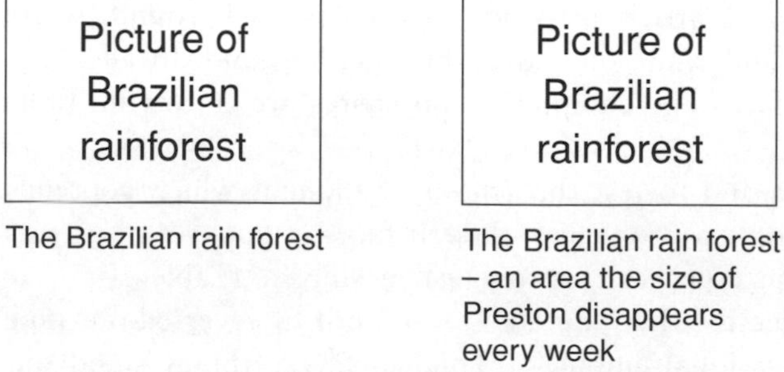

Picture of Brazilian rainforest

The Brazilian rain forest

Picture of Brazilian rainforest

The Brazilian rain forest – an area the size of Preston disappears every week

Figure 10.3 Making captions work harder

found it could increase the effectiveness of a fund-raising leaflet simply by rewriting the captions. The left-hand caption was the one they originally used; the right hand one was much more effective (Figure 10.3).

Which of these conjures up a more realistic picture for you? Incidentally, this would be a good example of how you could vary your text to suit segments of the audience. The example of Preston could be used for donors with a Lancashire postcode, whereas Reading may be substituted for those living in Berkshire.

Supporting pieces

Sometimes, when mailing a general list, you may not have enough data (or enough budget) to enable you to separate your audience into discrete segments, yet you want to make sure that you leave no question unanswered for those who have not heard about you.

Additional leaflets

In this case, you may opt for a multi-piece mailing. Instead of putting everything into the letter and perhaps 'overselling' to someone who is already convinced, you could introduce a couple of additional leaflets, for example:

- 'About our services' – a leaflet giving some background for those who like the sound of your services, but have reservations because they are not familiar with your company name.
- 'What our customers say about us' – an additional leaflet carrying testimonial statements from well-known or credible customers to reassure those who like the sound of your offer, but are not quite sure whether they should trust a company they do not know.

Newspaper and magazine reprints

If you have been lucky enough to get a good review in a newspaper or magazine, you should use it for all it is worth.

The publication is assumed to have an independent point of view, and if it says your product is good, it carries much more weight than the same claim made by you. You are expected to say yours is the greatest product ever, so the reader discounts your claims a little. Newspaper reprints are sometimes even more powerful than testimonials.

Do not forget that in each of the above cases you need to get the permission of the authors before reproducing their comments.

Now you have done all you can to 'sell' your proposition and reassure your prospect that you are a worthy supplier, you need to think about closing the sale, or in a two-stage situation, generating a response.

The essentials of a good response device

First, you should make it easy for the respondent by giving a choice of reply options (telephone, post, fax, e-mail and Web site). Let them decide which is most convenient. Some claim that offering a choice of response methods can confuse respondents, but the fact remains that responses tend to increase when a choice is offered.

Put yourself in the respondent's place. How would you like to respond? A large percentage of people, perhaps 60% or more, responding to advertisements for financial products such as loans do so on the telephone. That means that 40% do not use the telephone – perhaps because:

- they have a speech problem
- they have a hearing problem
- they have a name which no one can spell or pronounce
- they just do not like using the telephone.

Most of these people would prefer to return a coupon by mail or fax, or use e-mail or a Web site.

More than 20% of UK households have a fax. Many people who use e-mail, previously used the fax to send letters, copy and queries to clients and friends. One consumer mail order company still receives some 10% of all its Christmas orders by fax.

The use of e-mail and the Web site will depend very much on your audience. Those with home computers, often younger people, are quite comfortable with the Internet and they actually like responding this way. IT professionals also tend to do so. A letter written to IT professionals generated more than 12% response, 40% of which came via the Internet.

Make sure that you do as much of the work as you can. Try to fill in the prospect's name and address on the response form as:

- you will get more back – in some cases up to 15% more
- you will be able to read and process all the coupons you receive – a surprising number of people fail to include their post town and postcode (when the item they sent for does not arrive, you will get the blame!)
- you can print a customer reference number on the form so you only have to key in a few digits and your computer will automatically pull up the full address – this could save around 60% of your order-input time.

The second essential is to repeat your address and the main details of the offer on the order form. Some people will keep just the order form until they have time to send it. If the details are not repeated, those who cannot remember will not return it. Others may pass it on to a friend or colleague, who will not always see the full mailing.

Third, pay for the reply. You pay only for those who reply, and it is a small extra amount to pay for a warm lead.

Checklist

Here is a summary of the things to remember when designing your mailing.

- Gain attention.
- Consider your envelope – will an overprint be appropriate? You do not have to use an envelope message, but you should certainly test it. A high percentage of long-term successful mailings carry explicit envelope messages. Think carefully about your prospects – the more mail they receive, the more likely they are to find a message helpful. Some successful mailers find larger, longer, or thicker envelopes tend to work well.
- Start with your strongest benefit statement or main item of news. Do not save it, as they may not get to the end unless you have excited their interest. News headlines are invariably more successful than humour, curiosity or other gimmicks. Make sure your headline links closely to your envelope message.
- Use 'real' numbers – £294.70 sounds more 'real' than £300.
- Use a headline on your letters – this is one of the key factors in persuading people to read on.
- Try to create visual interest, but avoid irrelevant gimmicks.
- Do not assume that others share your tastes. This is especially important when considering humour. Keep things in good taste.
- Confirm the relevance of your offer by linking your claims to the reader's situation where possible, and demonstrating the product benefits and showing how it fits into the buyer's situation.
- Tell the full story. Do not be afraid of using long copy if necessary. There is no merit in long copy or short. Copy should be long enough to tell the complete story, and it will vary according to your objective.
- Use sub-headings, especially if the copy is long. Many readers will scan these first before deciding whether to read the entire letter.
- Make it easy for the reader with careful layout and display of key points.
- Keep to a logical sequence.
- Use short words, short sentences and short paragraphs.
- Involve your reader – enclosures that do something (such as tapes and videos) often work well.
- Convince the reader by selling the benefits not the attributes. People buy products because of what they do for them, not because of what they are.
- Use testimonials, as they are always more believable than your own claims.
- Quote research data, as it carries greater authority.
- Provide reassurance, such as 'no obligation' or 'strong guarantee'.

- Take the order. Make sure your letter has a powerful final paragraph, summarizing the benefits and the action required.
- Use a strong benefit-oriented P.S. Remember Siegfried Vogele's findings that 90% read the P.S. first.
- Use a time close, such as 'Offer closes in 7 days.'
- Summarize what you want the reader to do. Do not be vague. Give clear and concise instructions.
- Repeat the offer on the response form.
- Fill in as much of the response form as you can.
- Offer all response options.
- Try a follow-up. If you want to maximize the response to your mailing, consider following it up by telephone or mail.

Direct mail follow-ups

A mailed follow-up, arriving about 7–10 days after the original, will typically add around one-third to your response. Thus, it would increase a 3% response to 4%. You need to test this technique and work out the cost-effectiveness of the gain. Mail follow-up techniques that work include the following.

The carbon copy mailing

The terminology may be dated, but the technique still works. Before PCs, we used to send just a carbon copy of the letter with a little additional note at the top saying something like: 'In case you missed this when I sent it to you last week.' The updated version still tends to send just the letter, but we may add a yellow post-it note with a similar message. Alternatively, we could use a yellow highlighter to draw attention to the key benefit points in the letter.

The escalating discount series

This works well for a number of companies selling to prospects that have enquired from a press advertisement. One well-known self-improvement advertiser sends out up to ten follow-ups before giving up on an enquirer. The incentive or discount improves every second or third time the prospect is mailed.

This is another technique that requires careful testing and evaluation, but the simple rule is to continue to send follow-ups until the latest one loses money. The loss on the last mailing will generally be well covered by the additional gains from earlier follow-ups.

Escalating discount follow-ups must be approached with extreme caution when mailing to regular customers. You will soon 'train' them to wait for the best deal, and the net result can often be a reduction in your margins.

A large US company selling to businesses measured the performance of its entire staff on their quarterly sales figures. If they reached or beat their targets they got a bonus; if they failed, heads would roll. People would actually be fired if they missed their targets for two successive quarters.

Of course, this led to a bizarre situation where, in the final 3 weeks of every quarter the sales people would offer the most amazing discounts to make sure they got the order in before the end of the quarter.

Within a year of this policy taking effect, customers got the message. Sales in the first 10 weeks of every quarter reduced and there was always a boom in the final 3 weeks. Of course, margins were being decimated and the UK management was soon facing another head office purge for failing to reach their profit targets.

Example

The annual anniversary follow-up

This is typical for insurance companies. When a prospect enquires after details of insurance cover, they indicate that they are in the market now. Many companies send an offer but then forget it if they do not make the sale. Yet now the renewal date is known, we should always mail them another offer around the same time next year.

Following up by telephone

Many companies have had great success by using the telephone to follow up their mailings. The approach varies from the classic mail follow-up. The follow-up is made earlier (ideally within 3 or 4 days of the mailing arriving). In a mailed follow-up you can repeat the details in hard copy so 7–10 days' delay is not detrimental. But how much of the mail you received last week is still on your desk?

The telephone follow-up does not simply repeat the details, it is more of a general enquiry call. For example, 'Did you receive my letter? Do you have any questions about it? Is there any further information you would like? Should it have been addressed to one of your colleagues instead?'

Such follow-up calls are proving immensely successful as the following examples show.

A major international software company found that using a rapid telephone follow-up (within 3 days of the mailing arriving) increased the number of leads generated from 2% to 19%.

Using the same technique targeting solicitors, a UK charity changed a 2% into a 72% response.

Example

A charge card company mailing retailers to persuade them to accept the card as payment had 4% of prospects sign up to their proposal. Of the sample that received the rapid telephone follow-up, 26% accepted.

A small provincial insurance broker mailed existing policy-holders with a 'cross-selling' offer (motor clients were offered buildings or contents insurance, and so on). Response to the mailing was 5%. Then 7 days after the mailing touched down, the broker's office staff started telephoning non-respondents. The eventual sales uptake was 50%.

This technique clearly works in both business and consumer marketing. A final reminder. The telephone call should not be a hard-sell approach, but simply a friendly enquiry. This can be an advantage, of course, as the calls can be made by office staff rather than highly trained (and more expensive) telemarketers.

SUMMARY

This chapter began with the assertion that if the creative is targeting the wrong market the promotion is likely to fail.

It went on to elaborate on a pro forma for executing successful creative work:

1 objectives
2 target audience
3 offer
4 timing
5 medium
6 creative approach
7 implementation
8 response forecast
9 follow-up.

The way this process works was explained through the use of examples.

We have seen the need to manage any response generated and that successful implementation generates a regular and manageable supply of leads.

When designing a direct marketing communication, we noted that the desired sequence of events is:

• attract attention
• establish relevance
• convince the prospect of benefits

- close the sale
- confirm the action to be taken and take the order.

The three types of advertising were described and we distinguished among awareness advertising, direct response advertising and dual-purpose advertising.

The critical factors in creating successful direct response advertising were described as:

- targeting
- the offer
- timing
- the creative
- the response mechanics.

Each of these elements was discussed in detail.

The chapter went on to explore the fifteen rules for the creation of a successful direct response advertisement.

1 Place the headline below the picture.
2 The picture should be striking and action oriented.
3 Photographs work better than drawings.
4 Make the headline work.
5 Copy length is not critical.
6 Promote benefits not features.
7 Include a coupon.
8 Make the call to action prominent.
9 Repeat the benefits near the response device.
10 Include a second response device.
11 Smaller space is generally more cost-effective.
12 Avoid sans serif type for body copy.
13 Avoid reversed-out body copy.
14 Use right-hand pages.
15 Buy early positions in media.

The construction of the mail pack was examined, beginning with the outer envelope. The envelope should make an impression and if an envelope message is used, it must be highly relevant.

The following five popular myths about direct mail letters were destroyed:

1 a letter should be no longer than one page
2 a letter is not always necessary in a mailing
3 personalization does not work

4 you should start with a gentle introduction
5 the P.S. does not work.

There was a summary of the techniques that work in letter writing:

- the use of long copy
- good headings
- Johnson-boxed headings
- a suitable typeface – Courier is worth a try
- avoiding reversed-out copy
- the use of additional enclosures.

The response device should make it easy for the respondent to reply. The key factors were described as:

- prospects should be offered a choice of reply options, including the telephone, fax, e-mail and Web site
- do as much work as you can to remove barriers to response, for example try to fill in the respondent's name and address
- repeat your address and the main details of the offer on the order form
- pay for the reply.

The chapter concluded with a useful direct mail checklist that emphasized the value of the follow-up by letter or by telephone.

REVIEW QUESTIONS

1 What is the key success factor in creative execution?

2 What are the benefits of long copy and when should long copy be used?

3 What is the nine-stage process for the creative process?

4 What is the impact of creative on response management?

5 Outline the communications planning process. What is the desired sequence of events in any direct communication?

6 Outline and describe the three types of advertising.

7 What are the key factors in creating a direct response advertisement?

8 How do we select the right medium to target customers?

9 What is a one-stage and two-stage communication process?

10   What is the best typeface to use for body copy?

11   Why should reversed-out body copy not be used?

12   How can we make envelopes more impactful?

13   List the five myths of mail letters.

14   What is the role of the sub-heading in a letter?

15   How do additional enclosures help build response?

16   What are the characteristics of a good response device?

17   What is the role of follow-up in boosting response?

EXERCISES

Select a direct response press advertisement. Using the fifteen rules for successful direct marketing write a critique of the advertisement.

How would you improve the advertisement?

Chapter 11

The importance of testing

Introduction
- Test objectives
  - Media types
  - An individual medium
  - Position
  - Timing
  - Size
  - Frequency
  - Offers and creative
  - Response methods
- The hierarchy of testing
  - How does testing work?
- Testing with loose inserts
- Direct mail testing
  - An important reminder
- How to develop a test programme
  - Testing lists
  - Isolate the variables
- The statistics of testing
  - Sample sizes
  - Randomization
- Selecting samples for testing
  - Using formulae
  - Using tables rather than formulae
  - A few final comments
  - The hierarchy of testing
Summary
Review questions
Exercises

One of the key differences between direct marketing and other forms of marketing is the precise measurability of direct response activities. Of course, a traditional advertiser can measure the general effectiveness of a campaign simply by careful monitoring of sales before, during and after the advertising has run. However, there are limitations to this. No broadscale advertiser can tell you the precise effect of any individual insertion or medium.

Even in broadscale advertising it is possible to set up tests where one factor is added or dropped from the mix. This is most commonly done geographically – an area can be left without television, press could be added to another area and so on.

Unfortunately, this can set up other biases. Perhaps this offer does not appeal so much to people in the North-East, or there may be stronger competition in the South-West. So such test results are not totally reliable.

The beauty of direct response advertising is that every reply can be attributed not only to a general media category, such as press or television, but to an individual insertion. Thus, you can measure not only copy changes but also position or time slot differences, size or duration of advertisement – a whole range of variables.

By setting up test cells and exposing a different message to each, you can evaluate the relative performance of each approach. Alternatively, by exposing precisely the same message, on the same day in two different media you can make meaningful comparisons of their relative values.

Direct marketers, therefore, tend to use testing first, whereas traditional marketers have to rely on broader market research which helps them track attitudinal changes, and campaign-wide sales.

As we saw earlier, direct marketers use market research too, but generally to answer the question 'Why?' rather than 'What?' The first issue for direct marketers is cost-effectiveness, so tests will be built to answer such questions as the following.

- Is the *Daily Mail* as cost-effective in gaining new customers as the *Daily Express*?
- Is the cost per reply from television higher or lower than that from press?
- Will a longer letter produce more replies than a shorter one?
- Is the long-term buying performance of customers recruited through loose inserts better or worse than that of television respondents?
- Does our new creative idea produce more or less response than the previous treatment?

Testing is a crucial part of any major direct marketing campaign, although of course not all tests will produce a positive result. However, a well-planned test programme will generally produce enough information to enable you to more than recover your investment over the longer term. Even if several new ideas do not produce better results than your old faithful, at least you have the satisfaction of knowing that your existing advertising is as effective as you can make it.

A word of caution: testing is not an exact science as it deals in probabilities. The rules of statistics are not exact, so it is necessary to understand how to read a test result and how confident you can be in applying your findings to future activities. We will return to this point later in this chapter.

Test objectives

The purpose of testing is to enable the direct marketer to reduce risk by restricting the amount of budget exposed until alternatives have been evaluated. Many companies manage to trade very profitably without testing, but this does not disprove the case. Who is to say that they could not produce even better results? It is not unusual for one variant in a test to produce dramatically more response than another, which appears to be equally good.

Example

A UK publisher offered the same subscription incentive for 5 years and was quite satisfied with the results of its advertising.

Its marketing consultant eventually persuaded the publisher to test an alternative incentive that produced 100% more subscriptions.

Assuming it had done this test 5 years earlier and got the same result, its advertising would have been twice as effective and it would have made twice as much profit!

We can test:

- media type
- medium
- position
- timing
- size
- frequency
- offer
- creative treatment
- response methods.

Media types

Here we will be evaluating the use of, for example, press advertising against direct response television or direct mail. Our tests will be evaluated in campaigns rather than by individual insertions or spots. We will typically be looking to judge the amount of business generated by each media type for a fixed budget. We will try to keep the messages as similar as possible to reduce the amount of bias inherent in such a test.

An individual medium

In this case, we will have decided on our broad media type and now need to decide between, for example, the *Daily Mail* and the *Daily Express*, daily papers versus Sunday papers, terrestrial television versus satellite, two or more rented mailing lists and so on.

This sort of testing is quite common and although we will not always obtain a totally reliable comparison from a single test, we can easily compare the cost per enquiry; conversion rate; cost per order and so on. The reason it is not always possible to obtain a totally reliable comparison is that we do not have control over the surrounding material, for exaple other advertisers appearing at the same time and the gravity of news appearing at the same time. Thus, we must be careful not to make major decisions based on a single test comparison – especially where we are testing two different media.

Supposing our press advertisement produces more customers than our direct response television. Does this mean we should in future place our entire budget in press? It may do, but before we make such a decision we should examine the test scenario very carefully.

We may find that on the day we ran our test advertising an investment product, the newspaper ran an article commenting very favourably on such products, whilst the television station ran a programme 'exposing' another financial services company for misleading customers whilst selling a similar product. These would certainly affect response in both media and could present us with a highly misleading result.

If in any doubt about a bias affecting one or both halves of the test, it is advisable to re-test at a later date. If both results show the same pattern, you can feel more confident in making your decision.

This is less of a problem when testing two alternative rented mailing lists, as your mailing will be in a 'semi-solus' position. You cannot guarantee that any individual mailed will not receive a competitive mailing on the same day, but you can be fairly certain that the same mailing list will not have been mailed with a competitive product. A good list owner or broker will make sure this does not happen.

Position

In newspapers and magazines this relates to whether we go early or late. Early means at the front of the publication and late means at the back of the publication.

It might also relate to special positions such as the front page, the football results page, the television programmes page, alongside the crossword and the readers' letters page.

Testing positions within the same publication can be quite complicated, as it generally requires a 'partner'. We cannot simply run an advertisement on the front cover this week and the same advertisement on the sports page next week and expect the comparison to be meaningful. There could be a number of factors affecting the validity of such a test, including:

- competition – a major competitor may advertise in the same paper on one of our test days – this could seriously affect our response
- importance of the news – if a major crisis breaks on the day one of our advertisements appears, this is likely to affect response.

Nor can we simply run both advertisements in the same paper on the same day. This produces another set of problems. Even though we could put different response codes on each, we could not be sure that a response was solely attributable to the particular advertisement carrying the reply code.

What if someone saw both advertisements and only responded to one? What if seeing both advertisements stimulated more people than normal to respond – this would be quite probable.

How can we avoid these problems? The first thing to do is to make sure that the publication in question takes A/B split runs. (Split runs are explained in detail on p. 232.)

We could then set up a split-run 'cross-over' test with a 'partner' advertiser which takes the other half of the test. It works like this. We buy two split runs on the same day, one in the front half of the paper and the other in a later position. On the early split, we may take the A half with our partner taking B. On the later page we will run our same advertisement in the B half with our partner placing theirs in the A position. In this way, we can test each position without any bias creeping in from people seeing both advertisements in the same copy of the paper.

A word of warning: with this technique, only half of the newspaper readers will see each advertisement. This will reduce the response to each half of the test by 50%. This is no problem if the responses are large, but you must be sure that the response figures are statistically significant, that is large enough to enable a valid comparison between the two advertisements. (Statistical validity is explained on pp. 242–50.)

Timing

Many advertisers find that results from daily newspapers vary according to the day of the week on which their advertisement appears. Others find that advertisements run in March, say are more cost-effective than those appearing in May.

There are additional timing considerations in broadcast advertising. Here we may also be selecting breaks within specific programmes or at least time segments that promise to deliver a certain type of audience. We could, for example, set up a test to compare off-peak versus peak time, running the same commercial in the middle of the afternoon and during 'Coronation Street'.

The cost and response calculations will then be done to identify the most cost-efficient time for future exposure. Remember that statistical validity may require you to run this test more than once – especially to get a reliable reading on the off-peak slot.

The position within the time slot can be very important. In a very popular programme viewers are reluctant to leave the room during the show and tend to rush off to bathroom or kitchen as soon as a commercial break begins. Advertisers taking the first spot in a break may well lose a substantial part of the audience. The audience will be highest for the spot immediately before the main programme re-starts.

Size

Although traditional media planners try to dominate a page or publication with large advertisements, the precise measurability of direct marketing tells us that cost-efficient response is easier to achieve with small spaces. In fact, the smaller the space, the more cost-efficient it will be.

As we saw in Chapter 7, p. 132, Philip Sainsbury who analysed the results of hundreds of direct response advertisements and came up with his square root principle demonstrated this some years ago. Sainsbury's square root principle states that advertisement response does not increase in proportion to an increase in size, but merely by the square root of the increase. Sainsbury's research showed that smaller spaces were progressively more cost-efficient and spaces larger than a page progressively less cost-efficient. So if cost-efficient response is your main consideration, the smaller the space the more effectively you are spending your budget.

There are, of course, some situations when one may opt for a larger size:

- in dual purpose advertising (see Chapter 10, p. 199), where the main objective is to generate awareness with the amount of response being a secondary requirement

- where the advertiser wishes to impress potential partners and stockists and so on with the amount of advertising money being put into the campaign
- where the advertiser is able to negotiate an exceptionally large discount (easier with larger spaces), thereby increasing the cost-effectiveness of the larger space.

The problem of size tests

Testing the size of advertisements can be even more complicated than testing position. In order to test a full page against a half page, for instance, one would have to buy a full-page split run and make up, or persuade the publication to find, some additional editorial, running the test as outlined in Figure 11.1.

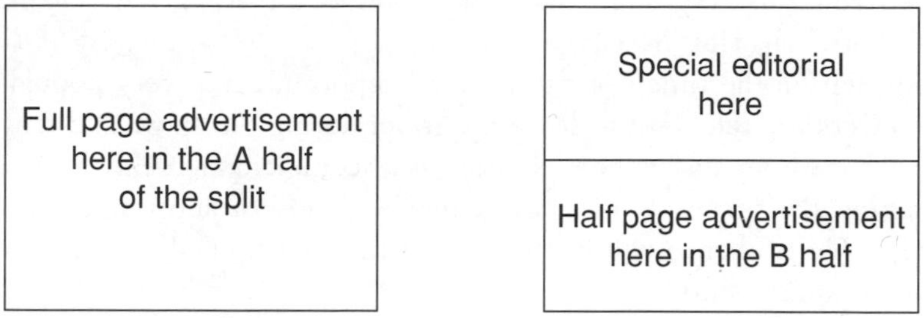

Figure 11.1 Testing the size of advertisements

As an alternative to producing special editorial, some companies trying this test find a partner advertiser, often a sister brand, to take up the spare half page.

Having pointed out the difficulty of such a test, it may well be worthwhile. According to Sainsbury's research, we would expect to achieve 71 replies from the half page for every 100 we receive from the full page. Therefore, if we can buy a half page for less than 70% of the cost of a full page, we should find the half page more cost-efficient.

This same technique could be used to test any combination of sizes, though the smaller the size the more difficult, or expensive, it would be to persuade the publisher to co-operate. Remember too that there will come a point when the space is too small to contain your entire message comfortably – changing the content of the advertisement will of course invalidate the test.

Frequency

As we saw in Chapter 7, the traditional awareness advertiser seeks to maximize impact by running multiple insertions in a very short space of time.

Based on readership data and 'opportunities to see', theoretically this optimizes the media spend.

Thus, the objective of the traditional media planner is to achieve maximum coverage as rapidly as possible. This means that high audience duplication across media and rapid repetition in the same medium are considered to be beneficial.

A direct marketer has a totally different approach, mainly driven by knowledge of what happens to responses if there is too much duplication or too rapid repetition.

When, through our direct response mechanisms, we are able to measure the effectiveness of each individual appearance of an advertisement we find that each successive insertion is slightly less efficient that its predecessor.

Furthermore, the time gap between insertions is critical. If we repeat the same advertisement in the same publication with too short a gap, our response will decline even more rapidly. The optimum length of gap can only be determined by testing, but it would typically be a minimum of 3 weeks in a daily paper.

We also see a marked fall off in response when the same advertisement appears at the same time in two publications that have a high cross-over of readership. For example it would not be wise to run the same advertisement on a Saturday in the *Daily Mail* and then the following day in the *Mail on Sunday*.

Offers and creative

These aspects are covered in Chapters 9 and 10.

Response methods

Tests can be set up to measure the effectiveness of reply coupons compared to telephone and fax numbers or e-mail and Web addresses. You can measure the effect of paying the reply postage or telephone charges, and, in direct mail, the effectiveness of pre-printing the addressee's name on the response form.

The hierarchy of testing

To repeat an earlier comment, there is no use spending time on tuning up our creative treatment, or the mechanics of obtaining a reply, until we have targeted the right person, decided on the most relevant offer or message for that person, and identified the right time to approach them.

Once we have these elements in place, we can start to tune up the performance of our advertisements and mailings through creative development and response devices.

How does testing work?

A/B split runs in newspapers and magazines

A number of publications offer the facility of split-run testing. Many newspapers and magazines are printed on very large cylinders, so large in fact that two copies of the publication are printed simultaneously side by side.

If an advertiser wishes to test two alternative creative treatments, these can be placed one on either side of the printing drum as in the example below.

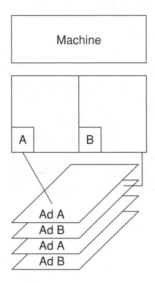

As the printed paper comes off the end of the press, it is cut in half so that the individual copies can be folded and assembled. This process finishes with alternative copies being stacked one above the other on a pile.

The finished 'ream' thus contains precisely the same number of copies carrying each alternative advertisement, in other words, in a pile of 500 papers every alternate copy would carry either advertisement A or advertisement B.

This process is called an A/B split run (or A/B split).

Figure 11.2 How an A/B split works

'Telescope testing'

Telescope testing is a technique used by large advertisers who wish to test a number of variables quickly. It makes use of both A/B splits and geographic splits at the same time.

Telescope testing is a technique used by large advertisers who wish to test a number of variables quickly. It makes use of both A/B splits and geographic splits at the same time.

Consider the *TV Times*. This is produced in several separate regional editions to match the television regions. They also allow A/B splits. This enables us to test several advertisements at the same time.

We book an A/B split in each region and our control advertisement 'Ad 1' appears in the A part of each region. We can vary the content of the B half of the split in each region as Table 11.1 shows.

Subject, as always, to statistical validity, we can now compare every 'new' variation against our control (Ad 1). Comparing results to Ad 1 with each other will give us an idea of regional variations and, with certain reserva-

Table 11.1 Telescope testing – format of text

Region	A half	B half
London	Ad 1	Ad 2 – lower priced option
South-East	Ad 1	Ad 3 – free gift
Midlands	Ad 1	Ad 4 – discount option
South-West	Ad 1	Ad 5 – use of personality
Wales	Ad 1	Ad 6 – shorter copy and bullet points
North-West	Ad 1	Ad 7 – long copy version
North-East	Ad 1	Ad 8 – cartoon strip copy
Scotland	Ad 1	Ad 9 – copy only version

Table 11.2 Telescope testing – response data

Region	Copy	No. of replies	Copy	No. of replies
London	Ad 1	300	Ad 2	450
South-East	Ad 1	200	Ad 3	280
Midlands	Ad 1	200	Ad 4	180
South-West	Ad 1	150	Ad 5	105
Wales	Ad 1	180	Ad 6	90
North-West	Ad 1	220	Ad 7	330
North-East	Ad 1	150	Ad 8	195
Scotland	Ad 1	180	Ad 9	108

tions, we will be able to compare (by interpolation) the results of each of the new versions with each other. This is where we must be very cautious.

Let's look at some imaginary results for each cell, as shown in Table 11.2.

To be honest, this does not tell us a huge amount in this raw state. We need to do two things to make these results more meaningful. The first is to express the number of replies to Ad 1 as a percentage of the circulation in each region. This will highlight any strong regional biases. The second is to express the replies in index form, so we can compare more easily the results of the new advertisements (Table 11.3).

Before we attempt to read anything from these results, we need to check the numbers for statistical validity. We are using indices to make comparisons simpler as each test has been exposed to a different-sized audience. However, the overall response numbers in each cell are a major factor too. This is explained in detail on p. 234.

Table 11.3 Telescope testing – using indices

Region	Copy	Response index*	Copy	Response index	Total responses
London	Ad 1	100	Ad 2	150	750
South-East	Ad 1	100	Ad 3	140	480
Midlands	Ad 1	100	Ad 4	90	380
South-West	Ad 1	100	Ad 5	70	255
Wales	Ad 1	100	Ad 6	50	270
North-West	Ad 1	100	Ad 7	150	550
North-East	Ad 1	100	Ad 8	130	345
Scotland	Ad 1	100	Ad 9	60	288

* In this example, it is assumed that every region would produce precisely the same percentage response. There is virtually no chance of this happening, but it makes the explanation easier. In other words, no significant regional biases have been found.

Table 11.4 Evaluating the significance of a test result

Total response, i.e. A + B	Significance factor*	Winner	Loser	% gain
50	70%	35	15	133%
100	65%	65	35	86%
500	57%	285	215	33%
1000	55%	550	450	22%
10,000	52%	5200	4800	8%

*% for result to be significant.

When we check these results against Table 11.4 showing significance factors in split-run testing (95% confidence level), we find that one of these 'results' is clearly not statistically valid.

Table 11.4, based on sound statistical formulae, enables a quick check of whether a result is reliable. The full process is explained later (see pp. 242–50), but what it shows here is that in the Midlands test, where 200 replies were received to one half and 180 replies to the other, the difference between the two results is not sufficiently large for the result to be significant. Interpolating in Column 1 (total response, that is A plus B) between the two response numbers of 100 and 500, we see that with a total of 380 replies, in order for this test result to be reliable, the difference between winner and loser would need to be about 49%. Our loser is only 10% less responsive, so this clearly is not enough for statistical validity.

Furthermore, the results from the South-West (Ad 5) and North-East (Ad 8) regions are only marginally valid. The performances of the Ads 4 and 5 are not encouraging anyway, so we can probably forget these two. The figures from the North-East region are just valid and the performance looks promising, so we may opt to retest Ad 8.

The remainder of the results are statistically valid and they show us that Ads 2, 3 and 7 have performed well against control. A re-test may well prove Ad 8 to be another winner. So we seem to have some promising new approaches.

Apart from Ads 4 and 5, we can probably also forget about versions 6 and 9. From here, we have two main tasks.

1 To re-test the 'winners' across other areas to ensure we are not simply seeing some strong regional preferences towards the new advertisements. We have already checked this on control. The re-tests will also confirm that we have not suffered from some statistical freak.
2 To watch carefully the sales performance of the customers produced by the new versions – we do not want to find later that we have simply produced a greater number of lower grade customers, with little long-term potential.

What if the test had produced no 'winners', but merely another advertisement that produced the same response as control? In one sense such an advertisement could be termed a 'winner', despite only producing the same response as our existing advertmisement. We said earlier that if we run the same advertisement too frequently our response will show a marked decline. Having an alternative but equally strong advertisement enables us to shorten the gap without paying such a high penalty in lost responses.

Furthermore, having a second equally good advertisement is like an insurance policy. No advertisement continues to work indefinitely – sooner or later it will become 'tired' and response will fall. Our second, newer advertisement will often continue to pull responses at the original level for some time to come, giving us time to run another test programme to find another reliable alternative. We may also find that the original advertisement will start to work well again after a rest.

Machine splits

Not all publications offer the A/B split facility, so a less attractive alternative is to find publishers who print using two separate machines, as shown in Figure 11.3.

In theory this sounds fine, but in practice it is not possible to guarantee statistical validity for the following reasons.

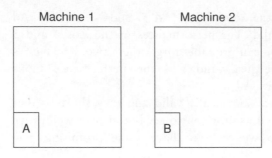

Figure 11.3 Layout of a 'machine split-run'

1 If there is a breakdown or a temporary hold-up on one of the machines, for example during a paper reel change, the second machine keeps on running, thus reducing the chances of the quantities being matched.
2 The output from each machine may be sent to different regions or whole-salers, thus introducing area or socio-economic variables.

A variation of the machine split is the 'geographic split', where the publisher prints in two centres, say London and Manchester.

Briefly, a cross-over test involves running Ad A in London on the same day that you run Ad B in Manchester. Two or three weeks later you reverse ('cross-over') the sequence so that Ad B runs in London and Ad A in Manchester. By adding the two results together you get a fair approximation of the comparative strength of the two advertisements.

A variation of the machine split is the 'geographic split', where the publisher prints in two centres, say London and Manchester.

Tests run in this way are much more difficult to read because of the twin biases of geography and volume (the number of copies printed for the Manchester edition is probably less than for the London edition).

It is possible to overcome the volume problem by weighting the figures according to the respective circulation numbers. We can tackle the geographical problem by running a 'cross-over' test, but, in attempting to eliminate the bias introduced by the above variables, this introduces another bias in the form of time.

Briefly, a cross-over test involves running Ad A in London on the same day that you run Ad B in Manchester. Two or three weeks later you reverse ('cross-over') the sequence so that Ad B runs in London and Ad A in Manchester. By adding the two results together you get a fair approximation of the comparative strength of the two advertisements.

Many advertisers run both machine splits and cross-over tests, but neither is as reliable as a genuine A/B split, which theoretically at least gives two perfectly matched samples.

Testing with loose inserts

One thing we may wish to evaluate is the performance of display advertising compared to loose inserts. Note that as discussed earlier, we would not simply compare on a single measure, such as cost per reply, as this could lead us to some dangerous conclusions.

For example, it is generally accepted amongst direct marketers that loose inserts produce considerably more response than display advertisements in the same medium. However, it may well be that quality of respondents will vary – so we must continue to measure performance after the initial enquiry has been generated.

Apart from comparing inserts with display advertising, loose inserts offer a number of benefits for testing offers, creative approaches and even individual media.

Although there are some variations in response patterns compared to display advertising, loose inserts are a very valuable test medium. One benefit is their power. An insert can easily produce three, five or even ten times as much response as a colour full-page advertisement in the same publication.

The chief advantage of inserts is that they are loose. This means that they do not all have to be the same and that you do not have to place one in every copy of the publication. This gives you flexibility in several ways.

- Design – you could vary your design, thus testing a variety of creative and offer treatments simultaneously. For example, in a magazine with a circulation of 100,000, you could try four alternative inserts each to 25,000. These could be randomized across the circulation to avoid geographical bias.
- Distribution – you could insert in only a proportion of the circulation. For example, you could place your inserts in only the subscription copies or only the newsstand copies, enabling a targeted message, such as a subscription offer to that segment of the readership for which it would be relevant. Another use of this facility would be with a multi-national publication. You could choose to insert in only the UK editions or perhaps vary the language of your message for each country.
- Targeting – many local newspapers and freesheets take loose inserts at quite low rates, and this enables you to target even local promotions. Some national newspapers (such as the *Mail on Sunday*) allow you to insert down to the level of a local wholesaler. This could be very interesting for a local business, as the leaflet would carry the cachet of arriving inside a national newspaper, whilst you would only have to pay for a local campaign. (Please refer to the section on statistical significance starting on p. 242 before attempting to evaluate tests with such local campaigns.)

- Size – there are few limits on space; you can insert anything from a single A5 leaflet to a 64-page catalogue. The greater the weight, the more you pay. However, something as small as an 8-page leaflet can carry a lot more copy than a single page advertisement.

Note that each publication has its own rules regarding weight, size, folds and so on. It is important to be aware of them before finalizing your design. Remember too that not all publications will accept loose inserts.

Direct mail testing

This can be very reliable because you can:

- select precisely matched test cells from a list
- ensure that the quantities and the timing are precisely controlled
- vary the length, size and design of your packages to a degree controlled only by the size of your budget and the number of names available.

You can also vary your message:

- by segment (perhaps making one offer to people living in detached houses and another to those living in flats)
- by individual (by, for example, varying the copy according to whether you are communicating with a company chairman or a shop assistant). This is not a matter of snobbery or discrimination – it simply makes sense to talk to people in the language they would use themselves.

Note that although many test programmes concentrate on new business activities, such as lead generation and conversion activities, they are not restricted to these areas. It is just as important to test alternative approaches to existing customers. In many cases, the payback from a successful test to customers will be much higher.

An important reminder

When we first get involved in the excitement of running and evaluating tests, it is easy to become 'test-happy'; in other words, we can get carried away by raw response statistics and take our eye off the main aim, which is to develop profitable long-term business. Response evaluation is only the beginning – the true measure is the long-term quality of the business generated by the activity.

How to develop a test programme

Let's examine the procedure for designing, implementing and measuring tests. The process is to establish your control and to decide what to test. Your control is the base or 'yardstick' against which your new ideas will be measured.

Your control is the base or 'yardstick' against which your new ideas will be measured.

It is your best-performing existing package, insert or advertisement (or at the least one that you know has worked previously to this market segment). It is the approach you would choose to run if you were unable to test alternatives. Of course, if you are new to the market and simply trying to find a cost-efficient way of attracting business, you will not have a control.

When deciding what to test, there are numerous possibilities, but (as discussed earlier) your test priorities should be worked out according to the hierarchy on p. 250.

If you have some previous results, an analysis of them will help you decide which of the potential new tests looks the most promising.

It helps to draw up your test strategy. This will have many uses including briefing creative people, mailing houses and internal colleagues, estimating costs and obtaining quotations. It is also a useful matrix for developing an evaluation report.

Table 11.5 shows an example of a test strategy for a mailing campaign.

Table 11.5 A typical test strategy

ACQUISITION TEST STRATEGY

Project: Autumn 2001 new customer recruitment mailing campaign
Issued: 4 June 2001
Control: C4 window envelope, 2 page letter, standard brochure and reply card

Test	Objectives	Method
1 Format test: C5 vs C4 envelope	Achieve same response at lower cost	Internal elements same as control, folded to C5
2 Free gift offer included – low key presentation	Improve response by offering free gift. No change to basic tone and structure of control pack	Mention free gift in the letter copy and the PS
3 Free gift offer included – with heavy emphasis	Improve response by featuring free gift heavily throughout pack	Separate four-colour gift 'flyer'; refer to gift in letter copy and PS; show on order card
4 New creative approach	Achieve a 'break-through' against control	New design to be briefed and discussed

Testing lists

Where several lists are available, your test strategy should also include the testing of lists. Equally sized randomized samples of each list should be mailed with the same pack. This is very important, as to mix alternative creative themes or presentations within a list test would leave you without a readable result.

Isolate the variables

Any segment of a test can incorporate any number of variables, but if we want to measure a specific factor we must make sure that no more than one variable appears in any single test cell.

Let's go back to our acquisition test strategy. In evaluating Tests 1, 2 and 3, assuming that our list cells have been produced correctly, we will know that any changes in response are the results of the individual changes made to the packs. The objective for Test 1 is not an increase in response, of course, but if we can attain the same response with the cheaper pack this will in itself make a significant contribution to the cost-efficiency of future campaigns.

Tests 2 and 3 are intended to increase response over control and if this happens we can say with confidence that it is due to the free gift. Comparing Tests 2 and 3 will enable us to judge the desirable level of promotion of free gifts in future.

However, when we compare the results of Test 4 with the control, we will know only the performance of the overall pack and not which element of the pack is responsible for the change. Was it the larger envelope, the fact that it had a message on it, the longer letter or a more effective free gift? We will not be able to judge this and, thus, cannot apply this detailed learning to our other packs.

Testing requires common sense. A good general rule is to isolate variables where you can bearing in mind your budget and the facilities available. You cannot carry out multi-cell testing if the total universe numbers 5000 names. Nor can you use multiple split runs if the publications you want to test do not accept them.

The statistics of testing

Sample sizes

Testing is designed to help you make sound judgements, but it is not an exact science. Test results will help you reduce risk by following the route that offers the greatest probability of success. The word 'probability' is very important – no test result can offer a guarantee that when repeated the same activity will produce the same result.

When using press advertising split runs, the process means that your sample sizes are virtually identical (every alternate copy of the paper carries Ad A or Ad B). This fact, and the large circulations of many publications means that for a straight A/B split-run test, given a sizeable difference between the two results, statistical validity is not difficult to achieve. We need to be more careful when using 'telescope testing' as we saw earlier (p. 232) as the individual response numbers can be quite small.

With loose inserts, you can control the precise number of each leaflet you deliver to the newspaper, and again ensure your samples are matched for size. It is still important for you to ensure that distribution is randomized to avoid area bias.

Sample sizes are equally crucial with direct mail and, therefore, it is necessary for you to understand a little about statistics. This is so that:

- you will know how many people you need to mail in order for a test result to be 'significant' and thus be a reliable predictor of what will happen when you 'roll out' the chosen mailing to the full list
- you will be able to decide, after the event, whether a particular test result is reliable.

Direct mail tests are conducted on samples from the various lists available. For comparative tests to be reliable, you must ensure that you are testing 'like with like'. In other words, the samples used for each test cell must be:

- matched with each other in terms of composition and characteristics
- the same size, or at least each of a known size so that you can allow for size variances in evaluation
- randomized, so that they are entirely typical of the universe they represent, so that you can predict the eventual performance of a 'roll-out' from the test data
- large enough to give a 'statistically significant' reading.

Randomization

To ensure that samples are truly representative of their total 'universe', they would typically be systematic, that is 1 in n samples. In other words to select a sample of 7500 names from a list of 300,000 you would instruct the computer to select every 40th name. This ensures randomization across the list, eliminating bias caused by keeping the list in, for example, chronological or geographical order.

Confidence level (also known as significance or reliability) – this is the number of times out of 100 that one could expect the test result to be repeated in a 'roll-out' (the levels commonly used in direct marketing testing are between 80% and 95%).

Note that although the simplest and quickest way of extracting 7500 names from a list of 300,000 would be to take the first 7500 records, if you used this method with a list held in chronological order, you would extract the 7500 newest or oldest names, which would not be typical of the list as a whole.

There are three basic statistical concepts involved in planning tests.

1 Confidence level (also known as significance or reliability) – this is the number of times out of 100 that one could expect the test result to be repeated in a 'roll-out' (the levels commonly used in direct marketing testing are between 80% and 95%).
2 Limits of error (also known as error tolerance) – as statistics is not an exact science, a test result is subject to a plus or minus correction according to sample size and response level.
3 Statistical significance – this is whether the difference observed is sufficiently large for it to be outside the variances expected due to the limits of error. If the answer is 'Yes', the result is significant. If the answer is 'No', it is not significant.

Selecting samples for testing

Limits of error (also known as error tolerance) – as statistics is not an exact science, a test result is subject to a plus or minus correction according to sample size and response level.

Statistical significance – this is whether the difference observed is sufficiently large for it to be outside the variances expected due to the limits of error? If the answer is 'Yes', the result is significant. If the answer is 'No', it is not significant.

A question asked by many people new to direct marketing is 'How many names do I need in a sample?' There are several possible answers to this question. The minimum sample size can vary according to whether you are planning to simply test a single list or pack, or whether you wish to compare alternatives. It will also vary according to how precise you want the results to be.

The reason for this apparently confusing statement is that sampling relies on the laws of statistics and these are not exact. In order to be able to 'read' a test result with confidence, we need to know how statistics work.

Our first consideration is the confidence level (also called 'significance' or 'reliability'). How confident do we need to be in the answer? We generally work to a confidence level of between 80% and 95%. In other words, what we have experienced in the test is likely to happen when we roll out to the larger list eight times out of ten (80% confidence level) or nineteen times out of twenty (95% confidence level).

Note the use of the phrase 'likely to happen'. Even after our test, we are only able to say what is 'probable'. Thus, confidence level is sometimes also referred to as 'probability' or 'significance', for example 80% or 95% probability or significance.

Unfortunately, even this is not the whole story. We also have to consider error tolerance (limits of error). This is the allowable error, which is a plus or minus amount we have to allow when reading our test results. In other words, because of the imprecision of statistical laws, a 2% response to a test cannot be taken as exactly 2%, but as 2% plus or minus an amount which is determined by the number of responses we have received. This, of course, is a simple function of the number of names we have mailed multiplied by the response rate.

What this means in general is that the more names we mail in our test sample, the more we can rely on the result.

Using formulae

We need to consider the formula for calculating sample size, error tolerance and reliability of results.

As regards sample size, it is not unusual to hear experienced marketers say things like: 'You should always test 10% of the list' and 'I never use test cells of fewer than 15,000 names.' The first statement is clearly nonsense; the second can often be wasteful (although, as we will see, such an approach may sometimes be prudent).

There is a formula for calculating sample size. To use it you need to have an idea of the likely response you are expecting and the degree of error you are prepared to tolerate. Whilst this may seem onerous, you would not really wish to embark on a mailing, even a test mailing, without some idea of what sort of response you expected. On a positive note, it does enable you to measure the result in retrospect with great precision, and thus decide how reliable your test has actually been.

The formula for calculating sample size is:

$$\text{Sample size} = \frac{(\text{confidence level})^2 \times \text{expected response} \times \text{non-response}}{(\text{error tolerance})^2}$$

Confidence level is expressed as a number of standard deviations from a normal distribution, for example:

- 95% confidence = 1.960 standard deviations
- 90% confidence = 1.645 standard deviations
- 80% confidence = 1.281 standard deviations.

Expected response and non-response are simple percentages, such as 2.5%, expressed as 2.5, and 97.5%, expressed as 97.5.

Error tolerance is the plus or minus amount you are prepared to accept, for example 0.5% (0.5).

Thus, allowing for a 95% confidence level, if we anticipate a response of 2.5% and we are testing two creative treatments (that is we are not sure how much more effective one will be than another), we will be wise to try to keep the error allowance fairly small. If we limit it to 0.25%, we see the following:

$$\frac{(1.960 \times 1.960) \times 2.5 \times 97.5}{(0.25 \times 0.25)} = 14,982$$

Let's require a sample of 14,982 names (rounded to 15,000) for each test cell. Although, as mentioned earlier, this may be a 'safe' sample size, if we want to measure several things in the same test programme we will soon run up a very large bill. What can we do to reduce the sample size and, thus, the cost?

Let's consider our confidence level. We have worked to 95% (nineteen times out of twenty). What would happen if we were prepared to accept a 90%, or even an 80% confidence level? Let's work out the numbers.

For a 90% confidence level:

$$\frac{(1.645 \times 1.645) \times 2.5 \times 97.5}{0.25 \times 0.25} = 10,554$$

This reduces the sample size to 10,554 per cell.

For an 80% confidence level:

$$\frac{(1.281 \times 1.281) \times 2.5 \times 97.5}{0.25 \times 0.25} = 6400$$

There is a further reduction to 6400 names per test cell.

Nowadays with costs so high, it is quite normal for marketers to work to an 80% confidence level. Indeed, you could argue that, allowing for the law of averages, an 80% confidence level could be taken as 90% given the following probable scenario.

A confidence level of 80% means that during 'roll out':

- eight out of ten will come in at the same level of response (plus or minus the error limit)
- one out of ten is likely to produce less response
- one out of ten is likely to produce more response.

So, given that you are not concerned about repeating exactly the result, but simply doing at least as well, you would probably be prepared to accept 80% confidence for most test programmes.

What else could we do? If we were prepared to go to a 0.5% error tolerance, what difference would this make to the sample size? We can work it through on 90% and 80% confidence levels again.

For a 90% confidence level:

$$\frac{(1.645 \times 1.645) \times 2.5 \times 97.5}{0.5 \times 0.5} = 2638$$

This is better, as our samples now reduce to a mere 2638 per cell.

For an 80% confidence level:

$$\frac{(1.281 \times 1.281) \times 2.5 \times 97.5}{0.5 \times 0.5} = 1600$$

Now we need only 1600 names per cell.

Clearly, the increase in error tolerance is a major factor in reducing sample sizes, so we can try one final calculation. If we want to be very confident that our test result is likely to happen on roll-out, we can do a final calculation based on a 95% confidence level and a 0.5% error tolerance:

$$\frac{(1.960 \times 1.960) \times 2.5 \times 97.5}{0.5 \times 0.5} = 3746$$

Now our required sample size is 3746 (round to 3800 for simplicity).

Table 11.6 shows how we might construct a test matrix from a test campaign.

Table 11.6 A mailing test matrix

	Control offer	Offer 2	Offer 3	Total
Control list	3800	3800	3800	11,400
List B	3800	3800	3800	11,400
List C	3800	3800	3800	11,400
Total	11,400	11,400	11,400	34,200

The sample sizes used here would enable us to compare list with list (across all offers) and offer with offer (across all lists) with a fair degree of confidence. Our total sample for each of these is 11,400 and at 2.5% response this gives us an error tolerance of 0.3% (0.287% to be exact) at a 95% confidence level.

Of course, what we would really like to do is to compare what happened in each of the individual cells and, if we do this, we will find that the error tolerance will change because the sample sizes are smaller.

A response rate of 2.5% to a sample of 3800 requires an error tolerance of plus or minus 0.5% (if you work this out, you will find it is actually 0.496%). This is not a problem in itself, but, as we have seen, it means that only larger differences in response will be significant.

Can we reduce test costs still further? If we are prepared to take a slightly increased chance of our results not being totally reliable, the easiest thing is to use a lower confidence (or significance) level. We can take a look at another text matrix, shown in Table 11.7, this time using smaller samples.

Table 11.7 Test matrix using smaller samples

	Control offer	Offer 2	Offer 3	Total
Control list	1300	1300	1300	3900
List B	1300	1300	1300	3900
List C	1300	1300	1300	3900
Total	3900	3900	3900	11,700

As before, this will probably tell us which list and which offer were more successful overall (a sample size of 3900 gives error tolerance of 0.49% at 95% confidence level). Trying to compare individual cells at this level is not recommended. The error tolerance for samples of 1300 at 2.5% is huge (0.85%), making such comparisons dangerous.

Even if we reduce our confidence requirement to 90%, the error tolerance level is still 0.71%.

Using tables rather than formulae

It can be easier and quicker to work with tables rather than formulae and the following tables may be helpful.

Table 11.8 is based on a 95% confidence level and shows required minimum sample sizes for range of responses from 0.5% to 10%, and a range of plus or minus error limits from 0.1% to 1%.

The key factor is that minimum sample size increases when we want smaller tolerances. For example, if we expect a 5% response and are prepared to accept a result of 5% plus or minus 0.5% (that is, our result can only be relied upon to produce between 4.5% and 5.5% when remailed), a sample size of 7299 will be adequate. On the other hand, if we want the error limit to be halved to 0.25%, the minimum sample size must be four times as large.

Table 11.8 Minimum sample sizes – 95% confidence level

	0.10%	0.25%	0.50%	0.75%	1%
	0.1	0.25	0.5	0.75	1
0.5%	19,112	3058			
1.0%	38,032	6085			
1.5%	56,760	9082	2270		
2.0%	75,295	12,047	3012		
2.5%	93,639	14,982	3746		
3.0%	111,791	17,886	4472	1987	
3.5%	129,750	20,760	5190	2307	
4.0%	147,517	23,603	5901	2623	
4.5%	165,093	26,415	6604	2935	
5.0%	182,476	29,196	7299	3244	
7.5%	266,511	42,642	10,660	4738	2665
10.0%	345,744	55,319	13,830	6147	3457

Table 11.9 Minimum sample sizes – 80% confidence level

	0.10%	0.25%	0.50%	0.75%	1%
0.5%	8151	1304			
1.0%	16,220	2595			
1.5%	24,207	3873	968		
2.0%	32,113	5138	1285		
2.5%	39,936	6390	1597		
3.0%	47,677	7628	1907	848	
3.5%	55,337	8854	2213	984	
4.0%	62,915	10,066	2517	1118	
4.5%	70,410	11,266	2816	1252	
5.0%	77,824	12,452	3113	1384	
7.5%	113,664	18,186	4547	2021	1137
10.0%	147,456	23,593	5898	2621	1475

Table 11.9 is a similar table, but this time based on an 80% confidence level.

As we can see, being prepared to accept a lower confidence level makes minimum sample sizes much smaller.

Let's look at a couple of examples to see how these tables can be used. For simplicity we will work these using only the 80% confidence level table.

We can take a sample size of 5000 names and a response rate of 2%. What can we predict from this? Looking this up in the 80% confidence table, we see that a response rate of 2% from a sample of 5138 (the nearest number quoted to our sample size) means we have to allow for error tolerance of 0.25%. This means that our test that produced a 2% response, can only be relied upon to deliver somewhere between 1.75% and 2.25% when repeated (or 'rolled out').

Allowing for our 80% confidence level, we can say that when rolled out to the larger list (of which our sample was truly representative), we can expect to experience a response rate of between 1.75% to 2.25%, eight times out of ten. So far so good. If 1.75% is sufficient to give us an acceptable business result, we can confidently proceed with the roll out.

However, things are rather more complicated when we are running more than one test at a time (which would often be the case). When comparing the results from two test cells we use a slightly different formula.

The significance of each result is carefully evaluated using the following statistical formula, which uses response data from both the control and the test cell to define an expected limit of error. If the actual difference between the two cells is the same or less than the expected limit of error, the result is not significant. If the actual difference is greater than the expected limit of error, the result is significant.

The formula for calculating the expected limit of error is:

$$\text{Confidence level} \times \sqrt{\frac{(\text{Response} \times \text{non-response})}{\text{Sample size}} + \frac{(\text{Response} \times \text{non-response})}{\text{Sample size}}}$$

So, whether you opt for the 90% or 95% confidence level, you are dealing with a high degree of probability, but subject to that limit of error.

Now we will run these calculations at both the 95% and the 90% confidence levels to show how they vary.

To demonstrate how this process works, we are using a typical mailing response. Here the advertiser is testing his standard incentive against an alternative. The data is as shown in Table 11.10.

Putting these data into the formula gives us:

$$\frac{(6.94 \times 93.06)}{12,500} + \frac{(6.35 \times 93.65)}{12,505} = 0.0516669 + 0.0475551 = 0.099222$$

Table 11.10 Test response data

Incentive	Mailing quantity	Response rate (%)	Response index
Standard – control	12,500	6.94	100
Alternative incentive	12,505	6.35	91

The square root of 0.099222 is 0.3149952 – multiply this by 1.96 to give an expected error limit of 0.6173905 at a 95% confidence level. We can round it to 0.617. The actual or 'observed' difference between the two results is 0.59 that is 6.94 minus 6.35. This is less than the expected error limit, so at the 95% confidence level this result is not significant.

Now we can try it at the 90% confidence level. To check this we simply take the same figure (0.099222) from the equation and multiply it by 1.645 (the figure for the 90% confidence level). This gives us:

$$0.099222 \times 1.645 = 0.5181671$$

So, the expected error limit is 0.518. Our observed difference at 0.59 is greater than this, therefore, at the 90% confidence level the result is significant.

What this means is that the test should not be relied upon if we want to be 95% sure that the same result will happen again (that is nineteen times out of twenty).

If, on the other hand, we are prepared to accept a slightly greater risk (nine times out of ten) we could take this result as significant.

Now, let us look again at the table we showed earlier. It is based on the same statistical formula but is somewhat 'rounded'. Nevertheless, it can be used as a good 'rule of thumb'.

Note that if your results are on the margins of these figures, you must work out the precise numbers using the formula. In other words, if in a test you received 65 replies to Sample A and 35 replies to Sample B, you should use the formula to work out the exact error tolerances before assuming you have a valid result.

Table 11.11 shows us that if we get 100 replies in total (that is the total from both test cells) and Mailing A pulls 65% of that total (65 vs 35 replies), the result is significant, but only just. If it is repeated (rolled out) to the larger list of which this was a truly representative sample, we can expect (nineteen times out of twenty) Mailing A to produce the same level of response (plus or minus an error tolerance that can only be defined if we know what the size of the test sample was). If it pulls fewer than 65 out of the total of 100 replies, it is not a significant (or reliable) result.

Table 11.11 Statistical significance at 95% confidence level

Total response i.e. A + B	Significance factor*	Winner	Loser	% Gain
50	70%	35	15	133%
100	65%	65	35	86%
500	57%	285	215	33%
1000	55%	550	450	22%
10,000	52%	5200	4800	8%

*% for result to be significant.

A few final comments

1 Test sample sizes are a matter for statistical calculation rather than guess-work, or broad 'rules of thumb'.
2 If we have an idea of likely response, we can use the formula to select a suitable sample size and, once we have the response data, to assess the degree of reliability of any given test.
3 It is often easier to find a good marketing statistician than spend too much time learning and practicing with formulae.
4 It is easier and quicker to work with tables rather than formulae.

Measurement of response is only the start, of course. You must continue to monitor the ongoing behaviour of respondents to ensure that an apparently successful new idea is not simply producing a large volume of poorly quali-fied enquiries.

The hierarchy of testing

Table 11.12 is a summary of the results of a major mailing test programme with more than 1000 test cells.

Table 11.12 Most important factor for success

Factor	Difference between best and worst responses
List	× 6
Offer	× 3
Timing	× 2
Creative	× 1.35
Response mechanics	× 1.2

Other studies have produced slightly different figures, but all agree on the general hierarchy, namely medium or list, offer or main message, timing, creative approach and response devices.

SUMMARY

This chapter has explored the central role of testing in direct marketing management. Whilst testing is carried on in mass marketing, the strength of testing in the direct marketing environment is that response can be tracked from an individual insertion and a far greater range of variables can be evaluated.

Direct marketing uses testing first to create cost-effective campaigns. Testing does not eliminate risk but will reduce risk through the evaluation of alternatives. We have seen that we can test a range of key variables, including:

- media type
- medium
- position
- timing
- size
- frequency
- offer
- creative treatment
- response methods.

We have explored each of these in detail and have seen that there is a standard hierarchy in testing and that this allows a logical sequence of testing activity.

The chapter then explored the methods of testing in various media looking at:

- A/B split runs in press and magazines, including telescope testing
- machine splits
- geographic splits.

It went on to look at the testing of loose inserts and identified the benefits – inserts are generally more responsive than advertisements placed in the same publications and they are a highly flexible medium in terms of design, distribution, targeting and size.

We have seen that testing in direct mail is reliable due to the fact that we can select matched test cells for a list, quantity and timing can be controlled, and there is flexibility in copy length, design and size of mailings.

We have looked at the process of developing a test programme, namely to:

- establish the control
- decide what to test
- set objectives
- isolate variables
- implement the test
- evaluate the results.

When testing, we must ensure that we are comparing like with like. Samples must be:

- matched in terms of composition and characteristics
- of a known size
- taken at random across a list by a 1 in n selection
- large enough to ensure validity.

The chapter has explored the statistical basis of testing and looked at confidence levels, limits of error and significance.

The process of selecting a sample was explored in detail. We saw that the required sample size depends on the level of confidence and the limits of error acceptable in any results. We have seen that it is not right to say you should always test a certain percentage of the list or a certain number of names.

We have looked at the formula required to calculate sample size. There are three key decisions to make:

- what is the likely response?
- what confidence level do we wish to work to?
- what are the acceptable limits of error?

A worked example was provided that showed the impact on sample sizes of changing the error tolerances to which we work.

Using tables, we selected a sample size and worked through the implications for a business.

We went on to look at the measurement of difference between a two-cell test. Again, a worked example was provided.

The section finished with the following important observations:

- Test sample sizes must be statistically based.
- If we know likely response, we can assess the suitable sample size. Once we have response data, we can assess the degree of reliability of any test.
- Use a statistician if you are unsure.
- It is easier to work with tables rather than formulae.

Finally, we looked at the hierarchy of testing and considered the relative importance of each element:

- targeting
- offer
- timing
- creative
- response mechanics.

1   Why is testing in direct marketing so important?

2   What can we test?

3   What is the most important factor to test?

4   At what level is media type testing evaluated?

5   Define position testing.

6   What is the hierarchy of testing?

7   List three methods of testing press and magazine advertisements.

8   Why are loose inserts a powerful testing medium?

9   Why are direct mail tests reliable?

10   How do we develop a test programme?

11   What is a control?

12   What are the four requirements of a statistically valid test?

13   What are the three statistical concepts involved in planning tests?

14   Define each of these concepts.

15   List the five elements of the hierarchy of testing in order of importance.

16   Why is targeting so important?

What is the formula for calculating sample size?
What is the sample size required when we anticipate 2% response and the acceptable limit of error is 0.5% at a 95% confidence level?
How does this change at 80% confidence level?

Chapter 12

Evaluation, measurement and budgeting

Introduction
- Evaluation
- Measurability
- Acquisition or retention – finding the balance
• Marketing measurement techniques
• Evaluating campaigns
- Two-stage selling
- Limitations
• How to calculate and deal with marketing costs
- Variable costs, fixed costs and overheads
- How to handle overheads
  Budgeting
- The benefits of budgeting
- What makes for successful budgeting?
• Creating a campaign budget
• Customer lifetime value analysis
- Using lifetime value modelling to evaluate marketing strategies
- Comparison of lifetime values with and without the retention programme
- Common questions
- Predicting lifetime value by customer segment
- How to develop lifetime value calculations
- Lifetime value analysis – summary
Summary
Review questions
Exercises

Evaluation

Direct marketers can evaluate many activities before making major investments.

Evaluation is the continuous measurement of marketing activities with a view to deciding whether they should be continued, amended or abandoned.

Every marketing activity can be budgeted for, measured as it proceeds and evaluated. This high level of control means that by studying the results of our activities, we can continually improve our performance, even whilst the campaign is in progress.

Evaluation is the continuous measurement of marketing activities with a view to deciding whether they should be continued, amended or abandoned.

Measurability

Unlike general advertising, most direct marketing communications are designed to elicit a response from the recipient and, thus, they can be measured very precisely. As we saw in the previous chapter, this enables us to identify good and bad publications, mailing lists, creative treatments and, indeed, types of prospect very quickly and without spending large amounts of money.

Acquisition or retention – finding the balance

As we know, developing relationships is one of the key concepts of direct marketing – some of the elements of direct marketing, database development for example, require serious investment before any sort of payback is possible. It is only by developing longer-term relationships and so ensuring a continuing flow of repeat business that such investment becomes viable.

However, companies are mainly in business to make money and it is important to find the correct balance between investing in new customers who will later become profitable and getting a satisfactory return on our expenditure in time to stay in business.

This balance is a critical success factor and the point of balance will vary according to the nature of the business.

Consider a company having a small range of products that it sells through single product advertisements in national newspapers. Once a customer has bought, they are sent a catalogue or leaflet carrying details of the other products in the range.

The primary objective of the company is to make a profit from the orders received from each advertisement.

The secondary objective is to build a 'list' and make subsequent sales (and profit) from future mailings to these customers.

Should this company stick to its policy of making profit from the first transaction or could it do better in the long term by 'breaking even' or even making a small loss on the first sale and thus generating more customers for its database?

Although the answer is not certain, it is likely that in most markets the 'investment route' will eventually yield more profit. However, only a carefully planned programme of testing and evaluation will enable the right balance to be found.

If a business has not been running very long it is likely to have only limited funding so it will not be able to afford to go flat out for later payback. However, some element of investment is probably advisable. In order to reach sensible and affordable decisions, it is necessary to make constant comparisons between these options.

Marketing measurement techniques

In direct marketing, although it is not necessary to be a statistician, some familiarity with numbers is very helpful. It is all too easy when we are under pressure to hit the wrong key on a calculator and, if we are not able to do an approximate calculation in our heads, we will not know until it is too late that the result shown on the calculator is wrong.

In marketing we deal with a wide range of numbers from television audiences or newspaper readerships that are expressed in millions to response rates which are often expressed in fractions of 1%. Thus, we have to be comfortable with both very large and very small numbers.

Much of our analysis is involved in making comparisons between two or more results or response rates. To make such comparisons easier we use standard measures and the following are some of the most common.

- Cost per thousand – this is used to compare media rates (these are usually expressed in 'cost per thousand' readers, names, viewers and so on) and print quotes (we compare the cost per thousand of two or more quotations for leaflets or brochures). It is all too easy to make basic errors when comparing costs on a cost per thousand basis. For example, second-class postage is currently 21 pence and when building this into a total mailing budget many people cost in £21 per thousand. Of course, 21 pence is actually £21 per hundred or £210 per thousand. This simple error occurs time and again and makes a nonsense out of many mailing budgets.

- Cost per response, reply, enquiry and lead – most direct marketing activities can be measured by activity generated and the results expressed in terms of cost per something.
- Cost per order or per sale – this goes a stage further and measures the actual amount of business produced by the activity. The ultimate short-term activity measurement is cost per pound turnover.
- Response rate – there are two common expressions of response; cost per response as mentioned above, and response percentage. We tend to use response percentage when dealing with mailings and cost per response when evaluating broadscale media, such as press and television. However, for a full comparison of activities both are helpful. Response percentages are used when forecasting demand and comparing results from test cells, and cost per response is used when evaluating results over a longer period.

Evaluating campaigns

One of the simplest measures used to evaluate direct marketing activity is the allowable cost per order, an approach which has been around for many years. This originated when most direct marketing activity was concerned with selling direct by mail order and is a very conservative approach to building business.

Allowable cost per order is reached by building a mini profit and loss account for an average sale including the desired profit but excluding promotional costs. The calculation shows the amount we can afford to spend to secure a sale – our allowable cost per order. This is also sometimes called allowable cost per sale.

The costing shown in Figure 12.1 indicates that we can afford to spend £25 to sell this product, and that each sale achieved at this cost will give us a profit of £30 to help fund business management and growth.

We can use the allowable cost per order to calculate the required response rate from a mailing. For example, we can work out the cost of mailing to 30,000 prospects at, say, £19,500 (at £650 per thousand), including print, postage and so on.

Dividing the £19,500 cost by our £25 'allowable cost' shows that 780 orders will be needed, that is a 2.6% response from our 30,000 prospects, to give us our required payback of £30 profit per order.

We can take this costing a stage further by calculating how many orders we will need to 'break even', that is to get the investment back without any profit. In the above model we simply divide the £19,500 cost by the £55 'contribution' to show that 355 (in fact, 354.55) orders would recover our investment. This represents 1.18% of the total mailed.

Allowable cost per order is reached by building a mini profit and loss account for an average sale including the desired profit but excluding promotional costs. The calculation shows the amount we can afford to spend to secure a sale – our allowable cost per order. This is also sometimes called allowable cost per sale.

Calculating the allowable cost per order		
Order value – gross revenue		£90
Manufacturing costs	£25	
Order processing, packaging and despatch costs	£10	
Total costs	£35	£35
Contribution		£55
Profit required		£30
Allowable cost per order		£25

Figure 12.1 Calculating the 'allowable' – one-step selling

If we were mailing for the first time, we would need to use our judgement to decide whether this looks achievable. Alternatively, we may run a test, but without any previous experience we would have to take a chance on achieving a statistically valid number of responses (see Chapter 11).

Two-stage selling

Although much traditional mail order is 'direct sell' or one-stage selling, there are many occasions when this is not appropriate, for example when selling more expensive items or when advertising a large catalogue with many available choices for the prospective buyer.

The process of advertising to attract enquiries for a catalogue or brochure is called two-stage (or two-step) selling. When using this method, there are some additional costs to be built into the model.

The process of advertising to attract enquiries for a catalogue or brochure is called two-stage (or two-step) selling. When using this method, there are some additional costs to be built into the model.

If we expect to receive one order from every four people who enquire (a 25% 'conversion rate') and it costs £1.50 (including despatch postage) for every information pack we send, and 25 pence postage for every reply we receive, the costings would now be as shown in Figure 12.2.

We also need to build the conversion calculations into the estimate of response required to hit the target and to achieve break-even.

First, to see what is required to hit the profit target, we divide the £19,500 cost by the £18 'allowable' giving a target of 1083 orders. At one order per four enquiries, this means we need to attract 4333 replies, which is a response rate of 14.4%. This is considerably higher than the one-stage route and it does not look particularly viable.

However, experienced mail order operators know that order values from two-stage selling are often considerably higher than from one-stage, so it will

Calculating the allowable cost per sale

Order value – gross revenue		£90
Manufacturing costs	£25	
Order processing, packaging and despatch costs	£10	
Cost of information packs: four per order @ £1.50	£6	
Freepost on replies, e.g. 4 × 25p	£1	
Total costs	£42	£42
Contribution		£48
Profit required		£30
Allowable cost per order		£18

Figure 12.2 Two-stage selling – allowing for conversion costs

probably be worth testing this method. Some mail order operators find that average orders from two-stage advertising are almost double those from direct selling or 'off-the-page' advertising.

Now let us rework the two-stage numbers on the assumption that average order values will increase to £150, an increase of 66.66% over the one-stage average (Figure 12.3).

Calculating the allowable cost per sale

Order value – gross revenue		£150.00
Manufacturing costs	£41.50	
Order processing, packaging and despatch costs, e.g.	£13.00	
Cost of information packs: four per order @ £1.50	£6.00	
Postage on replies, e.g. 4 × 25p	£1.00	
Total costs	£61.50	£61.50
Contribution		£88.00
Profit required		£50.00
Allowable cost per order		£38.50

Figure 12.3 Calculating the 'allowable cost' – higher order values

Dividing the £19,500 cost by the new 'allowable' cost per order of £38.50 gives a requirement of 507 orders and a response requirement of 2028 enquiries. This is 6.8% of the total mailed and looks more achievable.

Next we see what our base requirement is, that is, what we need to break even. Dividing the £19,500 by the £88.50 contribution shows that 220 orders are required to get our money back. At the expected conversion rate of 25%, we need 880 enquiries, that is a 2.93% response.

Again, we must use our judgement to decide whether this looks achievable. We will return to this point later when we consider again the issue of whether it is essential to make a profit on our first transaction with a new customer.

The above demonstration has deliberately been kept very simple. Do not forget to reduce your sales revenue to allow for such things as products being returned, replacements for items damaged in transit, bad debts and so on. Remember to allow for all costs, including, where relevant, design, photography, artwork, printer's charges, any response costs (postage, telephone and so on).

Although the allowable cost approach is very simplistic, it does help to give a better feel for the point of balance between acquisition and retention. If you feel confident that your new customers will buy further products in the future, and you have sufficient funding to enable you to wait for profit, you can be more relaxed about the amount of profit you achieve from your first transaction. You may perhaps aim for a simple break-even or even be prepared to accept a small loss.

Limitations

The allowable cost approach is very useful, but it has limitations too.

1 It requires sales, returns, damages and bad debts to be estimated in advance to enable realistic forecasting of net sales revenue.
2 It assumes that costs are fixed, thus they will not change with volume of sales.
3 It leads to decisions being based not on profit maximization but on profit satisfaction. It can become a self-fulfilling prophecy. If our target is to achieve 20,000 orders and our calculations show an allowable cost of £50 we have £1 million to spend. However, if that were our own money would we think differently? It is all too easy to spend this budget when we should be trying to achieve our 20,000 orders for as little as possible.
4 It does not take into account any future purchases by a new customer – 'forcing' a fixed profit from the first transaction can bias our judgement towards quantity rather than long-term quality. This is the most important limitation of this process.

The first of these concerns cannot be avoided. We will have to estimate these items in advance in order to calculate and justify the budget requirements so the calculation is not an idle exercise.

Overcoming the assumption that costs are fixed

This problem is easily addressed. All that is required is to re-run the numbers based on different levels of cost.

It is assumed for the purposes of this example that we are planning to offer a 'free gift' to make our advertisement more attractive.

All other things being equal, an incentivized offer will produce a higher response rate and, thus, more sales from the same mailing or advertisement. It may also affect the conversion rate from enquiry to sale. If the gift is given for simply enquiring, it will increase response dramatically but lower the conversion rate.

If the gift is given in return for an order only, it may increase the response rate a little, but improve conversion quite substantially. Only testing will show precisely what effect the gift will have.

Let us assume that we have decided to offer a free gift to customers who place an order. This gift has a retail value of £30, but costs just £10 on a sale or return basis. It is reasonable to assume that the free gift will improve both response rate and conversion rate.

Calculating the allowable costs and required response using different offers		
Mailing quantity	30,000	
Mailing cost	£19,500	
Cost per test segment	£9,750	£9,750
	Basic offer	Gift offer
Product price	£300	£300
Costs	£140	£150 (inc gift)
Contribution	£160	£150
Required profit	£100	£100
Allowable cost	£60	£50
Sales needed to achieve profit targets	162.5	195
Conversion rate	1 in 4	1 in 3.5
Responses required	650	682
Response rate	4.33%	4.55%

Figure 12.4 Comparison of allowable costs – basic offer v. free gift

What will be the precise effect on response rate and costings? We will not really know without testing it, but what we can do at this stage is to calculate what it will need to do to be equally cost-effective with the existing offer (Figure 12.4). We can then use our judgement to decide whether the test looks worthwhile.

(Note that to simplify this demonstration we have assumed that the net sales revenue per order is a standard £300.)

This costing shows that if, based on previous experience, the response rate of 4.33% and conversion ratio of one in four seem reasonable, we need only a 5% gain in response rate ($\frac{3.2}{650} \times 100$) and an improvement in conversion of 14% to make the free gift offer viable. If it works out, we shall gain 32 additional customers, some of whom will continue to buy in the future.

Note that these calculations do not tell us what *will* happen. This only tells us what the profit and loss situation will be under various circumstances. We still need to use considerable judgement – these cost exercises simply enable us to make better-informed 'guesstimates'.

We could use similar calculations to examine the effects of, for example, selling a higher volume or reducing the profit margin to enable us to make better offers.

Taking a wider view

The third limitation of allowable cost calculations is simply that they encourage complacency. They encourage us to stop when the calculation works out at our estimated profit. In real life, we should be seeking to maximize profit rather than simply achieve our estimates.

This issue can be tackled by moving up a level in the evaluations. Rather than using a single sale as the base level, we can move up to the campaign level.

Rather than judging a required response rate against experience, we will use our best estimate of response rate and judge whether to proceed or not on the profit likely to be generated. We can work out individual sales profitability from the overall campaign calculation, as the example in Figure 12.5 shows (which takes the same costs as in the previous example).

This analysis shows one of the shortcomings of restricting our view to a profit and loss account of a single transaction (the basis of the allowable cost process). At that level there is nothing to choose between the two approaches – each would deliver a contribution per sale of £100. If we made our decision at this point, we may well decide on Campaign A, as it saves us the trouble of sourcing and offering a gift.

However, when we base our decision on the overall campaign contribution, we see that the gift offer delivers an additional £3250 of profit and an additional 32 customers to whom we can sell again in the future.

Note that the above calculations are hypothetical, but if you run your campaign plans against these models you will get a much clearer view of your own costs and profitability.

Campaign based budgeting

	Campaign A	Campaign B
Net revenue per order	£300	£300
Costs	£140	£150
Gross margin	£160	£150
Number mailed	15,000	15,000
Response %	4.33	4.55
Responses	650	682
Conversion ratio	1 in 4	1 in 3.5
Sales	162.5	195
Gross profit	£26,000	£29,250
Cost of promotion	£9,750	£9,750
Campaign contribution	£16,250	£19,500
Contribution per sale	£100	£100

Figure 12.5 Campaign based budgeting

How to calculate and deal with marketing costs

Before we look at budgeting and decision-making more closely, it is important to understand costs – what they are and how they affect budgeting and evaluation.

Costs in marketing, as in every area of business, fall into two basic groups – fixed costs and variable costs. In building a budget, we need to be concerned with the costs we will incur, whether these costs are fixed or variable, and if variable, on which elements they depend.

Variable costs, fixed costs and overheads

The definition of costs depends on the level being addressed. Some costs may be fixed when looking at an individual campaign, but variable in the context of a year's-worth of campaigns.

Variable costs are defined as costs that vary with the amount of a given activity. For example, the cost of an advertisement will vary according to the newspaper we choose (rates are based on the number of copies the paper sells), and on the size and position of the space we buy.

The cost of a mailing list will vary according to the quantity of names we decide to rent and perhaps the quality too, if we are intending to segment

Variable costs are defined as costs that vary with the amount of a given activity. For example, the cost of an advertisement will vary according to the newspaper we choose (rates are based on the number of copies the paper sells), and on the size and position of the space we buy.

Fixed costs are costs that are not influenced by changes in activity. For example, the cost of artwork for a mailing is fixed at the campaign level – the cost is the same whether we print 1000 or 10,000.

Overheads (indirect fixed costs) are costs that are incurred whether or not an activity takes place. For example, property rental is likely to be a cost that is not only independent of the size of a campaign, but also independent of the number of campaigns in a given period (within reason).

the list by profiling factors. Outward postage will be directly proportional to the number of items mailed. Reply paid postal costs, charges for free telephone response numbers and the cost of data capture of responses will vary according to the number of people who respond.

Fixed costs are costs that are not influenced by changes in activity. For example, the cost of artwork for a mailing is fixed at the campaign level – the cost is the same whether we print 1000 or 10,000. However, it could be seen as variable at the strategic level, for example we can decide at the start of a year whether we are going to produce expensive glossy mailings or low cost ones.

Overheads (indirect fixed costs) are costs that are incurred whether or not an activity takes place. For example, property rental is likely to be a cost that is not only independent of the size of a campaign, but also independent of the number of campaigns in a given period (within reason).

How costs vary with quantity

In general, marketing costs increase with quantity. For example, overtime charges can result from an unexpectedly high response to a mailing or advertisement. On the other hand, some costs such as the unit cost of printing, can be dramatically reduced with increases in quantity – as is demonstrated by the example in Table 12.1 for a fairly standard mailing pack.

From this example, it can be seen that a straight extrapolation from test mailing costs would seriously distort the financial implications of a roll-out: the cost of the 100,000 roll-out mailings projected from the costs of the 5000 test would be £65,000, rather than the £50,000 it would actually cost.

However, if we were to 'run on' a further 100,000 copies, there might not be much further reduction for quantity, as we would already have amortized the set-up costs and used most of the 'economy of scale'.

Understanding the effect of quantity is important if the correct inferences about the financial implications of a roll-out are to be drawn from a test campaign. The basic rule is to base the evaluation of a test campaign on the level of costings that would have been incurred if we had mailed the larger (roll-out) number.

Table 12.1 How costs vary from test to 'roll-out'

Effect of quantity on print costs (C5 mailing)

Quantity		Total cost	Cost per pack
Test –	5000	£3250	65 pence
Roll-out –	100,000	£50,000	50 pence

One of the main reasons for spending so much time and energy on defining costs is that it is vital to have as clear a view as possible of the true profitability of each activity. The main aim is to attribute as many costs as possible to the activities for which they are incurred.

Most variable costs can easily be attributed to an activity – if we had not done the mailing we would not have rented the list, bought the envelopes and so on.

Many fixed costs can also be attributed to an activity – advertisement artwork is a good example. However, there is one category of fixed costs called indirect fixed costs or overheads, which can create many problems for marketers.

How to handle overheads

The handling of overheads is probably one of the most difficult areas of budgeting. We can attempt to allocate overheads to products or campaigns, but there are problems. For example, if an assistant has planned twelve campaigns for the year, we could allocate one-twelfth of his or her salary to each campaign. Yet what if two of the campaigns take twice as much time as the others? Or what if one of the campaigns is cancelled (after most of the work has been done) or another campaign is added during the period?

One answer is to instigate a method of decision-making that allows us to consider the success or otherwise of an activity (proposed or completed) before overheads are allocated, and then make decisions based on the level of overhead this activity would support. This is the contribution or relevant costing approach.

The contribution approach

The most useful level for decision-making is the contribution level. This takes into account all the revenue and costs directly associated with an activity, including those costs and revenues which are only incurred/generated because the activity is being undertaken.

The following example of the contribution approach shown in Figure 12.6 considers whether or not to undertake a mailing to 7500 businesses. Net sales revenue is £200 per order and expected response is 4%.

According to this calculation, the above activity makes a loss. However, there are two indirect costs (overheads) included which are going to have to be paid whether or not the campaign goes ahead. These are staff costs and office costs. Together these costs add up to £13,833.

The most useful level for decision-making is the contribution level. This takes into account all the revenue and costs directly associated with an activity, including those costs and revenues which are only incurred/generated because the activity is being undertaken.

Expected costs are:

Cost of goods	£80
List rental	£150 per thousand
Artwork/agency fees	£12,500
Production and postage	£750 per thousand
Marketing Department handling	
12 campaigns per year	£100,000
Other overheads (management, rent, etc. allocated to this campaign by Finance Department)	£5,500
In-house order processing	£20 per order

Putting this together we can calculate:

Mailing quantity	7,500
Response	300 orders
Revenue	£60,000
Cost of goods	£24,000
	————
Gross profit	£36,000

Costs to be deducted:

List rental	£1,125	
Production, print and postage	£5,625	
Agency artwork, fees	£12,500	
Staff (1/12th of annual cost)	£8,333	
Office costs (allocated)	£5,500	
Order handling	£6,000	
	————	
	£39,083	£39,083
		————
Profit/(loss)		**(£3,083)**

Figure 12.6 How contribution costing works

A contribution approach would say that the campaign generates a net sales revenue of £60,000 and, as a result of undertaking the campaign, costs of £49,250 will be incurred (cost of goods plus promotion costs plus order handling charges). Taking these costs from the revenue generated leaves an income of £10,750 to contribute towards overheads; in other words if we do not do the mailing we will be £10,750 worse off at the end of the period.

This contribution (or relevant costing) approach, based on identifying the relevant costs associated with a campaign, looks to see if undertaking the campaign contributes towards the overheads (which will be incurred whether or not the campaign goes ahead).

It is important to remember that, although the contribution approach does not rigidly allocate overheads to a specific activity, which can be very difficult, overheads cannot be ignored. The contributions from all the activities that the overheads support must add up to more than the overheads if the business is to survive.

The benefit of the contribution approach is that it looks at what additional costs will be incurred, over and above those that will have to be paid anyway, and so helps to lead to decisions which maximize contribution to profit – as the above example illustrates.

Budgeting

Budgeting is building a 'picture' of a business in numbers. It provides a framework in which to make decisions, and examine the impact of those decisions on the business.

In building a picture or model, there are two major influences:

- External influences – the effect of external influences on likely performance, for example 'How will the launch of my competitor's new model affect my sales in the next 12 months?'
- Internal influences – the effect of internal procedures on each other, for example 'If we sell 5000 units instead of 2000 what effect will this have on our production and handling costs?'

Building a picture of the business does not have to be an all-or-nothing process. It is usually an accumulation of smaller pieces put together by individual managers or departments.

In simple terms, the annual marketing budget is the sum of all the budgets for marketing campaigns proposed for the year, plus a share of the overheads needed to run the business.

The benefits of budgeting

Budgeting should not be seen as simply a form of monetary control. Among the many non-financial benefits of proper budgeting are that it:

- forces us to plan ahead and define our future objectives
- gives us a useful overview and checklist of planned activities
- makes us highlight key actions and responsibilities
- forces us to define measurements of performance
- helps us make decisions about trade-offs and priorities
- gives early warning of problems enabling corrective action.

Budgeting is building a 'picture' of a business in numbers. It provides a framework in which to make decisions, and examine the impact of those decisions on the business.

In simple terms, the annual marketing budget is the sum of all the budgets for marketing campaigns proposed for the year, plus a share of the overheads needed to run the business.

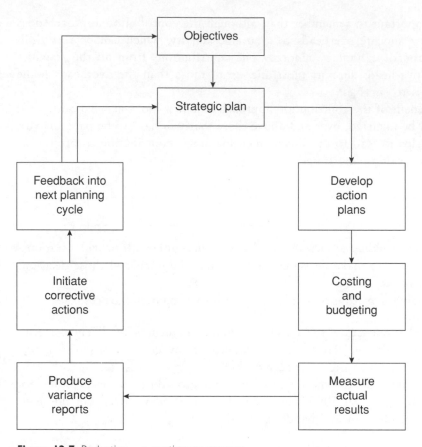

Figure 12.7 Budgeting – a continuous process

Budgeting should not be a one-off process. It is part of a cycle that helps manage a business and improve its performance. To make this happen results must be fed back into the budgeting process so that more accurate estimates (such as the likely response to our next offer) can be made.

The budget is a yardstick for performance measurement. It is a pre-event evaluation and should be the basis for continuous evaluation of actual performance during the budget period.

Providing the budget has been carefully constructed, we can use it to spot potential problems by comparing actual with expected performance.

The budget is a yardstick for performance measurement. It is a pre-event evaluation and should be the basis for continuous evaluation of actual performance during the budget period.

What makes for successful budgeting?

Successful budgeting depends on a number of factors. Failure to observe any one will jeopardize its usefulness and reliability. The main factors are as follows.

- Co-operation and communication between all the people concerned – office politics should be outlawed. Energies devoted to 'politics' could be used more usefully to plan better campaigns.
- Realistic targets – many plans fail because targets are unrealistically high or low. Both of these are de-motivating to staff.
- Consistent objectives – a business cannot be run like a speedboat. Frequent short-term changes in policy leave staff with a 'who knows/who cares' attitude.
- An easily understood format – budgeting is not just for accountants. If staff understand (and agree with) the business targets, they will be better able to tackle the tasks required. Better still, if they feel they have been consulted in fixing the targets they will 'own' them and work harder to help achieve them.
- Frequent reviews of progress and of the system itself – a manager or director who is open to suggestion and comment deserves, and usually gets, more committed employees. One of the best ways of improving your budgeting, forecasting and eventual performance is to get those at the sharp end involved at the planning stage.

Creating a campaign budget

The first step in creating a campaign budget is to define the structure of the campaign. Are we approaching existing customers or new prospects? If new, are we planning to use direct mail or advertising?

Having broadly defined the campaign we can then identify the various costs we are likely to incur, and the inter-relationships between them.

Figure 12.8 is a typical structure for a new customer acquisition campaign.

We can now look at each section of the campaign, start to build a detailed picture of what costs we are likely to incur and the various elements that influence the costs, and start to build budget models.

The typical cost components for an acquisition campaign are:

- press advertising – copy and design, artwork and media space
- public relations – expenses
- Web site – ad hoc development costs
- direct mail – design, artwork, print and production; list rental; and filling, despatch and postage
- bureau costs – lasering and de-duplicating; and data capture and data processing
- response costs – freepost, telephone and business reply service; handling costs; and data capture and de-duplication
- telemarketing – time, reporting and direct mail follow-up
- sales costs – sales calls and telephone calls

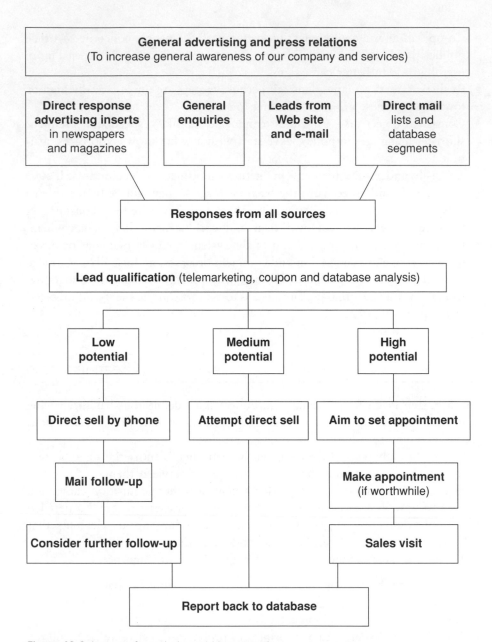

Figure 12.8 Layout of a typical acquisition campaign

- fulfilment material (enquiry packs and so on) – design and artwork; print and production; brochures; letter-headings; and envelopes
- other costs – such as premises and insurance
- overheads – allocated costs for staff and so on.

The final step is to draw up the individual campaign budgets and then to consolidate these into an overall annual marketing budget. Of course, each budget will have its own requirements and the details will vary according to the type of work involved.

Figure 12.9 shows an example of a budget for an acquisition campaign. In this example, a small net profit is made in addition to which:

- we will cover £24,000 of overheads
- we will have 9875 active customers, and 29,625 enquirers to follow up for future orders.

Press relations	Costs	£5000	**£5000**
Direct response advertising	Design fees, artwork, etc. Space costs	£10,000 £150,000	
Loose inserts	Artwork and print Inserting charges	£65,000 £65,000	**£290,000**
Direct mail (50,000 names)	Creative fees and artwork Print List rental Assembly and enclosing Postage (@ £0.20)	£10,000 £20,000 £6250 £750 £10,000	**£47,000**
Response costs (all media)	Postage (@ £0.22 × 17,500) Telephone costs (£1 × 17,000) Data capture and processing Handling @ £1.50	£3850 £17,000 £3000 £51,750	**£75,600**
Telemarketing costs	Direct mail follow-up test (£5 × 5000) Extra handling costs (2000 additional leads) Administration, management, etc.	£25,000 £3000 £2500	**£30,500**
Fulfilment materials (packs)	Complete (@ 50 pence)	£18,250	**£18,250**
Total costs of campaign			**£466,350**
Total sales value	9,875 orders – average gross margin £50		**£493,750**
Contribution			**£27,400**
Overheads Allocated proportion:	Staff costs Premises, etc.	£18,000 £6000	**£24,000**
	Net profit		**£3,400**

Figure 12.9 Example budget for an acquisition campaign budget

If these estimates are realized this will be considered a successful campaign.

Note that the above costings, whilst typical of those you may incur, are only hypothetical. You must use numbers that relate to your own business, taking the above as a framework only. You will also have to make a judgement regarding the balance between short-term profit and investment in future sales.

Customer lifetime value analysis

One of the key questions in developing customer acquisition plans is 'How much can I afford to invest in recruiting a new customer?' It is a very simple question, but is not an easy one to answer. If our planning process stops at the 'allowable cost' level, that is we expect to make profit from the first transaction, then the question answers itself. We are not prepared to invest anything, expecting all new customers to show profit from day one.

However, this may not be the best way to build a business. If we are confident that new customers will consider our products or services to be good value, and if we have the possibility of future orders, we can expect to receive a continuing flow of business for some time to come.

If we have confidence in the probability of this future stream of business, it makes sense to consider investing some proportion of future profits in order to maximize the number of new customers we recruit. So, now we can return to the question of how much to invest in recruiting a new customer.

In fact, this question cannot be answered with any degree of confidence until we can answer another question, which is 'How much will a new customer be worth to me in net profit over the time they continue to buy from me?'

This is another difficult question, but this and the earlier one can at least be tackled using a process called lifetime value analysis. Lifetime value analysis is a method of predicting the likely profitability of customers by modelling their future behaviour based on analysis of their (or other customers') previous actions.

Lifetime value analysis can also be used to measure the effects of marketing and loyalty programmes, but we should deal with the basic problem first.

Lifetime value analysis is a method of predicting the likely profitability of customers by modelling their future behaviour based on analysis of their (or other customers') previous actions.

Lifetime value is the net present value of the profit that a company will realize on a new customer during his or her 'lifetime' as a customer. 'Lifetime' is not to be taken literally – it really means over a number of years, typically 3, 5 or 10 years. A life insurance or mortgage company may choose to evaluate lifetime value over a longer period, but, as we shall see, there are reasons why this is not only difficult but also unsafe.

The best way of explaining the process of lifetime analysis is to take an example and work through it step by step.

Table 12.2 A 5-year 'Lifetime value' projection

		Year 1	Year 2	Year 3	Year 4	Year 5
A	Customers	1000	500	275	165	115.5
B	Retention	50%	55%	60%	70%	80%
C	Sales per annum	£600	£660	£720	£780	£840
D	Total sales	£600,000	£330,000	£198,000	£128,700	£97,020
E	Net profit 20%	£120,000	£66,000	£39,600	£25,740	£19,404
F	Discount rate	1	0.86	0.7396	0.636	0.547
G	NPV Contribution	£120,000	£56,760	£29,288	£16,372	£10,614
H	Cumulative NPV contribution	£120,000	£176,760	£206,048	£222,420	£233,034
I	Lifetime value at net present value	£120.00	£176.76	£206.05	£222.42	£233.03

Table 12.2 shows the projections for a group of new customers over a 5-year period. Note that 1000 has been chosen as an illustration. The actual number of customers can be more or less. The important point is that we need a sizeable group of customers to allow for attrition, that is the loss of some customers who do not continue to buy year after year.

Now we can work through this table row by row.

Row A shows how many of the 1000 original customers we expect to remain 'loyal', that is to continue to buy year after year. This expectation is based on an assumed retention rate. Note that in Year 5 we show 115.5 customers – we cannot of course have half customers in real life, but if we build these models on a spreadsheet we will often encounter fractions of customers. It is important to leave these in the model unchanged because when we multiply customer numbers by annual sales figures the differences caused by rounding can be quite significant.

After this point rounding has a less dramatic effect so, apart from the customer row and the final lifetime value calculation the numbers have been rounded to the nearest pound.

Note that if you work this table through with a calculator, you will also find odd anomalies due to the rounding effects inherent in Excel. For example, in Year 4 Row F the discount rate is shown as 0.636 and if you multiply the number in Row E (£25,740) by this you will arrive at a slightly different figure to the one shown. This is because Excel has rounded the figure 0.636 down from 0.636056. These small differences are not very important as the entire process is based on some major assumptions that we shall examine shortly.

Lifetime value is the net present value of the profit that a company will realize on a new customer during his or her 'lifetime' as a customer. 'Lifetime' is not to be taken literally – it really means over a number of years, typically 3, 5 or 10 years.

Row B shows the retention rate we expect – at the end of the first year we only expect to retain 50% because many new customers will be simply trying us out and will return to their regular supplier in future. However, the retention rate tends to increase year by year, as, by definition, customers who stay longer are more loyal.

Row C shows the average amount spent by each of these customers each year. In this projection it is estimated that sales will increase by £60 per customer per year.

Row D shows the total revenue each year from customers who remain out of the original 1000. It is simply the number of customers remaining (A) multiplied by the average yearly sales (C).

Row E shows the net profit. Costs can include raw materials, processing costs, overheads, marketing and so on. The total costs are assumed to be 80%, leaving a net profit of 20%.

Note that these numbers have been selected arbitrarily as an example. When using this process, you should use numbers that make sense in your own business. The only necessity is to keep this figure constant throughout the entire calculation. This is because one of the main uses of these calculations, apart from the basic one of showing how much a customer is worth over time, is to compare the effects of varying marketing strategies (for example the difference caused to long-term (lifetime) value by adopting a new marketing approach). In this case, there would be two or more cells of customers, one cell for each different programme.

So long as we keep to the same cost percentage throughout the evaluation, we can be sure we are comparing like with like. In this context, the precise profit figure is not necessarily of crucial importance so long as it is approximately correct.

Net present value

Net present value refers to the fact that in order to make sensible evaluation of future profits, we need to discount the amounts received in future years. This process is called discounted cash flow.

You may ask 'Why do we need to discount future profits?' This is the element of lifetime value analysis with which people have most trouble. The reason we need to discount profits is simply that money has a cost – the value of a pound received in 2, 3 or 5 years' time is not the same as the value of a pound received today. Put simply, if I have a pound now I can invest it and it will appreciate by the interest rate I can achieve from my bank. If you owe me £10 and you do not return it for 5 years, I have lost the potential earning power of that money. Its value is, therefore, £10 minus the interest it would have earned had you given it to me now. This reduced amount is the net present value of my £10.

> Net present value refers to the fact that in order to make sensible evaluation of future profits, we need to discount the amounts received in future years. This process is called discounted cash flow.

This is important because we will in many cases be considering investing money today (in customer recruitment campaigns, database developments and so on) to recruit customers whose sales will materialize over a period of years.

By how much should we discount future profits? The simple answer is to use the expected rate of interest. If we borrow £1,000 today and intend to repay it in 1 year's time, the lender will expect some interest. For the purposes of this example, the interest rate is assumed to be 7%. Whatever rate we use, the simple interest level will be sufficient for something so clear-cut as a loan. However, when we are dealing with less tangible factors, such as predictions of future sales, it will not be prudent to allow only today's interest rate.

Sensible marketers increase the discount rate to allow for the additional risks inherent in any long-term business relationship. Examples of such risks include that:

- our product could be superseded by a revolutionary new development
- interest rates may rise above our estimate of 7% – in the mid 1990s, UK interest rates were in double figures
- our competitors may prove to be better at marketing than we are and thus take market share away from us
- we may make mistakes – even with the most careful planning, this can happen.

For these and other reasons, it is sensible to base our discount rate on a higher figure, and in this example we have doubled the expected interest rate to 14% (the original 7% plus an extra 7% to reflect the additional risks outlined above).

This may seem very conservative, but as one of the main purposes of this analysis is to justify investment to create future profits, it is safer to be conservative. As with the net profit row, you should base this on numbers that make sense in your own business. Your accountant or financial controller will tell you what rate is used in your company.

Row F – once we have settled on the discount rate, we can apply it year by year. Each year will have a different discount rate, of course, as the numbers compound year by year. There are various ways of applying the discount but the easiest is simply to convert the rate to a decimal and multiply the net profit in Row E by that decimal.

Note that in Year 1 we do not discount profits. This is deemed to be earned within the same accounting period and, thus, is retained at its full value. So let's see the process in action in Year 2.

If the discount rate is 14%, the decimal we need to use is 0.86 (100 minus 14). We multiply our net profit (£66,000) by 0.86 to arrive at the net present value contribution of £56,760.

In subsequent years, the discount rate is simply 0.86 compounded. Thus, in Year 3 the rate is 0.86 multiplied by 0.86, which is 0.7396. Multiplying this figure by 0.86 again gives us 0.636056 for Year 4. (Excel shows this as 0.636, but actually calculates the net present value figure using the full decimal.) A similar rounding can be seen with Year 5 – try it on your calculator.

Row G – it is now a simple matter to calculate each year's net present value figure and then accumulate these year by year in Row H.

Row I, the lifetime value row, is simply derived by dividing the cumulative net present value contribution in Row H by the original number of customers (1000 in this model).

What this shows us is the lifetime value at net present value for each of the customers we recruited – regardless of the fact that some of them have stopped being customers. As we can see, to divide by the number of customers remaining would not answer the difficult question we posed a few pages ago of 'How much is a new customer worth to us over time?'

In this example, the lifetime value at net present value of those 1000 customers we recruited in Year 1 is predicted to total £233,034. Dividing this by the original number of customers in the cell (1000) means that each is predicted to be worth £233.03 over the 5-year period.

It is worth repeating that the final calculation (Row I in each year) is always the cumulative net present value contribution for that year divided by the number of customers we started with at the beginning of the model, not for that year.

Before moving on to the next stage, which will show how lifetime value analysis can be used to predict, and eventually compare, the effectiveness of different marketing strategies, we can summarize briefly the key elements of lifetime value modelling.

The entire success of these models depends on three factors:

• applying a sensible rate of discount
• the accuracy of our estimated retention rate
• how well we have predicted annual sales per customer.

The first, discount rate is a matter of judgement, but every company applies the principle of discounted cash flow, so your financial director will be able to tell you what rate your company considers appropriate. You should simply use that figure.

The other two are more difficult to predict, so most marketers, when using these models for the first time, base these factors on historical analysis of other customer groups.

The technique is simply to review the buying and retention patterns of a group of customers who started from a similar source to those you now wish to model, but who have been buying from the company for 2 years or more.

This analysis will enable you to calculate their retention rate and, of course, their average sales per year.

Where there are no previous customers, we are forced to build our own historical file before we can start. Thus, we can only start with customers who have at least 1 year's history with us.

It is important to remember that this analysis will be used to make invest-ment decisions, so we must be conservative in our estimates, especially in the early days. As time goes on, we can measure the actual retention rates and sales and adjust our model accordingly.

Using lifetime value modelling to evaluate marketing strategies

We can also use lifetime value analysis and, in particular, the retention and sales figures, as a measure of the relative effectiveness of alternative marketing strategies.

Let us assume we wish to test a new customer retention strategy. This strategy is to anticipate customers' needs by means of a sophisticated data-base system fed by information from detailed questionnaires. These questionnaires are gathered in various ways – via the sales force, telephone, post, Web site and e-mail.

The objective of this new strategy is to increase sales and retention rates by targeting our communications to increase their relevance and, thus, their acceptability and effectiveness.

The plan is to contact individual customers to make relevant offers at appropriate times.

The information on which this strategy is based must be accurate and up to date. This requires much effort by employees working in sales, marketing and telemarketing and those operating the database. Indeed, good database management is crucial. In each promotional cycle, the database identifies customers for whom a specific offer would be appropriate. In addition to identifying the individuals, the system should:

- match products to customer types and buying patterns
- indicate the potential value of each prospect enabling an appropriate offer to be made (for example, a firm selling catering foods to cafés and restau-rants would make a different offer to a café selling 50 meals a day than it would to one selling 1000 meals a day)
- produce the necessary personalized communications
- monitor results, produce reports and update customer records.

We can now produce some lifetime value models to see how effective the new strategy might be. The first step is to build a base table like Table 12.2 on p. 273. This is built on the basis that, apart from the despatch of the annual catalogue, for example, no additional customer marketing is carried out.

This table is the base against which we compare our predictions in the following table (Table 12.3) – the one that allows for the extra expenditure and its likely effects on our customers.

We develop our marketing ideas and build the likely effects into the second table. We then monitor closely to measure the actual effects of the new programme as it progresses.

We start with the assumption that if we treat our customers well, they will respond better – if we only communicate with them when we have an offer that is relevant to them, rather than simply mailing each customer with every offer, we will generate more sales at less cost. We will also retain more customers year to year.

Customer retention strategy (loyalty building) affects the following five things.

1 Recommendations – satisfied customers are more likely to recommend us to their friends and colleagues. We can also undertake positive marketing actions to encourage this.
2 Retention – building relationships by regular communication tends to increase customer retention.
3 Sales – targeted database activities can be expected to increase cross-selling, up-selling and frequency of purchase.
4 Profits – database activities can also help us reduce costs, in some cases, by changing distribution channels. Companies selling via resellers, for example, find they can dramatically reduce their costs when they sell further products by direct mail to their database customers (that is those who return warranty cards or register in some other way). Great care must be exercised with such a strategy, of course, so as to avoid alienating existing profitable business channels.
5 Marketing costs – the estimated costs of running the new communications programmes have also to be built into the lifetime value model.

Well-planned marketing campaigns, targeting only those prospects more likely to be interested, can actually achieve the same or even more sales at less cost. Furthermore, if the funds invested are transferred from another less cost-efficient form of programme, they can actually reduce overall marketing costs.

The objective of a retention strategy is to increase the first four factors, recognizing that costs will also increase, especially to the targeted segments.

A good example of this is the experience of a major high street bank. Before it started to segment customers, it sent out around 80 promotional mailings a year, with little customer targeting. Now it sends around 400 mailings a year, each to a tightly targeted segment of its customer file. Of course, this new policy has increased its costs, but the return on investment from the programme has grown by more than 300%.

We now develop a second model using our best estimates of the changes the new programme will cause. Table 12.3 shows how these factors can affect our calculations.

Again, we will work through the table row by row.

In Row A we have assumed that, by developing better relationships through making more relevant offers, we can encourage 5% of our customers to recommend someone to us. If this assumption is correct our customer base will increase by 5% each year. Thus, our Year 1 base of 1000 customers will bring in 50 additional customers during the year (Row B) and these can be added to our Year 2 customer strength.

Note that this is the only circumstance in which new customers can be added to the model during its life. Our objective is to track only the performance of the 1000 customers recruited in Year 1. However, the recommended customers are with us only because we recruited those 1000 in the first place so they can be added legitimately.

In Row D, we are assuming that better customer management and communications will increase our retention rate in Year 1 from 50% to 60% with

Table 12.3 A 5-year lifetime value showing the effect on the retention strategy

		Year 1	Year 2	Year 3	Year 4	Year 5
A	Recommend rate	5%	5%	5%	5%	5%
B	Customers gained		50	33	23	17
C	Customers	1000	650	455	341	273
D	Retention	60%	65%	70%	75%	80%
E	Sales per annum	£720	£800	£880	£960	£1040
F	Total sales	£720,000	£520,000	£400,400	£327,600	£283,920
G	Net profit (20%)	£144,000	£104,000	£80,080	£65,520	£56,784
H	Retention activities (£10)	£10,000	£6500	£4550	£3413	£2730
I	Net contribution	£134,000	£97,500	£75,530	£62,108	£54,054
J	Discount rate	1	0.86	0.7396	0.636	0.547
K	NPV contribution	£134,000	£83,850	£55,862	£39,504	£29,568
L	Cumulative NPV contribution	£134,000	£217,850	£273,712	£313,216	£342,784
M	Lifetime value at net present value	£134.00	£217.85	£273.71	£313.22	£342.78

a 5% increase in the rate each year. This is a very conservative assumption – many programmes have produced much better gains than this.

How much control do we have over the retention rate? We can control our marketing activities and, by careful testing, identify factors that increase or decrease the retention rate. We can also control the level of service we offer and, thus, our customers' perceptions of us as a supplier.

There are, of course, some things we cannot control directly:

- our competitors – they may make better offers than we do
- the economy – the UK recession in the early 1990s ruined many carefully constructed marketing plans
- world news – many well-planned marketing campaigns failed miserably during the early days of the Gulf War when many customers had a lot more on their minds than making buying decisions.

If we have estimated our recommends and retention rates correctly, we will see a considerable increase in the number of customers remaining with us year on year. So in Row C this time in Year 5, instead of having only 115 of our original 1000 customers we have 273 remaining. But there is more to come.

If we are going to spend more time and money communicating with our customers, it is reasonable to assume that they will buy more from us – we do not yet know how much but some increase is highly likely. We have estimated this at 20% in Year 1 (£600 plus 20%, which is £720), with a slightly better increase in subsequent years, as our experience grows.

This may not prove totally accurate, of course, but it is typical of what many retention programmes have achieved and careful monitoring will soon tell us how good our estimating is. Of course, we can adjust our model as time goes on to reflect actual achievements in the earlier years.

The improvements in customer strength and sales have a dramatic effect on our 'total sales' shown in Row F.

Row H is the cost of retention activities. We have allowed £10 per customer per year for this programme. This should be enough for some database work, and some customer communications.

Note that although based on fact, the figures in these models are hypothetical to demonstrate the process. You must calculate your own figures based on conditions in your own company and industry.

Rows I to M are calculated in the same way as rows E to I in Table 12.2.

Comparison of lifetime values with and without the retention programme

Table 12.4 compares the bottom lines of the previous two tables (lifetime value at net present value) on p. 273 and p. 279, and we can clearly see the difference between the values with and without the new communications programme (assuming our projections are correct).

This shows that if our assumptions are correct, our customer retention programme will increase the average lifetime value of each customer recruited (not just those remaining) by £109.75.

It means that if we have a total of 1000 customers, and we can increase their lifetime (5-year) profit by an average of £109.75, we will add £109,750 to the bottom line. With 5000 customers the additional profit would amount to £548,750.

Common questions

- What if the analysis predicts a drop in profits? Although the above example shows a worthwhile gain in net profit, not all retention building programmes will work so well. In effect, we are seeking a positive balance between the extra expenditure we need to implement the programme and the additional profit it produces. Sometimes the additional costs incurred in building the database and implementing programmes can be more than the gains. Costs, especially those relating to database development, must be allocated carefully and fairly, particularly if they can also contribute to future developments. However, even if the predictions are negative, the lifetime value analysis will give us early warning and prevent us from pumping further money into a redundant strategy.
- How long is 'lifetime'? In our example, we have used a period of 5 years, but is this correct? The answer is that the period varies according to business circumstances. A consumer mail order company, for example, may use a period of 5 years, whereas a life insurance company may consider 20 years the minimum. A bank may use 5 years for a current account customer,

Table 12.4 Comparison of LTV – with v. without the retention programmes

	Year 1	Year 2	Year 3	Year 4	Year 5
Table 12.2 (on p. 273)	£120.00	£176.76	£206.05	£222.42	£233.03
Table 12.3 (on p. 279)	£134.00	£217.85	£273.71	£313.22	£342.78
Increase	£14.00	£41.09	£67.66	£90.80	£109.75
1000 customers	£14,000	£41,090	£67,660	£90,800	£109,750
5000 customers	£70,000	£205,450	£338,300	£454,000	£548,750

but 25 years for a mortgage customer. It is sensible to work out models for a number of periods, then, in the light of prevailing conditions in your own market place, ask 'What is a sensible period for us?'

• Why not run the model through until there are no customers left? My answer is that, as this is a predictive technique, it is full of assumptions. Therefore, to stop when there are still a good number of customers in the model gives an additional margin of safety. Even if we have been optimistic in our sales estimates, the fact that some customers remain means that we will probably reach our profit target eventually even if it takes a little longer than we predicted.

Predicting lifetime value by customer segment

Lifetime value analysis is not just used to make investment decisions and compare retention strategies. Many companies also use it to compare the longer-term quality of customers recruited by different media or offers. For example, we may be able to increase the number of new customers by offering a free gift with first purchase, but this offer *may* attract a less committed customer whose future buying behaviour may be markedly different from the customer who first bought without an inducement.

Lifetime value is likely to vary according to the medium we used for recruitment, the product first purchased, the time of year that the first purchase was made and so on.

Where possible, we should segment customers by type (perhaps taking account of geo-demographic and lifestyle factors), product, source (such as mailings, press and television) and by the type of offer that originally attracted them.

We may then see that differing levels of investment are appropriate for each segment – perhaps ranging from thousands of pounds to zero. If we do not segment down to this level we will be ignoring one of the key strategic benefits of direct marketing, that is the ability to vary programmes, timing, even copy according to the response and buying patterns we predict or observe for each segment.

How to develop lifetime value calculations

Lifetime value predictions are not as difficult as they may seem. The essential steps are as follows.

1   Select the samples. Size is not critical, as long as there are enough of them to leave a significant sample in the final year of the model. They should have become customers at around the same time and, if this is the first LTV exercise in the company, more than 1 year ago. Unless there is at least 1 year's data, we will not be able to make sensible estimates of

annual sales and retention rates. It would be better to have 2 years' data.

2 Calculate the retention rate into Year 2 from Year 1. Estimate retention rates for the remaining years of the model. First year retention is likely to be lower than subsequent years.

3 Calculate annual sales.

4 Calculate costs and profit margins.

5 Decide on an appropriate discount rate. Be prudent and remember the risks.

6 Project the figures over the remaining years of the model, as in Tables 12.2, p. 273 and 12.3 p. 279. Build the model in a spreadsheet such as Excel. This makes it easy to make modifications and instantly see the results.

7 Plot the effects of various assumptions: 'What if I can increase retention by a further 5%?', 'Let's see what will happen if I spend £15 a head on the retention programme', 'Suppose I cut my predicted gains in half?' and so on.

8 Keep practising the technique. Do not stop experimenting and checking actual results against predictions.

Lifetime value analysis – summary

For many businesses, lifetime value analysis is a practical realistic technique for determining the effectiveness of various marketing strategies. It can be applied to a marketing plan to predict the likely outcome before a significant amount of money is spent.

Before acting on hunches and presumptions, we work hard to prove, at least in theory, whether any proposed programme has a chance of success, and if not, which factor needs to be improved.

The theory can be tested as the programme progresses, and the activity can be modified or even abandoned if the assumptions prove to be incorrect. The basic idea is to produce strategies that increase lifetime value by as much as possible. Once we have set up a model like Table 12.3, p. 279 it is possible, using theoretical 'what if' analyses, to see what we can do to increase lifetime value. The effect of each possible action can be estimated to determine whether the result is likely to be worth the investment.

As mentioned earlier, not all customer development programmes will prove to be cost-effective. Constant rigorous evaluation is necessary so that non-productive programmes can be identified and abandoned quickly.

SUMMARY

This chapter has looked at the process of evaluation, measurement and budgeting. We have seen that measurement and accountability are key advantages of response driven direct marketing.

One of the benefits of measurement is the understanding of where revenue comes from – is it from existing or acquired customers? This allows the company to focus its marketing activity on the most profitable source of business.

We have explored several key direct marketing measures, including the use of cost per thousand as a way of comparing different quotes; cost per enquiry, lead, reply, response, order or sale as a way of evaluating campaigns; and percent response rate.

We have seen the importance of the allowable cost per order. A mini profit and loss account was developed that allowed us to arrive at this key measure, and we saw how it helped us to work out required response rates to a mailing. We developed this model within a two-stage campaign.

The strength of the allowable cost approach was made clear from the example used, although we also saw some disadvantages:

- it requires sales and so on to be estimated in advance
- it assumes that costs are fixed
- it simply satisfies rather than maximizes profitability
- it does not take into account any future purchases.

We then looked at ways of overcoming these problems. These included the assessment of the contribution from multiple campaigns.

The examination of the budgeting process began by looking at fixed, variable and overheads or indirect fixed costs and defined each.

We looked at the behaviour of costs over large volumes and saw that, up to a certain point, they generally fall proportionately. However, we also saw that after a certain volume there were only limited savings available as the economies of scale had been used. The importance of understanding costs was stressed, as it is necessary to have a clear view on the profit of each activity.

We went on to consider how we should manage overheads and explored the contribution approach. This takes into account all the revenue and costs directly associated with an activity. We followed a detailed example, showing the value of the contribution approach to costs in looking at the additional costs incurred in carrying out any activity.

We have also looked at the internal and external influences on the budgeting process and explored the benefits of budgeting. These were seen to be that it:

- forces us to plan ahead and define our future objectives
- gives us a useful overview and checklist of planned activities
- makes us highlight key actions and responsibilities
- forces us to define measurements of performance
- helps us make decisions about trade-offs and priorities
- gives early warning of problems enabling corrective action.

We looked at the process of budgeting and saw that it was a continuous process to help manage and improve business performance.

We have seen that successful budgeting depends on several factors:

- co-operation and communication between all the people concerned
- the setting of realistic targets
- consistent and sustained objectives
- an easily understood format that is 'owned' by staff
- frequent reviews of progress and of the system itself.

We saw how to create a campaign budget and this was developed through a worked example of an acquisition campaign.

We went on to explore the key problem for all companies of how much to invest in creating a new customer. This question is answered in part through the use of lifetime value calculations. Lifetime value was defined as the net present value of the profit that a company will realize on a new customer during his or her time as a customer.

We saw that 'customer lifetime' for various companies will vary considerably. We explored the concept through a worked example. We explored each line in detail and saw that the key element in the calculation was of net present value and by how much we should discount future profits. In the example we used 14%, but the amount will vary according to the interest rates at the time, perceived risk factors and industry levels of return on investment.

The use of lifetime value depends on three factors:

1 a sensible rate of discount
2 the accuracy of the assumed retention rate
3 the accuracy of the predicted annual sales per customer.

The importance of conservatism in estimates was stressed, as we went on to consider the use of lifetime value analysis in evaluating marketing strategies.

The whole process is driven by good database management, enabling us to:

- identify individuals
- match products to customer types and buying cycles
- indicate potential value of each prospect
- produce personalized communication
- monitor results.

We can then produce a lifetime value analysis comparing the impact of alternative strategies.

We should see a loyalty strategy impacting in five areas:

1   recommendation rates
2   retention rates
3   sales
4   profits
5   costs.

A worked example enabled us to see this in practice.

We were able to compare lifetime value with and without the new communications programme.

We have seen that lifetime value analysis allows us to:

- evaluate expensive retention programmes
- focus on the long-term life of a customer and to answer the question of what is a sensible period for us to expect a customer to remain with us
- compare sources of recruitment or market segments to identify those offering the best business potential.

The chapter has finished with a summary of the process for the development of lifetime value calculations and the need to recognize lifetime value as a diagnostic tool to help business decisions.

REVIEW QUESTIONS

1   What is the benefit of measurability in direct marketing?

2   List three standard measures in direct marketing.

3   What is allowable cost per order?

4   How is allowable cost used in setting campaign budgets?

5   What are the strengths and weaknesses of the allowable cost approach?

6   What are the three types of costs in business?

7   Define overheads.

8   What happens to costs with quantity?

9   Why is it important to understand costs and the way they behave?

10   Define the contribution approach to costs.

11   List six benefits of the budgeting process.

12   What are the stages of the budgeting process?

13   What are the requirements for a successful budget?

14   What is net present value?

15   What is the role of lifetime value analysis in direct marketing?

16   What are the three requirements for successful lifetime value calculations?

17   What is a customer lifetime?

EXERCISES

You may wish to set up a spreadsheet for this exercise.

Develop a 5-year lifetime value calculation using the following figures:

- 1000 customers in Year 1
- retention 50% per year
- sales £600 per year, increasing at 5% per year
- net profit 15%
- discount rate 15%.

Then see what would be the impact of:

1   reducing the discount rate to 10%
2   spending an additional £60 per customer on a retention scheme that leads to a recommends rate of 5% and an increase in retention to 60% per year.

Chapter 13

Choosing and briefing suppliers

Introduction
- Mailing list suppliers
  - The rental contract
  - De-duplication
  - Lifestyle database companies
- Mailing and fulfilment houses
- Database and computer bureaux
- Web-site consultants and designers
- Printers
- Direct marketing agencies
- Using a consultant
- Where to find specialist suppliers
- Choosing the right supplier
  - The long list
  - The short list
  - Meet the account handlers
  - Tell them exactly what you want them to do
  - Asking for quotations
  - Expect a rapid acknowledgement
  - Take up business and credit references
  - Comparing quotations
- Writing a clear and effective brief
  - A briefing form

Summary
Review questions
Exercises

However good you are at writing letters or advertisements, organizing the despatch of mailings and so on, there will come a time when you have to consider using external suppliers.

Sooner or later you have to start prioritizing your time and there are many tasks which may be better, or more cost-effectively, done by specialists.

We will now start to discuss some of the specialist resources that you may need and how you can go about finding them. Once you have found them, you have to explain your needs very clearly. The more care given to this, the better the job will turn out. Over many years of using specialist suppliers, I have found that more often than not, when a job goes badly wrong, a good proportion of the blame lies with lax briefing.

By using outside suppliers in the early stages of building a business, you can learn many things, including how to avoid some costly mistakes. Once you have experienced a few campaigns, you will be better able to estimate the cost and implications of providing such facilities in-house.

One advantage of using outside suppliers is that you can expect them to keep their equipment and expertise up to date. This may not be so vital in the case of an envelope-filling machine but could be crucial in the case of data-analysis techniques.

There are many specialist suppliers, but those most frequently required are:

- mailing list suppliers – brokers and owners
- mailing and fulfilment houses
- database and computer bureaux – laser print shops
- Web-site designers and consultants
- printers
- direct marketing agencies or freelance design and creative teams
- consultants.

Mailing list suppliers

There are more than 5000 lists available for rent in the UK – split approximately 50/50 between business lists and consumer lists. It is also possible to buy lists outright, although this is expensive and not always the best option. Unless you have a product or service that will appeal to the majority on a list, you may simply buy a lot of data you will never use again.

The preferred option may be to rent first and make a good offer that encourages interest from the maximum number of good prospects. Once these people have responded, you can put them onto your own database and, subject to the provisions of the Data Protection Act, mail them as often as you like.

Most rented lists are available from list brokers and there are three main ways of finding brokers.

1 Read the advertisements in the trade press (*Precision Marketing, Direct Response, Marketing Direct* and so on). You will also find lists advertised in the business-to-business sections of national newspapers.
2 Contact the Direct Marketing Association and ask for its list of members who are list brokers. These brokers can suggest lists to reach your target audience.
3 Look out for directories that are produced periodically by trade publishers. A good example is the *Direct Marketing Guide*, published by Beyond Communications (the publishers of *Direct Response*). This contains details of many direct marketing suppliers in all fields from full-service agencies to plastic card manufacturers.

The rental contract

List rental contracts are quite specific and should be read carefully. Usually a rental covers a single use of the names and if the renter does not stick to this the broker will know through the use of 'seed' names, that is people who report to the broker when they receive a mailing. Using a rented list more than the agreed number of times is a breach of contract and brokers would be quite within their rights to sue offenders.

Tell the list broker who you are trying to reach. They should be able to offer a number of suggestions of suitable lists.

Lists are supplied in a variety of ways:

- online
- on a magnetic tape, which can only be used by those with access to fairly serious computer equipment
- on a floppy disk – some brokers will supply a disk for use in a PC mail-merge
- on sticky labels or continuous stationery.

Before the data is supplied, the broker or list owner will want to know:

1 how the addresses will be applied to the mailing piece
2 whether there will be a merge/purge (de-duplication) before mailing
3 what the contents of the mailing are – the usual terms of business give the owner the right to vet all material for its suitability.

Note that in some cases the list owner will not release the names at all and will demand that the prospective mailer simply sends all materials to a mailing house for assembly and despatch.

De-duplication

Even when renting a single list, it is worth considering a merge/purge or de-duplication run against your own customer file. This is helpful in a number of ways.

1 It will prevent you from sending people more than one copy of a mailing – saving much prospect irritation.
2 Analysis of the de-duplication run will tell you whether you have chosen good lists: the higher the duplication with your own customer list, the better the rented list will perform; the lower the duplication within a list, the better that list is managed, therefore the more up to date the data is likely to be.
3 You will avoid paying for the names of people already on your database.

Good de-duplication is a highly technical process and not something the average mailer should attempt. An off-the-shelf PC database package may claim to be able to de-duplicate records, but not in the way a good computer bureau would do it.

We do not need to go into the technical details here, but a bureau-operated de-duplication service is likely to be more accurate and more cost-efficient in the long term.

When a list de-duplication is planned, brokers can supply 'industry compatible' tapes. In other words, they will all send their data in compatible formats making the job of matching the lists easier.

Do not worry about having to find a computer bureau for this job yourself, as most list brokers will be able to recommend a suitable supplier.

Lifestyle database companies

We have mentioned lifestyle databases several times and we will now consider them in their role as list providers. All of them can supply good mailing lists, usually with a considerable amount of additional data enabling us to select prospects with great precision. On p. 15 we saw how an insurance company achieved a major increase in response by selecting only those motorists who were due to renew their insurance in the immediate future.

The following examples show what can be achieved.

Example

A leading financial services company wanted to improve the cost-efficiency of their lead generation, which had always been done through press advertising.

They asked Claritas to profile their existing customers and using this profile they selected 40,000 prospects from Claritas Lifestyle Selector. The direct mailings generated leads at half the cost of press advertising with response rates of up to 6%.

Profiling the responses from this test they further refined their selection criteria and this was so successful that they now use Claritas for a monthly mailing programme.

Example

Following their very successful advertising campaigns in the 1980s and early 1990s Zanussi boasts that one in three UK households owns a Zanussi appliance. The positioning adopted in those early advertisements had appealed strongly to younger consumers and the company now wished to replicate this successful approach.

The first step was to check the profile of current buyers and they were surprised to find that this was much older than had been believed. It seems that whilst the buyers of the 1980s were young when they first purchased Zanussi they had remained loyal but of course had grown older. Therefore, current buyers were mainly repeat purchasers rather than new customers.

Zanussi realised that they had a difficult task: 'We need to take action to ensure we build a steady stream of new, younger customers and convert them to similar levels of brand loyalty. However, at the same time, we must not alienate our traditional customers.'

Using PRIZM lifestyle segmentation Claritas identified three younger prospect groups for Zanussi to target and convert to customers. Using direct communications these prospects can be targeted discretely whilst not changing the positioning of communications to their traditional buyers.

Tim Banks, Account Director at Claritas comments: 'As brands evolve it is not unusual for their target markets to change over time. It makes a lot of sense to run regular profile checks to ensure that communications are delivering the right messages to the right audience.'

Mailing and fulfilment houses

A mailing house is an organization that can carry out most or all of the functions involved in assembling and despatching a mailing. These typically include:

- receipt and storage of materials
- assembly – folding, filling, sealing, sorting and bagging mail
- addressing in a variety of ways – sticky labels to laser printing
- letter and order form printing – often with laser addressing
- liaison with and despatch to Royal Mail.

A fulfilment house is an organization that can carry out all or most functions of a mail order company, such as:

- receipt of responses to promotions and mailings
- despatch of ordered goods or information packs
- receipt and storage of goods (including valuables)
- receipt and processing of mail orders
- banking of customer remittances
- picking, packing and despatch of goods
- customer service functions, often including helplines
- reporting of orders, despatches, stock, banking and so on.

Many companies offer all of the above facilities and several specialized add-ons, such as database development, printing and plastic card embossing.

It is important to 'shop around' using the same sourcing methods as described above for list brokers. Once a short list is identified, it is worth visiting a few to get a feel for their capabilities. Are they tidy or untidy? Is their security impressive? Can you speak to some of their existing clients?

The next step is to get a couple of quotations to help you choose. As with all suppliers beware of choosing solely on price. A few hundred pounds saved will not seem very good business if a vital part of the job is carried out badly.

A mailing house is an organization that can carry out most or all of the functions involved in assembling and despatching a mailing.

A fulfilment house is an organization that can carry out all or most functions of a mail order company

Database and computer bureaux

As we discussed in Chapter 6, a database bureau can take away a lot of the uncertainty of database development, especially for first timers. They generally use 'state-of-the-art' software and hardware and are aware of the latest techniques in data processing, analysis and management.

In addition, because they have a range of clients with a variety of problems, they have wider experience and can often develop a practical solution more quickly.

A good database bureau will sympathize with your desire to bring the operation in-house eventually and will help you work towards that goal with enthusiasm.

Computer bureaux are often the same companies as the database bureaux. However, the term 'computer bureau' generally implies a range of ad hoc services such as data capture and enhancement, analysis and output for mailings such as labels and laser letters.

They usually have up-to-date experience in the more sophisticated data analysis techniques such as CHAID, multiple regression and neural networks. Such techniques develop almost daily and no in-house IT department could hope to stay totally up-to-date. Bureaux often specialize in such things and, thus, are more capable of doing the job.

Most bureaux will be happy to demonstrate what they can do and a couple of days' research here will be time well spent.

Computer bureaux are often the same companies as the database bureaux. However, the term 'computer bureau' generally implies a range of ad hoc services such as data capture and enhancement, analysis and output for mailings such as labels and laser letters.

Web-site consultants and designers

In this highly specialized field it is vital to find the right advice. There are lots of 'nerds' about, but you do not want someone who is a wizard at surfing the Internet. What you need is someone who understands the business applications of the Internet and can give you sound commercial advice. In this new field it is even more important to shop around and take up references before committing yourself to a major development. See Chapter 8 for more information.

Printers

If your only requirements are for simple colour leaflets, plain envelopes and single page non-personalized letters, you could choose almost any printer from *Yellow Pages* and receive a good workmanlike job.

If, however, you want to take advantage of, or even simply find out about, the many specialized formats that have been developed by today's direct marketers, you must search a little more carefully.

There are thousands of printers in the UK, but not all of them understand direct marketing. There are many with the right experience, however, and it will usually pay to seek out the good ones.

It is a major mistake to wait until the job is fully designed before talking to printers. Like other specialists, printers have experience that can help you to get a better job more cost-efficiently.

Getting the printer to talk to the designer can pay huge dividends. You may make major savings on print by getting the printer and designer together at the start of the job. In some cases, just moving a fold can make a major difference to the cost. Very few designers have such detailed knowledge, so it makes good sense to take advantage of the skills and knowledge of a print specialist.

Printers can also advise on paper quality and availability, suitable weights, cost-efficient sizes and formats, artwork requirements and so on.

Direct marketing agencies

There are many agencies available, ranging from small 'hot-shops' to huge multi-nationals with offices all over the world. Your choice should be guided by a number of factors. It is important to find an agency that understands and can empathize with your needs and aspirations.

Many small companies seeking rapid success feel they should start at the top and hire a large agency such as Ogilvy One, Impiric, Craik Jones or WWAV Rapp Collins. However, large companies:

- have large overheads, which means their charges are likely to be high (an agency with a salary bill of more than £1 million a month cannot afford to charge small fees)
- have larger clients and it is difficult for a small client to command a high level of service against the demands of large multi-national companies.

On the positive side, large agencies:

- generally offer a wide range of services – apart from the normal media, creative and account management services, many large direct marketing agencies can offer sophisticated planning, research, database and other skills
- have more clients and, therefore, are likely to have a wider range of experience across many product fields.

Choosing an agency is a rather different proposition than choosing a mailing house or a list broker. Although all of them may hopefully be the start of a long relationship, the level of involvement expected with a mailing house or broker will be much less. An agency appointment is generally a much more complex relationship.

When choosing an agency, it is important to be very frank. Many agencies have taken on new clients on a loss-making or break-even basis on the promise of large billings to come. When this does not happen the entire relationship can go sour very quickly.

Many prospective clients have difficulty with the concept that an agency should act like a normal business. Yet, would you ask Tesco to give you your first week's groceries free as a gesture of their desire to have you as a customer? Do you give your own new customers free goods and services as a welcoming gesture?

When I ran Ogilvy & Mather Direct in London, we were often asked for, but almost never produced, speculative work. In fact, we would only agree to do so when my colleagues and I felt we were strong favourites to win a major account.

Of course, it is reasonable to expect some time and free advice about your business, but not finished ideas and creative work. If you are being offered free services from an advertising agency, you might ask how they have time to do this if they very busy. If they are producing free work for you, who is paying for it? If it is their other clients will they use the time you pay for to do the same for another company?

Many of the other considerations about choosing an agency are the same for most suppliers, so we will cover these collectively in the next section.

Using a consultant

It may be worth considering the use of a specialist consultant – either a general direct marketer or perhaps a database development specialist. Good consultants can be expensive, but they can sometimes help to avoid costly or embarrassing mistakes.

This decision should hinge on the overall advantage to the business and this is not a simple judgement to make. A consultant's charges could easily be more than the cost of hiring a full-time assistant, so the first thing to do is to make an objective decision about your existing resources and experience.

If you have plenty of experience but are simply short of time, a good assistant may well be a better investment. On the other hand, if your experience is limited, it can be very helpful to have a seasoned adviser available 'on tap'.

This is a list of some services you could reasonably expect an experienced consultant to provide:

- market analysis and strategic planning
- targeting of prospects and sales forecasting
- mailing list selection
- location and selection of specialist suppliers, such as advertising agencies, creative teams, mailing and fulfilment houses, computer and telemarketing bureaux and printers
- production of, and/or evaluation of creative work
- recruitment of staff

- specialized training for yourself and your staff
- product design and development.

There are many consultants available – subject them to the same careful selection procedure as you would an agency or database bureau.

Where to find specialist suppliers

As mentioned under 'Mailing list suppliers', a good starting point is the Direct Marketing Association, the address of which you will find in Chapter 14. Membership of the Association does not guarantee that a supplier will have a greater knowledge of direct marketing than a non-member will, but there is a better chance that this will be so.

Therefore, your first step should be to ask the Direct Marketing Association for its list of member suppliers in your required area. Amongst its members are direct marketing agencies, mailing and fulfilment houses, list brokers, database and computer bureaux and printers.

Among the advantages of choosing Association member companies are that they:

- subscribe to the Association's Code of Conduct, so you can be assured of certain minimum standards
- are likely to know more about the special requirements of direct marketers than non-members.

Do not forget the other routes:

- directories, such as the *Direct Marketing Guide* and even Thomsons and *Yellow Pages*
- trade press advertisements
- trade fairs and exhibitions – many suppliers take stands at the annual Direct Marketing Fair in the spring.

Choosing the right supplier

Once you have assembled your list of potential suppliers, you have to start evaluating them. This task can be broken down into stages to reduce your involvement at the start.

First, build a list of potential suppliers from the above sources. You can make some basic judgements from their advertisements or directory descriptions. Then write to those which look interesting asking them to tell you:

- what they can do for you, in other words what experience they have in your field
- who their clients are – the answer you receive will be the most revealing you get; as well as gauging their experience in your field, you can make sure they are not dealing with one of your major competitors
- their basis for charging – where possible you should look for project or 'menu' fees rather than hourly or daily rates
- why they should be given the job – their answer will tell you how keen they are to get your business.

This preliminary process can be completed without major time input on your behalf. The responses to your basic 'questionnaire' will give you enough information to draw up a 'long' list.

The long list

This is an intermediate stage that you may or may not use. It will vary according to whether you are placing a single project or looking for a long-term relationship with an agency or bureau. Briefly, you decide on, for example, the six or eight most interesting candidates and telephone them for a detailed discussion. Again, this is an economical use of your time, as there is no sense in travelling all over the country to ask questions which can just as easily be raised by telephone. The responses and perceived level of interest from each candidate simplify the job of producing your short list.

The short list

Now comes the labour-intensive work. You cannot complete this stage by telephone. However, as your list should contain no more than three or four 'probables', it is not an impossible burden.

The first task is to arrange to visit them at their premises. Many marketing executives insist on suppliers coming to them, but in the early stages (especially during the initial selection process) it can be useful to visit suppliers. How can you possibly get a feel for a business by meeting their people on your own, or neutral ground? You need to get a feel for the place, to look around and see if it looks efficient, and to talk to the workers to judge whether they seem happy and co-operative.

Meet the account handlers

During your visit, you should ask to meet the people who will be responsible for handling your business on a day-to-day basis. Senior management and sales people will impress you with their knowledge and experience, but if they will not be personally involved in managing your business, this may be irrelevant or even misleading.

Tell them exactly what you want them to do

Many suppliers make mistakes because they have not understood precisely what their clients want. Of course they should tell you they do not understand, but, unless you have actively encouraged this, they are often too embarrassed to admit it.

Once a mistake is made, many suppliers will try to cover it up – even though this can add to the problem in many cases. This is human nature and quite understandable. The best way to avoid this is to make sure that your brief is clear, complete and understood in full. You can make sure of this if you ask them to help you write your brief. Your suppliers are the best people to tell you what they need to know. They have been at the receiving end of many briefs – good and bad – and can help you avoid the worst pitfalls, but only if you encourage their input. Far from it being unprofessional to ask a supplier for help, it is in fact highly professional. By doing so, you are encouraging your suppliers to give of their best, and encouraging ownership of the project.

Asking for quotations

Once you have agreed on the brief you can invite quotations. Let them know you have asked for other quotations, but do not overdo it. Agencies do not mind quoting or pitching against a couple of others, but will rarely be prepared to get into major bidding contests.

Expect a rapid acknowledgement

The best suppliers are the busiest, so do not be surprised if they ask for a few days before they send you a full quotation. However, they should acknowledge your brief very quickly, either by telephone or mail. If they feel they are too busy to pick up the telephone what will happen when they have a problem on your job?

Take up business and credit references

No reputable supplier will hesitate to give you the names of existing customers. Naturally, they will put you in touch with their favourite clients. You can choose to contact them or you could 'go it alone' and ask some of their other clients. Whichever option you choose, this is an important part of the process.

It is also, sadly, important to run a credit check on a potential supplier. I once had a large mailing for IBM ready to be posted, when the mailing house, the UK subsidiary of a major international group, went into receivership. The receiver would not release our mailing and the whole programme had to be abandoned. That taught my colleagues and me two valuable lessons – one about references and the other about insurance.

Comparing quotations

When comparing quotations make sure you are comparing like with like. Suppliers will try to bend your requirements to fit their systems or experience. This is fine to a point, but if you do not want that extra report which only their unique system can deliver, then why pay for it. If you are not happy with 'extras' like these, simply tell the supplier to quote again without the trimmings.

Some will, some will not, but the time to argue about it is before you give them your business.

Once you have the quotations in a form that makes a comparison possible, you can start to make decisions. But remember that price should not be your only consideration. As with many other things, you tend to get what you pay for, and that £500 you saved will not be worth much if you have to spend several days sorting things out later.

You need to balance the price quoted with your assessment of their capabilities. Do they impress you with their systems and their staff? Do they seem the sort of people to take problems off your hands or to present you with new ones?

Writing a clear and effective brief

As your brief will vary according to the type of job and the type of supplier, the following is an example of a creative brief only. A mailing brief will be somewhat different; a database development brief totally different. Do not forget to make use of the supplier's experience too.

As an example of the depth of detail required, the following elements should be included in a creative brief to an agency:

1 Information – you cannot usually overdo this. Most inadequate briefs are short on vital facts and figures. Tell them everything about your product, your market, the sort of people who buy it and the number of competitors you have. If you do not feel you can trust them with your secrets you have probably chosen the wrong partners. One major direct marketing company actually produces totally spurious briefs for new suppliers to see

how they handle them and to check whether any of the 'confidential' information hits the streets. You may feel this is going a bit far, but it depends on how confidential you feel your data is.

2 Brief the right people. Make sure you talk to at least one of the actual people who will do the job. In a creative brief this means either the copy-writer or art director – preferably both. The questions asked by creative people are very different to those asked by account managers. The creatives write the copy and design the ad or mailing. The account manager's job is to make sure it is developed into the finished job accurately and on time. Ideally, both creative and account managers should be involved in the meeting. You will probably find this is easier to arrange when you go to the agency rather than asking them to come to you. Apart from the improvement in outcome, there is an additional bonus. Visiting the agency means you can have a chat with the research manager and the print buyer, call in the chairman for a bit of extra advice and so on. Unless you are a huge client, you will rarely get such a huge team visiting your office.

3 State a clear objective – a creative team, however brilliant, cannot generate a convincing advertisement or mailing unless they know what you want them to achieve. Do you want to attract orders or enquiries. If enquiries, do you want 'loose' or 'tight' enquiries? Loose leads respond when you mention benefits, but not price. Tight leads are told more in the copy. Tight leads are easier to convert to sales, but you do not get so many. Which should you go for? How good a salesperson are you? How easy is it to tell a full and convincing story in the advertisement or mailing? As with so many questions, the answer depends on your own business circumstances.

4 Prepare a positioning statement – this is an area that causes great concern, but again, without clear guidance, your creative team cannot hit the target. They need to know whether you are selling a Rolls Royce or a Lada. Positioning is discussed in Chapter 9.

5 Give an indication of the budget. It is up to you whether you tell them the exact amount you have available, but they will not be able to give you what you want unless they know whether you want a low budget execution or a high-quality prestige presentation.

6 Set a timetable – suppliers tend to operate to the 'just in time' principle. Once you have fixed the timetable, stick to it, from your own side too. If you have provided all the necessary information on time, you are entitled to expect the finished job to be on schedule. If your materials were provided late, do not be surprised to find your job is also running behind schedule. There may be a 'knock-on' effect. If you return the typescript copy 2 days late, the agency may have missed the appointed 'slot' they had at the studio. This could cause another couple of days delay. This makes the artwork late, which causes a problem for the printer. A small

delay of 2 days on your part could easily escalate into a delivery hold-up of more than a week. Prudent suppliers build in time for 'slippage', but the key message is do not hold things up yourself and then expect everyone else to stick to the original timetable.

7 Describe your prospect clearly. There is a saying in direct marketing, 'You cannot write to a list, only to a person'. An effective copywriter spends the first half hour of any job thinking up a description of the person to whom he or she is about to write. This description is hypothetical, of course, but it helps him or her to write believable, convincing copy. Which of the following prospect descriptions would you find it easier to write to? *(a) Parent*; *(b) Parent-owner of a fairly expensive detached house, professional, aged over 35, has two children at fee-paying schools and a sizeable mortgage. Is concerned about school fees. Wishes to maintain a good standard of living. Needs convincing that further investment is worthwhile and even affordable. Would probably listen to arguments supported by credible testimonial statements.*

8 Define the benefits of your product. Only a small number of people buy products because of their technical excellence – most buy because they deliver better end-user benefits. Make sure you tell the creative people how the attributes of your product deliver benefits to users. It will be helpful to explain how benefits vary for different types of prospect. For example, a man who travels a lot will like electric central heating because he can switch it on by telephone from anywhere in the world. His father, who is 83, may like it because it is so easy to turn on and adjust. If you do not know what the end-user benefits of your product are, seen from the point of view of your customers, you need to do some research before delivering your brief.

9 Explain your offer to the creative team. Expect them to question the power of your offer – listen to their arguments. Although they will not always be typical of your target audience, they will often produce good ideas that can improve your results.

10 Put your brief in writing. This seems obvious, but many important briefs are not confirmed in writing. When something goes wrong, who is to blame? When you are not available who can answer the questions?

A briefing form

Figure 13.1 shows a typical form for a creative brief. A jointly designed briefing form serves several useful functions:

- it forces you and your supplier to think through the job very carefully – in advance of work starting
- it reminds you to cover every aspect
- it is a valuable checklist when no one is around to answer questions

Creative Briefing Form	
Name of job: [for example spring mailing campaign]	
Date:	
Product/service description: to which this brief relates [for example new spring models]	
Background: market situation, competitive situation, any other similar relevant comments	
Positioning: a brief and simple statement describing the overall impression you wish to leave in the mind of the reader	
Communications objective: what are you trying to achieve – to attract enquiries, change attitudes, encourage trial or visit to dealer?	
Target audience: who are you talking to – large or small customers, prospects, decision-makers, influencers or purchasing departments?	
Media to be used: is this a stand-alone mailing or advertisement, or will the same theme be used across several media?	
Response mechanism: mailed coupon, telephone, fax, e-mail or Website	
Proposition: offer – what customer benefit does this product offer? This should be expressed very briefly – if all else fails, it may be used as the headline	
Rationale: why will this product provide these benefits?	
Secondary benefits: Are there any other benefits which should be included?	
Tone of voice: Authoritative, questioning or advisory	
Executional guidelines: any wider issues to be conformed to? Group logos or other design elements, terminology, and so on	
Promotional aspects: what sort of promotional offer is to be made – price, prize draw or incentive?	

Figure 13.1 A creative briefing form

- it helps when briefing other areas of the business, such as a telephone response team.

SUMMARY

This chapter has looked at the range of suppliers used by direct marketing and the process of briefing and managing them to get the best from them for your business or your clients.

The range of suppliers to the industry is significant and includes:

- mailing list suppliers – brokers and owners
- mailing and fulfilment houses
- database and computer bureaux – laser print shops
- Web-site designers and consultants
- printers
- direct marketing agencies or freelance design and creative teams
- consultants.

List brokers can be found through the trade press, the Direct Marketing Association or in a range of directories. They will make lists available in whatever format is required and will often help with de-duplication and if required the processing of the list.

The differences between mailing houses and fulfilment houses have been covered in detail and their operations were listed.

We have looked at the use of computer bureaux in database management and manipulation.

The commissioning of Web-site consultants and designers has been explored and we saw the need to take up references.

We have considered the role of the printer and the need to manage communications between the printer and the designer.

We then looked at the role of the direct marketing agency and explored the differences between large and small agencies.

There was a review of the range of services that consultants provide and where they can be found.

We defined a process for choosing suppliers:

1 build a list of potential suppliers
2 write to them
3 create a long list
4 drill down to the shortlist

5 visit them

6 meet their people

7 write the brief

8 ask for quotations

9 take up business and credit references

10 make your decision.

We considered how to write a good brief, including the need to:

- provide as much information as possible
- brief all concerned with the project
- give clear quantified objectives
- prepare a positioning statement
- give an indication of budget
- set a timetable
- describe the prospect clearly
- define the benefits of your product
- explain the offer
- put the brief in writing.

We have seen that a briefing form forces a supplier to think through the job in detail and is a valuable checklist if there are any problems.

An example of a typical creative briefing form can be found on p. 303.

REVIEW QUESTIONS

1 List the main suppliers with which a direct marketer may have to deal.

2 How many lists are available to rent in the UK?

3 Where can we find list brokers?

4 Why is de-duplication important?

5 List the functions of a mailing house.

6 List the functions of a fulfilment house.

7 What are the unique attributes of a database bureau?

8 What are the problems and advantages in using a large direct marketing agency?

9 How can the use of consultants help the direct marketer?

10 How do we choose good suppliers?

11 What are the stages in the briefing process?

12 What are the benefits of a good brief?

EXERCISES

Using the creative briefing form and the advertisement you selected in Chapter 10 write a creative brief outlining improvements you think should be made to the advertisement.

Chapter 14

Where to go for more information

Introduction

- Qualifications
- Training
- Education
- The skills you need to succeed
- Career opportunities
  - Client-side operations
  - Agencies
- [a] Bibliography
  - Direct marketing
  - Marketing
  - Database marketing
  - Marketing communications and branding
  - Relationship marketing
  - Statistics
  - Internet and e-commerce
  - Journals and periodicals
- Useful addresses

INTRODUCTION

There has never been more demand for the skills of the direct marketer. The following quotations show the huge opportunities that are opening up for direct marketers at all levels:

> The future of e-commerce depends on the know-how of direct marketers. We feel very strongly that this will be the highest demanded skill-set as more and more e-commerce players come into the market space.
>
> Gregory K. Jones, President/CEO, uBid.com

> Internet commerce will starve without the expertise of direct marketers.
>
> Forrester Research

Finally in the 1990s, direct marketing emerged from the engine room of the corporate ship, where we were busy helping to power the thing forward with our highly focused activity. It is now in its rightful place on the bridge. Direct marketing enables a company to use the intimate knowledge it has about its customers to take the whole organization forward.

There are direct marketers on the main boards of many FTSE 500 companies. The best direct marketing agencies are now ranked alongside their above-the-line colleagues in terms of creative and value added. The language of 'modern' marketing is the language direct marketers have used for years.

Marketing now is about:

- relationships
- loyalty
- lifetime value
- customer management
- one to one
- responsiveness
- real time
- interactivity.

Direct marketing and direct marketers are ready to take the corporate high ground as the custodians of company/customer relationships and the generators of long-term value for the organization.

Direct marketing is an essential part of the modern marketer's tool kit, embracing as Graeme McCorkell (1997) points out, the four cornerstones of profitable marketing and successful long-term business:

- targeting
- interaction

- continuity
- control.

Qualifications

So how can you learn more about direct marketing? You have started well by reading this book! However, the next place to go to is the Institute of Direct Marketing. It offers a huge range of professional qualifications taught by practitioners and academics with a vast body of industry experience.

It offers four certificate products:

1 a Certificate in Direct Marketing
2 a Certificate in Call Centre management
3 a Certificate in E-Commerce
4 a Certificate in Customer Relationship Management.

These courses teach the fundamentals of the subject.

The Diploma in Interactive and Direct Marketing takes the topics of the certificate courses and looks at their strategic application and integration in business. This Diploma is recognized around the world as the leading direct marketing qualification, and is seen increasingly as the most relevant marketing qualification to the modern marketer. The Diploma can be studied via distance learning, by evening class or in intensive mode.

Training

The Institute of Direct Marketing also offers a range of professional short courses and in-company programmes. These range from a complete direct marketing course to highly specialized statistical training. It also offers new training programmes in e-marketing. The Institute can be contacted at its Web site (www.theidm.com) or on 020 8977 5705. It has a range of useful services free to members and I thoroughly recommend that you join.

It is there to support the individual within the profession. The Institute's increasing overseas activity means that should you travel abroad to take up the range of opportunities that are available, it will be there to help you in your career.

Other training courses are available at the Chartered Institute of Marketing (www.cim.co.uk).

Marketing research training is handled well by the Market Research Society, which can be contacted at www.mrs.org.

Education

Some of you may be studying marketing or business studies courses at college or university, with a range of course options. If you are aiming to enter direct marketing, there are several points to make that should guide your choice of courses or options.

It is important to understand the role of technology in marketing particularly in order to be able to manage suppliers of technically based solutions. However, you also need to know the details of how to produce an effective advertisement or direct mail pack and how to manage a campaign. You should look to increase your IT skills and be aware that the Web is a tool that helps many companies deliver added value to the customers.

You need to understand how marketing is developed and delivered to customers. As George Bull said, 'Marketing is about making a difference' and the key difference is in the mind of the customer. Courses on consumer behaviour and research will be useful.

The Institute of Direct Marketing has worked with educators for many years and your college or university may well offer a specialist course on direct marketing. Even if you are not planning to go into specialist direct marketing, you would be advised to take such a course as an awareness of the role of direct marketing is now central to most organizations.

The Institute is committed to lifelong learning and the pace of change in industry means that none of us can afford to neglect new skills. It is currently looking at developing an MA in Direct Marketing – actually Kingston University already offers an MA in Direct Marketing and recognizes the Diploma in Interactive and Direct Marketing as an entry point.

Other universities, including the University of Greenwich, offer MAs in Marketing that recognize prior learning with the Institute. Kingston University can be contacted at www.kingston.ac.uk and Greenwich at www.gre.ac.uk.

The skills you need to succeed

The skills needs for the direct marketing industry exist at all levels. A 1998 survey carried out for the Institute showed that agency heads saw a requirement for planners and good strategic thinkers.

Recent research work has shown skills shortages in the technical side of database and e-commerce marketing.

There is always a requirement for individuals with strong interpersonal and management skills, tenacity and an eye for detail in project management.

Direct marketing is about measurement and accountability so numeracy is required.

Direct marketing also requires good literacy skills. There are often reports to write and to present, so written and oral presentation skills are important.

The Institute has summarized the skills set required of the direct marketer as:

- creative and imaginative
- highly computer literate
- people-oriented and people-focused
- analytical and problem-solving
- strategic and far-thinking
- technical and mathematically based
- off-the wall and lateral-thinking
- organized and process-driven people.

Career opportunities

There are a huge variety of careers available to the direct marketer.

The specialist areas of direct marketing include:

- list broking
- media buying
- database management and data planning
- research and proprietary profiling systems
- statistical analysis
- work in print shops, mailing houses or fulfilment houses
- call centre or contact centre work
- design and copy writing
- Web site management
- consultancy.

Client-side operations

This covers the direct marketing of brands in all sectors of industry. You may be managing direct marketing programmes that are integrated with other activities that support a brand, or alternatively managing a stand-alone direct marketing function. Recent moves towards integration have created opportunities for direct marketers to move easily between these areas.

Work in this area would usually start at executive level and can take you to board level responsibility in many organizations.

Agencies

Agency life offers variety and a fast pace – most account executives will work on a range of different clients' work. The complexity of the direct marketing task means that there are many deadlines to be met and some late hours to be worked. It can be a fascinating and rewarding career.

Entry is normally at account executive level and movement up to group account director and beyond can be very fast. Some agencies are prepared to take on more mature executives, especially those having strong client-specific experience.

In addition to general account management, agencies also offer specialist areas of work including planning and research, data planning, media buying, creative and new business generation.

The Institute offers a service to graduates to help them find a job in direct marketing. This is a free service open to all graduates and is often part of the recruiting programme of major employers. Graduates therefore gain access to a very wide range of career opportunities. It provides advanced notice of vacancies and it is easy to register on the Internet.

People have been placed at many leading companies including Ogilvy One (Ogilvy & Mather), Lowe Direct, Claritas, Miller Starr, The Computing Group, Aspen Agency, Commercial Union, Cornhill Direct, Freemans, General Universal Stores, Bank of Scotland, Mobil BP, National Geographic Society, JD Williams, Procter & Gamble, Legal & General, World Vision.

With whichever company you are working, direct marketing will provide you with a fulfilling and fascinating career.

Good luck!

Bibliography

The best place to go for more information is your library or the Internet. A number of excellent books have been published in the area of direct marketing. The following are recommended.

Direct marketing

The Direct Marketing Guide (1998). The Institute of Direct Marketing.
Bird, D. (2000). *Commonsense Direct Marketing* (fourth edition). Kogan Page.
Kobs, J. (1992). *Profitable Direct Marketing*. NTC Business Books.
McCorkell, G. (1990). *Advertising That Pulls Response*. McGraw-Hill.
McCorkell, G. (1997). *Direct and Database Marketing*. Kogan Page.

Nash, E. (1993). *Database Marketing*. McGraw-Hill.

Nash, E. (2000). *Direct Marketing Strategy, Planning and Execution* (fourth edition). McGraw-Hill.

O'Malley, L. *et al.* (1999). *Exploring Direct Marketing* (first edition). Thomson.

Skinner (1993) *Integrated Marketing*. McGraw-Hill.

Stone, B. (1996). *Successful Direct Marketing Methods* (sixth edition). NTC Business Books.

Tapp, A. (2000). *The Principles of Direct and Database Marketing* (second edition). FT Pitman.

Thomas, B. (1996). *The Royal Mail Guide to Direct Mail for Small Businesses*. Butterworth-Heinemann.

Vogele, S. (1992). *Handbook of Direct Mail*. Prentice Hall.

Watson, J. (1996). *Successful Creativity in Direct Marketing*. WWAV Rapp Collins.

Marketing

Adcock, D. Bradfield, R. Halborg, A. and Ross, C. (1998). *Marketing: Principles and Practice* (third edition). Pitman.

Baker, M. J. (1999). *The Marketing Book* (fourth edition). Butterworth-Heinemann.

Brassington, F. and Petitt, S. (2000). *Principles of Marketing* (second edition). Pearson.

Crouch, S. and Housden, M. (1996). *Marketing Research for Managers* (second edition). Butterworth-Heinemann.

Davidson, H. (1998). *Even More Offensive Marketing*. Penguin Books.

Kotler, P. *et al.* (1999). *Principles of Marketing* (second edition). Prentice Hall.

McDonald, M. (1993). *The Marketing Planner*. Butterworth-Heinemann.

McDonald, M. (1996). *Strategic Marketing Planning* (second edition). Kogan Page.

McDonald, M. (1999). *Marketing Plans: How to Prepare them, How to use them* (fourth edition). Butterworth-Heinemann.

Payne, A. (1996). *Marketing Planning for Services*. Butterworth-Heinemann.

Database marketing

Jackson, R. and Wang, P. (1994). *Strategic Database Marketing*. NTC Business Books.

Shepard, D. (1999). *The New Direct Marketing* (third edition). McGraw-Hill.

Marketing communications and branding

de Chernatony, L. and McDonald, M. (1998). *Creating Powerful Brands*. Butterworth-Heinemann.

Hallberg, G. (1996). *All Consumers are not Created Equal*. Wiley.

Hart, S. and Murphy, J. (1998). *Brands – the New Wealth Creators*. Macmillan Business/Interbrand.

Pearson, S. (1996). *Building Brands Directly*. Macmillan Press.

Schultz, D. E. and Tannenbaum, S. I. (1997). *Integrated Marketing Communications*. NTC Business Books.

Yeshin, T. (1998). *Integrated Marketing Communications*. Butterworth-Heinemann.

Relationship marketing

Burnett, L. (1992). *Relationship Fundraising*. The White Lion Press.

Christopher, M. (1993). *The Customer Service Planner*. Butterworth-Heinemann.

Gamble, P. Stone, M. and Woodcock, N. (1999). *Up Close and Personal?* Kogan Page.

McKenna, R. (1993). *Relationship Marketing*. Addison-Wesley (US).

Peppers, D. and Rogers, M. (1996). *The One-To-One Future*. Piatkus.

Peppers, D. and Rogers, M. (1999). *Enterprise One-To-One*. Doubleday.

Peppers, D. and Rogers, M. (1999). *The One-To-One Manager*. Doubleday.

Peppers, D. and Rogers, M. (2001). *One to One B2B Customers: Relationship Marketing Strategies for the Real Economy*. Doubleday.

Reichheld, F. (1996). *The Loyalty Effect*. McGraw-Hill.

Statistics

Diamantopoulis, A. and Schlegelmilch, B. (1997). *Taking the Fear out of Data Analysis*. Dryden Press.

Internet and e-commerce

Berners, Lee J. (1999). *Weaving the Web*. Orion.

Birch, A. Gerbert, P. and Schneider, D. (2000). *The Age of E-Tail*. Capstone Publishing.

Bowen, D. (1999). *Electronic Business Manual*. Net Profit Publications Ltd.

Chaffey, D. *et al.* (2000). *Internet Marketing* (first edition). FT Prentice Hall.

Collins, S. (1998). *Doing Business on the Internet*. Kogan Page.

Dell, M. (1999). *Direct from Dell*. HarperCollins.

Hagel III, J. and Singer, M. (1999). *Net Worth*. Harvard Business School Press.

Hanson, W. (2000). *Principles of Internet Marketing*. South Western College Publishing.

Kalakota, R. and Whinston, A. (1997). *Electronic Commerce: A Manager's Guide*. Addison Wesley.*

Seybold, P. B. (1998). *Customers.com*. Times Books.

Sterne, J. (1999). *World Wide Web Marketing* (second edition). John Wiley & Sons.

Strauss, J. and Frost, R. (1999). *Marketing on the Internet*. Prentice Hall.

Turban, E. *et al.* (1999). *Information Technology for Management*. Wiley.

Turban, E. *et al.* (2000). *E-Commerce: A Managerial Perspective*. Prentice Hall.

Wurster, T. and Evans, P. (2000). *Blown to Bits*. HBS Press.

Journals and periodicals

Never ignore the business journals; the direct marketing trade press is great for picking up on the latest trends in the industry, who is doing what, who is moving where, and there are usually some excellent special features. They also publish details of industry awards and they are really useful in order to get a view on new creative techniques and so on.

The academic journals, whilst hard-going in certain areas, are invaluable. Most articles are based on a sound research methodology and the insight that the best of these provide is often very useful.

The following is a sample of the many journals that are available. They are almost all accessible online and there are several useful online services. A useful source of marketing links on the Web is www.mousetracks.com. Anbar and other online directories are very useful. A huge range of Web sites offer excellent information on the industry. It would be worthwhile creating your own favourite list.

Trade and specialist press
Admap
Advertising Age
Campaign
Customer Loyalty Today
Customer Management
Direct Response
Direct Marketing (US)
Loyalty
Marketing
Marketing and Research Today
Marketing Business
Marketing Direct

Marketing Week
Net Profit
New Media Age
Precision Marketing
Research
Revolution

Academic journals
Colombia World Business
European Journal of Marketing
Harvard Business Review
International Journal of Advertising
International Journal of Customer Relationship Management
International Journal of Market Research
Journal of Brand Management
Journal of Database Marketing
Journal of Interactive Marketing (UK)
Journal of Interactive Marketing (US)
Journal of Marketing Management
Journal of Targeting, Measurement and Analysis
Sloan Management Review

Useful addresses

Advertising Association
Abford House
15 Wilton Road
London SW1V 1NJ
Tel: 020 7828 2771
Web Address: http://www.adassoc.org.uk

Advertising Standards Authority
2 Torrington Place
London
WC1E 7HW
Tel: 020 7580 5555
Web Address: http://www.ada.org.uk

Association of Household Distributors
Haymarket House
1 Oxendon Street
London SW1Y 4EE
Tel: 020 7321 2525
Web Address: http://www.dma.org.uk

BARB
18 Dearing Street
London
W1R 9AF
Tel: 020 7529 5531
Web Address: http://www.barb.co.uk

BBS
Kings House
Kimberley Road
Harrow
HA1 1PT
Tel: 020 8861 8000
Web Address: http://www.ipsos-rsl.com

British Advertising Gift Distributors Association
177 Bagnall Road
Basford
Nottingham
NG6 8SJ
Tel: 0870 6039195
Web Address: http://www.bagda.co.uk

British Market Research Association
16 Creighton Avenue
London N10 1NU
Tel: 020 8374 4095
Web Address: http://www.bmra.org.uk

British Printing Industries Federation
11 Bedford Row
London WC1R 4DX
Tel: 020 7915 8300
Web Address: http://www.bpif.org.uk

British Promotional Merchandise Association
Bank Chambers
15 High Road
Byfleet
Surrey KT14 7HQ
Tel: 01932 355661
Web Address: http://www.bpma.co.uk

CACI Ltd
CACI House
Kensington Village
Avonmore Road
London W14 8TS
Tel: 020 7602 6000
Web Address: http://www.caci.co.uk

Call Centre Association
Strathclyde House
6 Elmbank Street
Glasgow G2 4PF
Tel: 0141 564 9010
Web Address: http://www.cca.org.uk

Caviar:
Caviar can be contacted via Carlton Screen Advertising and Pearl & Dean
Carlton Screen Advertising
12 Golden Square
London
W1F 9JE
Tel: 020 7534 6368

Pearl & Dean
3 Waterhouse Square
138-142 Holborn
London
EC1N 2N7
Tel: 020 7882 1109

Chartered Institute of Marketing
Moor Hall
Cookham
Maidenhead
Berkshire SL6 9QH
Tel: 01628 427500
Web Address: http://www.cim.co.uk

Circular Distributors
1-3 Malvern Road
Maidenhead
Berkshire
SL6 7QY
Tel: 01628 771 232
Web Address: http://www.cdltd.co.uk

Committee of Advertising Practice Copy Advice Team
2 Torrington Place
London WC1E 7HW
Tel: 020 7580 4100
Web Address: http://www.cap.org.uk

Communication Advertising and Marketing Education Foundation
Abford House
15 Wilton Road
London SW1V 1NJ
Tel: 020 7828 7506
Web Address: http://www.camfoundation.com

Companies House
Cardiff:
Companies House
Crown Way
Cardiff
CF14 3UZ
Tel: 0870 3333 636

London:
Companies House
21 Bloomsbury Street
London
WC1B 3XD
Tel: 0870 3333 636
Web Address: http://www.companieshouse.gov.uk

Computing Services and Software Association
20 Red Lion Street
London WC1R 4QN
Tel: 020 7395 6700
Web Address: http://www.cssa.co.uk

Data Protection Registrar
Wycliffe House
Water Lane
Wilmslow
Cheshire SK9 5AF
Tel: 01625 545745
Web Address: http://www.dataprotection.gov.uk

Department of Trade and Industry
Consumer Affairs
Water Lane
Wilmslow
Cheshire SK9 5AF
Tel: 020 7215 5000
Web Address: http://www.dti.gov.uk

The Direct Mail Information Service (DMIS)
5 Carlisle Street
London W1V 6JX
Tel: 020 7494 0483
Web Address: http://www.dmis.co.uk

Direct Marketing Association Inc.
1120 Avenue of the Americas
New York NY10036 - 6700
USA
Tel: 00 1 212 768 7277
Web Address: http://www.the-dma.org.uk

The Direct Marketing Association (UK)
(DMA)
Haymarket House
1 Oxendon Street
London SW1Y 4EE
Tel: 020 7321 2525
Web Address: http://www.dma.org.uk

Direct Selling Association
29 Floral Street
London WC2E 9DP
Tel: 020 7497 1234
Web Address: http://www.dsa.org.uk

Experian
Embankment House
Electric Avenue
Nottingham NG2 1RQ
Tel: 0115 968 5333
Web Address: http://www.experian.com

Federation of European Direct Marketing Associations
439 Avenue de Terweren
B-1150 Brussels
Belgium
Tel: 00 322 779 4268
Web Address: http://www.fedma.org

Incorporated Society of British Advertisers
44 Hertford Street
London W1Y 8AE
Tel: 020 7499 7502
Web Address: http://www.isba.org.uk

Independent Committee for the Supervision of Standards of Telephone
Services
The Secretariat
3rd Floor
Alton House
177 High Holborn
London WC1V 7AA
Tel: 020 7240 5511
Web Address: http://www.icstis.org.uk

Independent Television Commission
33 Foley Street
London W1W 7TH
Tel: 020 7255 3000
(responsible for the code of advertising standards and practice relating to
television)
Web Address: http://www.itc.org.uk

Institute of Direct Marketing
No. 1 Park Road
Teddington
Middlesex TW11 0AR
Tel: 020 8977 5705
Web Address: http://www.theidm.com

Institute of Practitioners in Advertising
44 Belgrave Square
London SW1X 8QS
Tel: 020 7235 7020
Web Address: http://www.ipa.co.uk

Institute of Sales Promotion
Arena House
66–68 Pentonville Road
Islington London N1 9HS
Tel: 020 7837 5340
Web Address: http://www.isp.org.uk

List Warranty Register
Haymarket House
1 Oxendon Street
London SW1Y 4EE
Tel: 020 7766 4450
Web Address: http://www.dma.org.uk

Mail Order Protection Scheme
16 Took's Court
London EC4A 1LB
Tel: 020 7405 6806
Web Address: http://www.mops.org.uk

Mail Order Traders Association
40 Waterloo Road
Birkdale Southport PR8 2NG
Tel: 01704 563 787

Mailing Preference Service
Haymarket House
1 Oxendon Street
London SW1Y 4EE
Tel: 020 7766 4410
Web Address: http://www.dma.org.uk

Market Research Society
15 Northborough Street
London EC1V 0AH
Tel: 020 7490 4911
Web Address: http://www.mrs.org.uk

Newspaper Society
Bloomsbury House
74–77 Great Russell Street
London WC1B 3DA
Tel: 020 7636 7014
Web Address: http://www.newspapersoc.org.uk

NRS
42 Drury Lane
London WC2B 5RT
Tel: 020 7632 2915
Web Address: http://www.nrs.co.uk

Office of Fair Trading
Field House
15–25 Bream's Building
London EC1V 0AH
Tel: 020 7211 8000
Web Address: http://www.oft.gov.uk

Office of National Statistics
1 Drummond Gate
London SW1V 2QQ
Tel: 020 7460 5368
Web Address: http://www.statistics.gov.uk

OFTEL
Export House
50 Ludgate Hill
London EC4M 7JJ
Tel: 020 7634 8700
Web Address: http://www.oftel.gov.uk

Periodical Publishers Association
Queens House 28 Kingsway
London WC2B 6JR
Tel: 020 7404 4166
Web Address: http://www.ppa.co.uk

Postar
Summit House
27 Sale Place
London W2 1YR
Tel: 020 7479 9700
Web Address: http://www.postar.co.uk

RAJAR
Gainsborough House
81 Oxford Street
London W1D 2EU
Tel: 020 7903 5350
Web Address: http://www.rajar.co.uk

Royal Mail Customer Services
5 Almeida Street
London N1 1AA
Tel: 0845 7740 740
Web Address: http://www.royalmail.com

Royal Mail Sales Centre
35–50 Rathbone Place
London W1P 1AA
Tel: 0845 7950 950
Web Address: http://www.royalmail.com

Telephone Preference Service
Haymarket House
1 Oxendon Street
London SW1Y 4EE
Tel: 020 7766 4420
Web Address: http://www.dma.org.uk

Women in Direct Marketing
Wellers Yard
Brooks Road
Lewes
East Sussex BN7 2BY
Tel: 01273 480460
Web Address: http://www.wdm-uk.com

Glossary

There is much jargon in the marketing business and, although we have tried to keep this to a minimum, there will inevitably be some terminology that is unfamiliar to some readers. Therefore, the following glossary should explain some of the more specialized terms.

A/B split run – a method by which two alternative advertisements can be tested simultaneously in the same newspaper or magazine. See Split-run testing.

Above the line – a term applied to traditional (that is non-direct response) advertising.

ACORN – an acronym for A Classification of Residential Neighbourhoods. A marketing segmentation system enabling consumers to be classified according to the type of residential area in which they live.

Acquisition (of customers) – all activities related to the location of and marketing to new prospects.

Added value – some additional element provided to a customer for which no extra charge is paid, for example a free booklet explaining how to get extra miles per gallon. Also called an 'extra value proposition'.

Advance mailer – a simple mailing or postcard, mailed before the main mailing to increase awareness and response. Sometimes called a 'teaser'.

Advertorial – a paid-for space in a magazine or newspaper which is laid out in editorial fashion, giving the impression of being editorial rather than advertising.

Advocate – our best customer as he or he tells others how good we are.

Artwork – the finished layout of typesetting, drawings and photographs, made up in a form which is ready for the printer to turn it into plates or data for laser, ink-jet or digital printing.

Artwork studio – the place where artwork is made up from photographs, drawings, lettering and typesetting.

Awareness – advertising or other promotional activity (such as public relations) whose primary purpose is to increase general knowledge and understanding of the company, and to make people feel more positively towards it. Also known as 'image' activity.

Below the line – a term used to denote advertising activities other than awareness advertising. It includes direct marketing (incorrectly) and sales promotion.

Benefit testing – a telephone research technique, used to establish customer comprehension of, and preference for, specific promotional statements (headlines).

Bleed – printed matter running off the cutting edge of a page.

Block designs – a form of direct mail test matrix which reduces the number of names required.

Body copy – the main areas of text in an advertisement, brochure or leaflet, other than headlines and sub-headings.

Bound-in inserts – see 'Loose and bound-in inserts'.

Break-even costing – a method of costing used in direct marketing to tell us how much response we need to recover our costs without making any profit.

Brief – verbal or (preferably) written instructions to a supplier, such as an agency, mailing house or computer bureau.

Broadscale advertising – advertising using large circulation media, such as newspapers, magazines, radio and television.

Bromide (PMT) – Photo Mechanical Transfer. Laser-etched black text and screened images on light sensitive paper, used to make up mechanical artwork.

Business databases – databases compiled by organizations such as Dun & Bradstreet, the Yellow Pages (the Business Database) and CCN. Companies can have their own lists checked or profiled against these and also have data added to their own records. Mailing lists can also be bought or rented from these companies.

Business mailing – a mailing sent to a business (as opposed to a consumer).

Business to business – direct communication from one business to another.

Caption – a brief explanation of a picture or drawing.

Cheshire labels – labels produced by a Cheshire machine, which cuts up continuous stationery from a computer printer.

Chromalin – a method of proofing four colour work chemically on photographic paper, instead of using plates and ink.

Closed-face envelope – an envelope without a window.

Cold list – a list which has no affinity to the advertiser, nor any known buying history of the product or service.

Colour mark-up – specifications to a printer, showing the required colours for the item to be printed.

Communications action calendar – a detailed schedule of activities required to achieve the fulfilment of the communications action plan.

Compiled list – names and addresses derived from directories, public records, sales slips, trade show registrations and so on.

Computer personalization – printing of letters or other promotional pieces by a computer system using names, special phrases or other information based on data appearing in our database. The objective is to make use of the data to tailor the message to a specific recipient and to select only names for whom the message will be relevant.

Consumer list – A list of names and addresses of individuals at their home addresses.

Consumer mailing – a mailing to consumers at their home addresses.

Contact strategy – the process of deciding the exact details of customer contact – that is telephone and mail; press campaign and targeted direct mail and so on.

Control (package or advertisement) – our standard (usually pre-tested or previously used) design, against which new designs and offers are tested.

Controlled circulation – distribution at no charge of a publication to individuals or companies on the basis of their title, occupation or business type.

Conversion pack – material sent out in response to enquiries from prospects, with the intention of converting them into customers – also known as a 'response pack'.

Cookies – a file stored on your hard disk and used to identify your computer or your preferences to a remote computer. Cookies are frequently used to identify visitors to Web sites so that personalized pages can be served to them.

Copywriter – a specialist who writes copy for mailings, advertisements and so on.

Cross-selling – using a customer's buying history to select them for related offers, such as a car alarm for new car buyers.

Customer database – a record of customers' buying history and related information; usually, but not necessarily, held on a computer.

Customer lifetime value – see 'Lifetime value analysis'.

Customer profile – a collection of facts and characteristics about your customers, such as age, household composition, company size and number of cars.

Customer relationship management – the latest name given to the technique of managing customers by segmenting them according to their potential value to the organization. Previously known as 'relationship marketing' and 'dialogue marketing'.

Customer segmentation – the breakdown of customers into smaller groups of similar characteristics or propensities in order to improve targeting of mailings and offers.

Database – records of customer, prospect and market information. Used for many marketing, sales and business management purposes. Usually, but not essentially, held on a computer.

Data capture – the process of keying in (or scanning in) data to a computer.

Data protection – legislation to protect the interests of the individual by controlling the use of personal data for marketing or other business purposes.

Decision-maker – the person who makes the decision to buy or try a product or service. With expensive products or large contracts this person would generally be a member of a decision-making unit.

Decision-making unit – a group of people within a company (sometimes including outside consultants), who discuss the acceptance or otherwise of a business offer.

De-duplication – a computerized system of comparing data to identify names and addresses which appear in a list, or a group of lists, more than once.

Demographics – socio-economic characteristics of customers, such as gender and age, status.

Desktop publishing (DTP) – creating artwork and print from your computer. It requires special software and a fairly powerful computer, although most modern desktop machines have the necessary capability.

Die-cut – a shaped cut-out in a leaflet or brochure.

Digital printing – the latest form of printing that works like laser printing in that it generates images and text direct from data files. As there are no plates, each sheet is individually printed. Although expensive at present, it will ultimately enable brochures and catalogues to be truly personalized by 'matching in' information, images and so on from the database for each copy of the leaflet or brochure.

Digitized signature – a computer-printed simulation of a personal signature. This technique can also be used to simulate handwriting on envelopes, in letters and so on.

Direct mail shot – term used to describe a direct mail promotion. Also known as a 'mail shot'.

Direct marketing – marketing activity which is based on a direct relationship between advertiser and customer or prospect. Also known as 'customer relationship management', 'dialogue marketing' and 'relationship marketing'.

Direct response advertising – advertising carrying a response device of some sort (coupon, telephone or fax number). The primary objective is to generate enquiries or orders direct.

Display advertising – advertising which is 'laid out', often with illustrations, as opposed to lineage or classified advertising.

Door to door (door drops) – unaddressed 'mailings' delivered by Royal Mail and other companies. They can be targeted to small areas, making them suitable for small businesses. Royal Mail is the most expensive, but also most the responsive.

Dual-purpose advertising – advertising which, whilst carrying a response device, is also intended to generate awareness of a product or service.

E-mail – electronic mail is the facility that allows you to send and receive messages from anyone else on the Internet. This could include colleagues within your own organization, suppliers, clients and friends. Access to the Internet is provided by Internet Service Providers (ISPs), such as CompuServe. The recipient does not have to be present to take delivery of a message as the ISP holds an electronic mailbox that can be accessed at any time by the recipient. The majority of Internet traffic is associated with electronic mail. E-mail is more than a messaging service. Virtually any type of data file, a software program, text, graphics, sound or video, can be sent and received across the Internet.

External lists – mailing lists from outside sources, that is not from within one's own company records.

Extranet – an Intranet that extends access to selected customers or suppliers, allowing them access to parts of a company database, usually via the Internet. A good example of an Extranet is the Federal Express tracking system, which allows customers to find out where their package is 24 hours a day.

Firewall – a system designed to prevent unauthorized access to or from a private network on a computer. It sits at the entry to a corporate network and checks all the incoming and outgoing traffic. Firewalls come in both hardware and software forms and use a variety of security techniques.

Flyer – additional insert in a mailing package.

Follow-up – a second or subsequent approach to the same addressee to increase response. It usually reminds them of the original offer or makes a better offer. It can be made via mail, e-mail or telephone. Generally, the sooner it is done after the original mailing arrives, the better – especially when using e-mail or telephone.

FRAC – a form of analysis relating to buying behaviour. The letters stand for 'frequency' (how often they have bought), 'recency' (how recent their last transaction was), 'amount' (the value of their last transaction or all transactions to date) and 'category' (what sort of product they purchased). These are the four most powerful discriminators in selecting names from a database. See also 'RFM', which is a slightly less informative version of the same technique.

Fulfilment – the processing of an order or request for information.

Fulfilment house – see 'Mailing house'.

Galley proof – a proof taken before printing plates are made.

Gateholder – a member of the decision-making unit who has the power or authority to stop a purchase.

Gone-away ('Nixie') – a term used to indicate that a person mailed is no longer at that address.

GSM – stands for 'grammes per square metre' and is the standard measure of paper weight.

Guard book – a collection of mailings and advertisements, marked up with results information, improving capabilities for future campaign planning. It often contains details of competitors' advertising too.

Gum strips – strips of glue applied to a mailing leaflet or envelope, enabling it to be sealed when moistened.

Hand-enclosing – assembling and enclosing a mailing entirely by hand, as opposed to machine enclosing. It is also called 'hand-filling'.

Hardware – computer equipment including PCs, printers and modems. As opposed to software (the programs that make them work) and 'wet-ware' (a slang term indicating the brain, that is 'human involvement').

Imposition – the process of laying down artwork or negatives so that printing plates will print in the correct sequence for the finished job.

Influencer – a member of, or adviser to the decision-making unit.

Initiator – the member of the decision-making unit who sets the process in motion by perceiving or reporting the need.

Ink jet – a computer-controlled printing process using a jet stream of ink droplets. It is often used to 'personalize' leaflets or brochures with names and addresses.

Inserts – see 'Loose and bound-in inserts'.

Integrated marketing communications – the process of co-ordinating all our information and one or more communication media to deliver a powerful message to the right person at the right time.

Interactive – a communication method, such as telephone marketing or a face-to-face meeting, where the message can be varied according to the response of the prospect, and where the respondent can become involved by discussing and asking questions. Now, of course, this includes Web-site and e-mail interaction.

Internet – the Internet is a network of networks. It comprises of tens of thousands of interconnected computers spanning the globe. The computers that form the Internet range from huge mainframes in research establishments to individual PCs in homes and offices. The Internet grew out of US academic and military networks, until it gradually began to break up into separate networks, each one owned and funded by a different group of people. These separate networks were able to talk to each other because they spoke the same language, namely the Internet Protocol. Although there are advisory boards and standards committees, no single organization owns the Internet in its entirety.

Intranet – a private company network based on Web technology. The network can span all computer platforms and users access the information via a Web browser. An Intranet may be connected to the Internet and companies can, using software, monitor and control the access employees have to various sites.

ISO sizes – paper sizes based on a square metre and internationally accepted. The dimensions are such that when a sheet is halved along its long edge, the ratio of the long edge to the short edge remains the same. Generally, 'A' sizes are for printed work (for example A5 and A4), 'B' sizes for charts and 'C' sizes for envelopes. Thus, an A4 sheet fits into a C4 envelope.

Job bag – a large bag or envelope in which all elements of artwork, proofs, quotes and so on are kept together for easy reference.

Johnson box – a headline or offer statement at the top of a letter, above the salutation. Used to attract the immediate attention of the reader. So called because a US direct marketer called Johnson noticed that many successful direct mailers were adding a headline above the salutation. Drawing a box around this headline, he began the use of the Johnson box! Nowadays it is usually called a 'Johnson box' whether or not the line is actually drawn.

Junk mail – badly targeted mail which irritates the recipient because it is duplicated, irrelevant or both.

Key British Enterprises – published by Dun & Bradstreet, *Key British Enterprises* lists Britain's top companies, with additional data of interest to business-to-business marketers.

Key coding – printing a code onto a response device to enable the source of the enquiry or order to be traced.

Ladder of loyalty – a method of classifying customers and prospects, enabling us to decide how much information to send them, and what sort of offers they will find appropriate.

Laser printer – a computer-controlled printer which works on the same principle as a photocopier. An electrostatic impression is applied to a sheet of paper which then passes through a drum of charged grey particles. These adhere to the charged part of the paper and the powder is then baked onto the paper by heat. An alternative method known as 'cold laser' uses gas instead of heat to fix the impression onto the paper. As it is computer controlled, it is very flexible and is widely used to produce 'personalized' letters, varying name, address and text according the data in the computer.

Layout – drawing or sketch showing the relative positions of graphics and type in an advertisement or mailing.

Lead – an enquiry or interested prospect. Leads can be 'loose' or 'tight'. A loose lead is where the advertisement makes a large promise, but gives little information as to price or commitment required by the respondent. This maximizes response, but reduces conversion. A tight lead is where the advertisement gives full details and thus reduces response. However, conversion will be greater as respondents know exactly what they are sending for.

Lead generation – activity to produce enquiries (leads) which can then be followed up by telephone, sales force or direct mail.

Leading edge – the edge of the printed piece which is inserted into the envelope first.

Lead qualification – the process of evaluating the sales potential of a lead in order to decide on the optimum contact strategy.

Lettershop – see 'Mailing house'.

Lifestyle database – databases of consumers built by questionnaires, guarantee cards and so on. Several companies are involved, and between them they have several million records available for rental. Claritas the leading UK operator claims to have data on 75% of UK households.

Lifetime value analysis – the cumulative net worth of a customer to an organization over the actual or predicted transactional 'life' time.

Lift letter – an additional letter within a mailing package, often from an authoritative individual who endorses the product or service. So called because they generally increase (lift) response.

Linework – all type, lines and borders that make up the finished design.

List (mailing list) – names and addresses of individuals or companies having in common a specific characteristic (such as SIC code), activity (Workshop), or interest.

List broker – a specialist who arranges for a company to rent the list of another organization.

List building – the process of gathering names and addresses and compiling them into a list for mailing or other purposes (such as telemarketing).

List cleaning – the process of correcting or removing a name and address from a mailing list because it is no longer correct.

List exchange – some organizations are prepared to exchange names with other organizations that are promoting a non-competitive product or service to the same type of prospect. Of course, it is important that any names exchanged on this way have been given the opportunity to 'opt out'.

List rental – the process of renting a list from a broker or, sometimes, direct from the owner.

List selection – a sub-section of a list, enabling an advertiser to mail only the part of the list he or she considers to be more likely to respond. (For example in a list of company directors the advertiser may select only the financial directors or chief executives).

Literal – a misprint or mis-spelling within a printed job.

Loose and bound-in inserts – leaflets that can be inserted in newspapers and magazines to generate leads. Usually more cost-effective than page advertising in the same publications.

Loose Lead – see 'Lead'.

Machine folding – a process of mechanically folding printed paper.

Mailer – another name for a mailing pack or piece.

Mailing house – also called a 'mailshop' or a 'lettershop'. It is an organization that offers a range of services to the advertiser, including assembly and despatch of a mailing; receipt and fulfilment of responses; and laser printing and other computer work.

Mailing list – a collection of names and addresses with a common link which has been assembled for the purpose of despatching a mailing.

Mailsort – the Royal Mail discount service for direct mailings. Users pre-sort the mail into postcode areas in return for discounts on postage costs.

Market profile – selling history and other relevant information about a target audience.

Match code – a unique reference code, built from a name and address, enabling a computer to carry out a de-duplication run. See 'Merge/purge'.

Matched sample – when testing various types of offer, creative treatments and so on, each test is sent to a cell made up of the same type of people or companies (matched samples) to ensure that the results are truly representative.

Mechanical artwork – finished layout, comprising typesettings and photographs, which is ready for making printing plates.

Media – the plural of 'medium'. Media are carriers of advertising messages and include newspapers, magazines, radio, television and direct mail.

Media mix – the combination of media used in a single campaign.

Member get member (MGM) – a marketing device to encourage customers to introduce new customers or prospects. It is sometimes (but not always) accompanied by the offer of a free gift. It is also known as 'friend get a friend', 'recommend a friend' or 'referral schemes'.

Merge/purge – the process of matching lists (merging) to identify duplicate listings; these are then listed and can be removed (purged) before mailing. See 'De-duplication'.

Negative option – an offer where delivery to the customer is carried out unless the customer requests to the contrary within a specified period.

Negative pre-screening – see 'Pre-screening'.

Net names – names actually usable after a de-duplication operation.

Nth name selection – a method used in list testing to ensure a randomized sample selection, for example to select 1000 names at random from a list of 15,000 we would specify 'every 15th name'. This overcomes any bias that might arise if the list is held in chronological or value order.

Objective – a stated requirement (precisely quantified) for achievement, for example 'to increase our number of active customers to 2000 by June 2002.'

OCR – stands for 'Optical Character Reading (or Recognition)' and is a process using equipment that can 'read' specially formed characters to speed up the analysis of reports, questionnaires and so on.

Offer – what you do to attract the prospect to send for more details or order your product. It might be a 'special' offer, such as a discount or incentive.

Off-the-page – obtaining a lead or a sale directly from a press advertisement without additional follow up.

OMR – stands for 'Optical Mark Reading' and is similar to OCR, but the machine reads marks or bars rather than alpha and numeric characters.

One-shot – a solo mailing, usually promoting a single product, without a follow-up.

Origination – all the processes involved in the reproduction of original material, including creative work, photography, artwork, typesetting and colour separation.

Overprint – to run previously printed material through a press to print additional matter, such as adding the name and address to a previously (pre-printed) letter.

PAF – the Postcode Address File

Personalization – see 'Computer personalization'.

Piggy-back – additional promotion in a mailing package, usually from a different advertiser to the main offer.

PMT – stands for 'Photo Mechanical Transfer' and is a reproduction quality copy of an original piece of artwork.

Postcode – an alpha-numeric code that defines each part of a postal address.

Pre-paid – printing a mail mark or applying a stamp to a reply device to encourage response. Using Royal Mail Business Reply or Freepost services is more cost-effective, as advertisers pay only for those returned.

Pre-screening – originally used exclusively by mail order companies to cut down the wastage of expensive catalogues to non-orderers. A low-cost mailing is sent to each prospect 7–10 days in advance saying 'In one week we will be sending you our catalogue. If you do not want to receive this please return the enclosed postcard and we will take you off our list.' Typically, about 20% of cards are returned, saving the company a large amount of money in catalogues and postage. An additional benefit is that the remaining 80% tend to order more as the advance mailing generates more interest in the catalogue when it arrives. Today a similar technique is very useful in cleaning up a database. There are two versions – negative pre-screening and positive pre-screening. Negative pre-screening works like the catalogue technique above. The letter simply says 'We will continue to send you information (mailings) unless you return the card telling us not to do so.' Again, typically, 20% ask to be removed. This enables a large segment of non-interested people to be removed from the database. Positive pre-screening is used with much older data as it is a more aggressive cleansing process. Here the letter says 'Unless you return the card, we will take you off our list.' Again, about 20% of people respond, so this cuts down the database by 80%. However, the remaining 20% have positively opted in to receiving mailings and will respond much better than the average of the entire previous file.

Printed postage impression – a Royal Mail system enabling volume users to pre-print envelopes with an impression, instead of affixing stamps to each piece.

Profiling – the selection or clustering of customers or prospects according to specific characteristics. For example, profiling may indicate that our best customers are companies with more than 200 cars or are in heavy engineering.

Proof – a printed sample of work to be checked for errors in text, positioning or quality of colour reproduction.

Prospects – prospective customers who match our buying profile, but have never bought this particular product from us.

Qualitative research – research that is used to assess opinions, understanding of concepts, like or dislike of concepts, creative treatments and so on.

Quantitative research – research which sets out to answer the 'how many' questions. Requires much larger samples than qualitative research.

Rate card – publisher's details of advertisement rates, copy dates and artwork sizes.

Referral – see 'Member get member'.

Referral rate – the frequency or percentage of referrals we receive.

Reminder mailing – a mailing sent to customers reminding them of a significant date such as a renewal or cut-off date.

Rented lists – mailing lists which can be rented from owners or brokers.

Response devices – the various elements used to get a reply, such as order forms, telephone and fax numbers, e-mail addresses and Web site addresses.

Response rate – the level at which replies or orders are received as a result of a promotional campaign, advertisement or mailing. Usually expressed as a percentage of the number mailed or 'universe' promoted to (such as newspaper readership).

Retention (of customers) – activities to increase the loyalty of customers, that is to make them remain as regular buyers.

Retention rate – the percentage of customers who continue to buy from us from year to year.

Reversed-out type – type printed white out of black or any other dark colour. When used for body copy, this usually reduces comprehension and response quite dramatically.

RFM – an acronym for 'recency', 'frequency' and 'monetary value' – a form of analysis relating to buying behaviour. See also 'FRAC'.

Roll-out – a test mailing would normally be done to a sample of a list. If the results are satisfactory the mailing may then be 'rolled out' to the full list.

Rub-off – an involvement device where the recipient rubs or scratches off a surface coating to reveal a symbol or prize.

Run-on price – a price from a supplier for continuing to produce further supplies of a print job over and above the quoted quantity.

Salutation – the addressing of a letter to an individual, such as 'Dear Mr Brown'.

Sample – a representative sub-set of a list or 'universe', used in research and testing. See 'Matched sample' and 'Nth name'.

Sans serif typeface – a type faces with no serifs (short terminal stroke at the end of the main stroke of a typographical character). Although such typefaces look clear and easy to read, they can be a barrier to comprehension when used in body copy.

Seed names – names placed into a mailing list to enable the advertiser to establish when the mailing 'touches down', that is arrives. Also used as a control when renting lists to other organizations (enabling the renter to know whether the list has been used more than once).

Segment – a sub-section of a list that contains people or companies which have common characteristics.

Segmentation – the process of selecting and isolating segments from within a list or market.

Selection criteria – definitions of characteristics indicating segments within a list.

Self-mailer – a mailing piece where the outer envelope is an integral part of the piece. An attached, perforated response card or envelope may also be included.

Shoot – a photographic session.

SIC – stands for Standard Industry Classification. It is the government's numeric classification of businesses in the UK. Direct mailers can select companies of a specific type (industry) by using this coding.

Software – computer programs, that is the machine code which makes computers work, such as Microsoft Windows, Office and Lotus Notes.

Source code – a unique coding given to an advertisement or mailing response device, enabling precise allocation of the responses to source.

Speed premium – an incentive offered for an early reply. See also 'Time close'.

Split-run testing – testing involving alternative creative elements or offers to be tested in newspapers or magazines. Also known as 'A/B split runs'.

Split test – two or more matched samples from the same mailing list, that is the direct mail equivalent of the split run.

Strategy – the route or method by which an objective will be achieved.

Suppression file – a list of names and addresses that are not to be mailed.

Synergy – the working together of two or more elements (such as direct mail and awareness advertising) to produce an effect greater than would be achieved by the sum of their individual effects.

Tactics – the detailed actions involved in fulfilling a strategy.

Take one – a leaflet placed where interested prospects can 'take one'; often in a dispenser or display stand in retail sites.

Tandem communications – the use of simultaneous multiple mailings or other communications to target more than one member of a decision-making unit with messages relevant to their specific interests.

Targeting – the precise identification of an audience or target for a promotion.

Target Group Index (TGI) – an analysis of purchasing habits among consumers. It covers over 4000 brands and services across more than 500 product fields.

Telemarketing (telephone marketing) – the use of the telephone as a marketing medium. 'In-bound' is where the call is instigated by a customer or prospect; 'outbound' is where the call is made by you to a customer or prospect.

Telemarketing bureau – an independent organization offering telemarketing services on a project or campaign basis.

Telephone account management – the process of managing customers by telephone, usually with the addition of direct mail. Typically used for accounts which do not warrant regular personal calls by the sales force.

Telesales – the use of the telephone for selling. This is distinct from using the telephone to receive enquiries, develop customer relationships and manage accounts.

Testing – the process of evaluating alternative media, creative treatments, offers, timing, response devices and so on.

Tight lead – see 'Lead'.

Time close – an offer or special price which is said only to be open for a limited period, for example 'for 7 days only' or 'until 30 March'.

Tip-ons – a one-piece mailer or postcard which is attached by a dab of glue to a leaflet or advertisement.

The Times **Top Thousand** – a business register, giving names, addresses and general information about Britain's largest companies.

Typesetting – the assembly of body copy and headlines by keyboard, photo-setting or digital means.

Typo – slang term for 'literal'. It is the shortened version of 'typographical error'.

Unique selling proposition (USP) – that single proposition that sets your product or service apart in the minds of your prospects. In direct marketing it is common for USPs to be varied according to the status of the prospect within the buying process. See 'Decision-maker'.

Universe – the total audience within a certain specification, for example the 'universe' of company car drivers is all the company car drivers in UK.

Visual – a layout or 'rough', indicating the general design and the position of the various elements.

Window envelope – Envelope which has a portion cut out to reveal an address or other message printed on the material enclosed. Some mailers use two windows, enabling them to show personalized messages for even small segments by allowing the letter headline to show through this second window.

World Wide Web – the main driver of recent Internet growth, is a collection of millions of files scattered across computers around the world connected to the Internet. The Web was developed at the CERN research centre as a mechanism for scientists to share their work and access community information. For the business community and other organizations, the Web is providing a universal multimedia environment for publishing information on the Internet. As such, it provides access to millions of documents (called Web pages) stored on thousands of computers across the world (called Web servers). These Web pages are designed on a 'hypertext' system, so you can jump from one page to another with simple point and click links. They can also contain graphics, text, photographs, sound and even video.

Index

A/B split runs, 131, 228, 232–5, 241
Access, 111
ACORN, 78, 79–81, 128
Acquisition, 255–6
  costs, 40, 45
  customer lifetime value analysis, 272
  planning a campaign, 28–31
Added value, 31, 38, 44, 53, 182
Addresses, 316–24
ADSL *see* Asymmetric Digital Subscriber
  Line
Advanced Payment Programme (APP),
  99–100
Advertisements:
  planning and design, 27, 197–8,
    199–204
  size, 132–3
Advertising *see* awareness advertising;
  broadscale advertising; direct
  response advertising
Advocates, 83–4, 85–6
Agencies, 146–9, 295–6, 312
AIR MILES, 157
Allowable cost per order, 257–63, 272
Amazon, 161
Ambient media, 128
Annual anniversary follow-ups, 219
Apathy, 180–1
APP *see* Advanced Payment Programme
Argos, 161
Artificial intelligence, 97
Artwork:
  brochures for direct mailings, 214–15
  creative brief, 301

direct response advertisements, 202
  planning a campaign, 27
Asymmetric Digital Subscriber Line
  (ADSL), 165
Availability, offers, 181
Awareness advertising, 121–2, 123–5
  frequency, 230–1
  planning and design, 199
  press advertising, 130

B2B *see* business-to-business
Banners, Internet, 172–3
BARB *see* Broadcasters Audience
  Research Board
BBS *see* British Business Survey
Behaviour:
  integrated media campaign, 128
  regression analysis, 94
Bibliography, 312–16
BOGOF *see* buy one get one free
Bound-in inserts, 134–6
Brand awareness advertising, 121–2,
  123–5
  frequency, 230–1
  planning and design, 199
  press advertising, 130
Brand response advertising, 122–3
Break even, 148–9, 257–8
Briefs, suppliers, 299, 300–4
British Airways Holidays (BAH), 93
British Business Survey (BBS), 129
Broadcasters Audience Research Board
  (BARB), 129
Broadscale advertising, 7–8

costs, 18
  frequency, 230–1
  planning a campaign, 25–6
  relevance, 121
  suspects, 85
  testing, 225
Brochures, direct mailings, 206, 214–15
Budget, 254–87
  creative brief, 301
  marketing communications plan, 20
  planning a campaign, 29–30
Bureaux, 293–4
  data capture, 103
  de-duplication of data, 104–5, 291
Business information brokers, 60
Business models, 160
Business-to-business (B2B) marketing
  customer information, 59–60
  incentives, 187–8
  Internet, 155, 172
  press advertising, 130
  testimonials, 183
  timing, 26
  Web sites, 172
Buttons, Internet, 172–3
Buy one get one free (BOGOF), 180,
  185–6
Buying patterns, 92, 93, 94

CACI, 64, 81
Call centres, 138–9, 142–3
Campaigns:
  brand awareness, 123–5
  budgets, 269–72
  databases, 106–7
  direct response, 123–5, 144–9
  integrated media campaign, 15–17,
    126–9
  media selection, 130–44
  planning, 23–33, 106–7, 123–9
Caption, 214–15
Carbon copy mailing, 218
Careers, 311
CAVIAR see Cinema and Video Industry
  Audience Research
CCA see Continuous Credit Card
  Authority
Censuses, 79
CHAID, 94–7, 294
Charles Schwab, 159–60

Chartered Institute of Marketing, 309
Chord9, 164
Cinema, 127, 129
Cinema and Video Industry Audience
  Research (CAVIAR), 129
Cisco, 161
Claritas, 58–9, 79, 292
Client-side operations, 311
Cluster analysis, 94–7
Cold calling, 139
Cold mailings, 17
Communications see marketing
  communications
Companies House, 65, 103, 319
Competitions, 186–7
Complaints, 41–3
Computer bureaux, 293–4
Computers:
  databases, 10–11, 107–13
  statistical analysis, 97–8
Confidence level, 242–9
Considering, 83, 85
Consultants, 296–7
  direct marketing, 296–7
  Web sites, 294
Contact centres, 138–9, 142–3
Contact frequency:
  customer retention, 37, 42
  retention marketing, 47
Contact strategy, databases, 106
Continuous Credit Card Authority
  (CCA), 180
Contribution costing, 265–7
Conversion, 13
Copy:
  creative brief, 301
  creative outline, 195
  creative work, 191–223
  direct mailings, 206–14, 217
  direct response advertisements, 202–4
  planning a campaign, 27
Copywriters, positioning, 184
Cost per lead (CPL), 144–6
Cost per order/sale, 257
Cost per response, 257
Cost per thousand, 256
Cost-efficiency, 16–17
  direct mailing, 146–9
  direct response advertisements, 203
  press advertising, 131, 132–3

size of advertisement, 132–3, 229–30
television campaigns, 142
testing, 225–6
Costs, 18
    calculating, 263–7
    campaign budgets, 269–72
    customer retention strategy, 277–81
    databases, 10
    direct mailing, 140, 146–8
    direct response campaigns, 144–9
    evaluation of campaigns, 27–8
    information, 14
    inserts, 136
    magazines advertising, 133
    measurement, 256–67
    new customers, 40
    new prospects, 29
    press advertising, 130–1, 132–3, 136–8
    radio campaigns, 143–4
    retention marketing, 45–67
    television campaigns, 142, 143
Coupons, 202–3, 231
CPL *see* cost per lead
Creative, 191–223
    briefs, 300–4
    direct response advertisements, 200, 201
    outlines, 194–7
    plan, 26
    testing, 225
Credit cards, 167–8
Credit checks, 299–300
Cross-over tests, 236
Cross-selling, 37, 47, 49, 139
Cuddle calls, 50
Customer delight, 30–1, 38, 44
Customer life cycles, 41
Customer lifetime value analysis, 272–83
Customer relationship management, 34–55
    customer lifetime value analysis, 277–81
    databases, 98–108
    Internet, 156, 157
    see also databases
Customer relationship marketing, 3, 43–5, 314
Customer satisfaction, 30–1, 38, 39–40, 41, 42, 43, 106

Customer satisfaction surveys, 41, 42, 43, 106
Customers:
    acquisition, 28–31, 40, 45, 255–6, 272
    attributes for satisfaction, 39–40
    complaints, 41–3
    databases, 89–119
    demographics, 113–14, 115
    development, 34–7
    effective communications, 120–52
    information, 56–70
    ladder of loyalty, 83–4, 85
    lapsed, 99–100
    life cycles, 41
    lifestyle, 114–15
    lifetime value analysis, 272–83
    lost, 40, 42
    loyalty, 13, 30–1, 34–55, 83–4, 85
    retention, 28–31, 34–55, 255–6, 272–83
    sources of information, 158
    testing direct mail, 238
    welcome, 45, 47, 48–9
    see also profiling; segmentation

Daily Telegraph, 99–100
Data:
    accuracy, 13–14
    capture, 103
    cleaning, 159
    de-duplication, 103, 104–5, 290, 291
    demographic, 78, 79–82, 95–7, 113–14, 115, 128, 133
    demographics, 113–14, 115
    enhancement, 78
    external sources, 113–16
    gathering, 8–15
    individual, 17
    lifestyle, 58–9, 78–9, 114–15, 128, 129
    maintenance, 101, 103–4, 106
    measurement, 13–15
    personalization, 206–7
    sources, 101–3
    use of, 105–8
    which is needed, 100–1
    see also information
Data mining, 3, 115–16
Data protection, 5–6, 67

Data Protection Act 1998, 67, 103, 166
Data warehousing, 3, 115–16
Databases, 3, 6–7, 10–15, 89–119
    bibliography, 313
    customer development, 37
    customer lifetime value analysis,
       277–8
    data enhancement, 78
    demographics, 95–7, 113–14, 115
    Internet, 157
    market research, 9
    original research, 65–6
    outside bureaux, 293–4
    retention marketing, 47–8
    segmentation, 73–4
Dataquest, 154
De-duplication, 103, 104–5, 290, 291
Decision-making unit (DMU), 74–5
Definitions, 4–5, 325–38
Dell, 161, 163
Dell, Michael, 163
Demographics, 78, 79–82
    databases, 95–7, 113–14, 115
    integrated media campaign, 128
    magazines, 133
Design:
    planning a campaign, 27
    suppliers, 294–5
    testing, 237
    see also creative
Desk research, 63–5
Development potential, 30
Dialogue, 43–4, 47, 49
Digital age, 123
Digital certificates, 167–8
Diploma in Interactive and Direct
    Marketing, 2, 309
Direct Mail Information Service, 68
Direct mailings, 139–41
    cost per lead, 144–6
    costs, 145, 146–9
    follow ups, 218–20
    junk mail, 19
    negative response to, 189
    outside suppliers, 293
    planning and design, 198, 204–20
    testing, 238, 241
Direct marketing agencies, 295–6, 312
Direct Marketing Association, 297
Direct Marketing Centre, 2

Direct response advertising, 121–2,
    123–5
    building a mailing list, 65
    campaigns, 123–5, 144–9
    costs, 144–9
    planning and design, 199–204
    press, 130–3, 145, 200–4
    radio, 143–4, 145
    television, 141–3, 145
    testing, 225–38
Direct response ghettos, 132, 134
Discounts, 180
Disintermediation, 159–60
Distress buying, 130, 138
DMU *see* decision-making unit
Donoghue, Peter, 182
Door-to-door distribution (DTD), 66,
    141, 145
Door-to-door selling, 189
Drucker, Peter, marketing, 6
DTD *see* door-to-door distribution
Dual purpose advertising
    planning and design, 199
    press advertising, 130
    size, 229
Dunn Humby, 115–16

E-commerce, 155, 156
    bibliography, 314–15
    security, 165–9
    strategy, 169–70
E-mail:
    advertising of Web sites, 172
    responses to direct mailings, 216
    surveys, 67
Early bird offers, 180
EDs *see* enumeration districts
Education, 2, 310
Electoral roll, 64
Employees, information from existing
    customers, 60
Enclosures:
    third-party distribution of leaflets, 138
    see also brochures; leaflets; letters
Encryption, Internet, 167
Enumeration districts (EDs), 79–80
Envelopes, direct mailings, 204–5, 217
Error tolerance, 242–9
Escalating discount series, 218–19
European Union (EU), 64

Eurostat, 64
Evaluation, 254–87
    planning a campaign, 27–8
    press advertising, 136–8
    retention marketing, 47
EVP *see* extra value proposition
Experian, 64, 81
Extra value proposition (EVP), 53
Extranets, 156

Fax, responses to direct mailings, 216
Fixed costs, 263–5
Follow ups, 15–16
    creative outline, 195
    direct mailings, 218–20
Forecasts, 19, 20
Forrester Research, 154, 155
FoxPro, 111
Free gifts, 52, 179, 187–8, 261–2
Frequency:
    customer retention, 37, 42, 47
    testing, 230–1
Fulfilment houses, 293
Funding, new business generation, 30

General advertising *see* broadscale
    advertising
Geodemographics, 78, 79–82, 128
Geographic split runs, 232–5, 236
Geographic testing, 237
Gerstner, Lou, 3–4
Gifts, 52, 179, 187–8
Glossary, 325–38
Graveyards, 132, 134
Great Universal Stores, 158, 161
Guarantees, 181–2
Guard books, 27–8
Guard files, 27–8

Hard sell, 188–9
Hardware:
    databases, 10–11, 107–10, 107–13
    statistical analysis, 97–8
Headlines:
    direct mailings, 217
    direct response advertisements, 202
    envelopes, 205
    letters for direct mailings, 209–10
    planning and design, 197–8
Heinz UK, 52

Helplines, 50–1
Hierarchy of testing, 231–7,
    250–1
Holder, Derek, 2
Hot-spots, 134
Household composition, 58
Humour, direct mailings, 217

IBM, 3–4
Incentives, 187–8
Industry statistics, 64
Information, 6–7
    accuracy, 13–15
    collecting, 56–70
    gathering, 8–15, 91
    Internet, 158
    personalization, 206–7
    using, 71–88
    see also data; databases
Information brokers, 103
Inland Revenue, 158
Inserts, 66, 134–6, 145, 201
    cost per lead, 146
    testing, 225, 237–8, 241
    third-party distribution of leaflets,
        138
Institute of Direct Marketing, 2, 309,
    310
Integrated media planning, 126–9
Integration, 15–16, 121–3, 126–9
Internet, 3–4, 123, 153–77
    bibliography, 314–15
    collecting information, 66–7
    consultants and designers, 294
    improving business processes, 156,
        163–4
    marketing tool, 156, 157–60
    responses to direct mailings,
        216
    security, 165–9
    selling tool, 156, 161–2
    television campaigns, 142
    see also e-mail; Web sites
Interstitial advertising, 173
Intranets, 156, 163–4, 169–70

Johnson box, 210
Jones, Gregory K., 308
Journals, 315–16
Junk mail, 19

Ladder of loyalty, 3, 82–6
Lead processing, databases, 106
Lead times, 131, 133
Leads:
    offers, 179–90
    positioning, 185
Leaflets:
    direct mailings, 214–15
    door-to-door distribution, 141
    third-party distribution, 138
Letters, direct mailings, 205–14, 217
Level of service, 30
Lifestyle data, 58–9, 78–9, 114–15
    integrated media campaign, 128
    list providers, 291–2
    magazines, 133
    media research sources, 129
Limits of error, 242–9
List brokers, 65, 159, 227, 289–92
List rental contracts, 290–1
Lists *see* mailing lists
Loose inserts, 66, 134–6, 201, 225,
    237–8, 241
Love letters, 53
Loyalty, 13, 30–1, 34–55, 82–6

McCorkell, Graeme, 308–9
Machine splits, 235–6
Magazines:
    direct response advertisements, 200–4
    inserts, 134–6
    integrated media campaign, 127
    media selection, 133–4
    position, 228
    reprints of reviews, 215
    testing, 228, 232–5
Mail order companies, 138
Mailing houses, 293
Mailing list brokers, 65, 159, 227, 289–92
Mailing lists:
    original research, 65–6
    planning a campaign, 26
    rented, 65
    suppliers, 65, 159, 227, 289–92
    testing, 240
Mailing preference service (MPS), 189
Market research, 8, 9–10
    collecting information, 63–6
    reliability, 67–8
    retention marketing, 47

Market Research Society, 309
Marketing, definition, 6–7
Marketing communications
    accuracy of data, 104
    customer care, 43–5
    customer information, 57
    effective, 120–52
    planning and design, 197–8
    retention marketing, 46–7, 47
    sales-orientated, 44–5
    timing of, 52–3
    two-way, 43–4
Marketing communications planning, 13,
    15–16, 20
Measurement, 19–20, 254–87
    Internet, 173, 174
    planning a campaign, 27–8
    testing, 14–16
Media:
    booking, 26
    cost per thousand, 256
    creative outline, 194–5
    integrated campaigns, 126–9
    planning a campaign, 25–6
    selection for campaign, 130–44
    testing, 227
Media buying agencies, 137–8
Member get member (MGM) offers, 66,
    84
Metcalfe's law, 155
MGM *see* member get member (MGM)
Millington, Roger, 15
Moments of truth, 41, 43, 45
Moore, Gordon, 11
Moore's law, 11
MOSAIC, 78, 79–81, 128
MPS *see* mailing preference service

National Census, 79–82
National Readership Survey (NRS), 129
Nestlé, 50
Net present value, 274–7
Net ratings, 154
Neural networks, 97, 116
New business models, 160
Newsgroups, 172
Newsletters, 51–2, 172
Newspapers:
    campaigns, 130–3, 145
    cost per lead, 146

design of advertisements, 201–4
direct response advertisements, 200–4
frequency, 201, 230–1
inserts, 134–6
integrated media campaign, 127
position, 136–8, 203–4, 228
readership research, 129
reprints of reviews, 215
size of advertisement, 132–3, 203, 229–30
testing, 225, 227–38
timing, 201, 229
Niche markets, 162
Nielsen, 154
NRS *see* National Readership Survey
NUA, 154

Objectives, 24–5, 192–4
Offer, 178–90
creative planning and design, 194, 198, 301
direct response advertisements, 200, 201
Office of National Statistics, 64
Ogilvy & Mather, 9–10, 126, 130
Ogilvy, David, 198, 202
One-stage campaigns, 25
creative work, 193
magazines, 133
Online shopping, 155, 161–2, 164–5
Opt out statements, 5
Opt in statements, 5
Order forms, 216, 218
Original research, 63, 65–6
Outline creative plan, 26
Outserts, 134
Outsourcing, 146–8, 288, 306
Overheads, 263–7

Pareto's principle, 18, 92
Pass-on readership, 133
Pedigree Foods, 157
Per inquiry deals (PI), 66, 141–2
Periodicals, 315–16
Personal computers (PCs) *see* computers
Personalization, direct mailings, 206–7
PI, 66
PI *see* per inquiry
Pictures:
brochures for direct mailings, 214–15

creative brief, 301
direct response advertisements, 202
Planning:
advertisements, 27, 197–8, 199–204
campaigns, 23–33, 106–7, 123–9
creative, 198
direct response versus brand awareness, 123–5
marketing communications, 13, 15–16, 20
Portals, 160
Position, 136–8, 203–4, 228
Positioning:
creative brief, 301
offer, 183–5
POSTAR, 129
Posters, 127, 129
Press:
buying advertising, 136–8
direct response advertisements, 130–3, 145, 200–4
inserts, 134–6
position, 136–8
testing, 225, 227, 229–38
see also magazines; newspapers
Price, promotional offers, 185–6
Primary research, 65–6
Printers, suppliers, 294–5
Printing, Internet, 158
Privacy, 5–6, 165–6
Prize draws, 186–7
Profiling, 4–5, 18, 75–8
customer information, 59
demographics, 113–14
information from existing customers, 62
integrated media campaign, 128
lifestyle data, 78–9, 114–15
reciprocal linking of Web sites, 172
retention marketing, 46
Profits, customer lifetime value analysis, 272–83
Promise, 30
Promotional devices, 180–1
Promotional offers, 185–6
Property type, 58
Prospecting, 13
Prospects:
building a mailing list, 65–6
creative brief, 301

direct mail, 140–1
e-mails, 172
effective communications, 120–52
ladder of loyalty, 83, 84–5
offer, 179–90
regression analysis, 94
segmentation, 72–5
Psychographic data (lifestyle data), 58–9,
  78–9, 114–15
  integrated media campaign, 128
  list providers, 291–2
  magazines, 133
  media research sources, 129
Public domain data, 64
Public relations, 158
Publishing, 158
Pyramid of Propensity, 3

Qualifications, 309
Quality, offer, 181
Quality control, 136
Questionnaires:
  customer information, 60–2
  customer retention, 53
  customer satisfaction surveys, 41, 42,
    43, 106
  lifestyle data, 79, 114
  retention marketing, 47
  statistical analysis, 97–8
Quotations, suppliers, 299–300

Radio:
  audience research, 129
  direct response campaigns, 143–4,
    145
  integrated media campaign, 127
  per inquiry deals, 141–2
RAJAR, 129
Random access memory (RAM), 110
Randomization, 241–2
Reactivation, 13, 47
Reassurance, offer, 181–2
Reciprocal linking, Web sites, 172
References, suppliers, 299–300
Referral offers, 66
Register of electors, 64
Regression analysis, 94
Relevant costing, 265–7
Rented mailing lists, 65, 227, 289–92
Reply paid, 217

Research:
  reliability, 67–8
  targeting the right person, 74–5
  see also statistical validity
Response devices:
  coupons, 202–3, 231
  direct mailings, 216–17, 218
  planning a campaign, 27
Response management, 27
  creative outline, 197
  databases, 106
  television campaigns, 142–3
Response rate, 257
Responses, 121–2
  creative work, 191–223
  direct response campaigns, 144–9,
    200
  inserts, 136
  measurement, 257
  offers, 188
  planning a campaign, 27
  press advertising, 130
  testing methods, 231
Retention, 34–55, 255–6
  customer lifetime value analysis,
    272–83
  planning a campaign, 28–31
Rewards, 52
Rolls Royce, 184
Royal Mail, 141
Run of week, 136
Run-of-paper, 131–2

Sainsbury, Philip, 132–3, 229–30
Sainsbury's square root principle, 132–3,
  229–30
Samples, testing, 242–51
SAS, 97, 111
Scaife, Jack, 162
Search engines, 170–2
Secondary research, 63–5
Secure Electronic Transaction (SET),
  167–8
Secure Socket Layer (SSL), 167
Security, Internet, 165–9
Segmentation, 8, 17–18, 72–5
  CHAID, 94–7
  cluster analysis, 94–7
  creative planning and design, 198
  customer development, 37, 38, 39

customer information, 57
customer lifetime value analysis, 282
databases, 13, 93–8
direct mailings, 215
direct response advertisements,
    200
retention marketing, 45–6, 278–9
Tesco's, 115–16
testing direct mail, 238
Selectivity, segmentation, 73–5
Semi-solus position, 137
SET *see* Secure Electronic Transaction
Seybold, Patricia, 155
Shell, 158
Signatures, Internet, 167–8
Single minded proposition, 7
Size, 132–3, 229–30, 238
Skills, 310–11
SMART, 24–5
Smart cards, 168
Sodastream, 91–2
Software:
    databases, 10, 110–13
    statistical analysis, 97–8
Solus position, 137
Spam, 67
Specialists, 288–306
Split runs, 134, 228, 232–5, 241
SPSS, 97, 111
SSL *see* Secure Socket Layer
Standing orders, 180–1
Statistical analysis, 97–8
Statistical significance, 241–2
Statistical validity:
    machine splits, 235–6
    telescope testing, 232–5
    testing, 228, 229
Statistics:
    bibliography, 314
    measurement, 256–7
    testing, 240–2
Stickers, 204–5
Strategy:
    Internet, 169–70
    marketing, 277–80
Subscriptions, 99–100, 180–1
Sun Microsystems, 164
Superprofiles, 78
Superstitial advertising, 173
Suppliers, 288–306

Supply chain management, 163
Suspects, 83, 84–5

Target Group Index (TGI), 129
Targeting:
    creative brief, 301
    creative outline, 194
    databases, 93–8
    direct mailings, 140–1, 204
    direct response advertisements, 200–1
    integrated media campaign, 126–7
    Internet, 157
    planning a campaign, 25
    profiling, 75–8
    television campaigns, 142
    testing loose inserts, 237
Telephone:
    account management, 39
    costs, 145
    follow ups, 15–16, 219–20
    integrated media campaigns, 138–9
    responses to direct mailings, 216
    television campaigns, 142
Telephone directories, 66
Telephone preference service, 139
Telephone selling, 189
Telescope testing, 232–5, 241
Television:
    audience research, 129
    direct response campaigns, 141–3,
        145
    integrated media campaign, 127
    testing, 225, 227, 229
    timing, 229
Terminology, 3, 4–5, 325–38
Tesco, 115–16, 161
Testimonials, 181–3, 215, 217
Testing, 14–16, 19–20, 224–53
    costs, 264
    direct mail, 140
    frequency, 230–1
    inserts, 135–6
    loose inserts, 237–8
    loyalty programme, 38
    magazine advertising, 133–4
    media, 227
    position, 228
    press advertising, 131
    radio campaigns, 144
    retention marketing, 47

samples, 242–51
segmentation, 74
size, 228–30
statistics, 240–2
timing, 228
TGI *see* Target Group Index
Third-party offers, 52
Timing, 16–17
   communications with existing
     customers, 52–3
   creative outline, 194
   direct response advertisements, 200,
     201
   door-to-door distribution, 141
   inserts, 136
   integrated media campaign, 126–7
   planning a campaign, 26
   relationship programmes, 45
   segmentation, 73
   testing, 229
Tip-on cards, 134
Training, 309
Transactional information, 58
Two-stage campaigns, 25
   creative work, 193
   direct response advertisements, 201
   evaluating, 258–60
   magazines, 133
   press advertising, 130
Typefaces, 203, 211–14

Unique selling proposition (USP), 7, 8
Unsolicited e-mails, 67
Up-selling, 37, 47, 139
UpMyStreet.com, 160
USP *see* unique selling proposition

Value, 181
Variable costs, 263–5
Variable Direct Debit Mandate (VDD),
   180–1
VDD *see* Variable Direct Debit
   Mandate
Viral techniques, 173
Virtual retailers, 161–2
Vogele, Siegfried, 207, 209

Web sites, 3–4, 156, 157
   consultants and designers, 294
   privacy, 166
   promotion, 170–4
   responses to direct mailings, 216
   strategy, 169–70
Welcome, 45, 47, 48–9
Wheildon, Colin, 211–14
Wise and Loveys Information Services,
   159
World Wide Web *see* Internet
World Wildlife Fund, 193

Zanussi, 292

r before the last date shown below.